THE
IRON
ROAD

THE IRON ROAD

THE ILLUSTRATED
HISTORY OF THE RAILWAY

CHRISTIAN WOLMAR

**LONDON, NEW YORK, MUNICH,
MELBOURNE, DELHI**

Editor	Hugo Wilkinson
Senior Art Editor	Phil Gamble
Editorial team	Andy Szudek
	Georgina Palffy
	Alison Sturgeon
	Richard Gilbert
Designers	Paul Drislane
	Katie Cavanagh
	Stephen Bere
Senior Editor	Angela Wilkes
Picture Research	Luped Media Research
Jacket Designer	Mark Cavanagh
Jacket Editor	Maud Whatley
Jacket Design Manager	Sophia M.T.T.
Producer, Pre-production	Rebecca Fallowfield
Production Controller	Mandy Inness
Managing Editor	Stephanie Farrow
Senior Managing Art Editor	Lee Griffiths
Publisher	Andrew Macintyre
Art Director	Phil Ormerod
Associate Publishing Director	Liz Wheeler
Publishing Director	Jonathan Metcalf

First published in Great Britain in 2014
by Dorling Kindersley Limited
80 Strand, London WC2R 0RL

Penguin Group (UK)
2 4 6 8 10 9 7 5 3 1
001–196353–May/14

Copyright © 2014
Dorling Kindersley Limited

A CIP catalogue record for this book is
available from the British Library.

ISBN 978-1-4093-4799-6

Printed and bound by
South China Printing Company, China.

Discover more at
www.dk.com

Contents

Introduction

Of all the great inventions of the Industrial Revolution, the railways had the most impact. In a world before rail, travel over any distance was a major undertaking. Regions of even small countries, such as France or England, could be up to seven days' journey from the capital, while large countries like the United States, China, or Russia could take months to cross. Until the early 19th century, most people lived their whole lives within the confines of the town or rural area in which they were born, and no-one had ever gone faster than a horse could gallop. Travel was simply too difficult and too expensive for the vast majority of people, which in turn limited the spread of ideas and technology.

Lack of mobility was a major barrier to economic and social development. In the absence of rapid transport, people could starve within only a few hundred kilometres of plentiful food supplies. The slow transit of goods by horse and cart, or along rivers and canals, meant that perishables had to be consumed very rapidly. Sending a letter across the country took days, and newspapers were a misnomer, since they were effectively full of old information. It took months for people to learn the fate of loved ones at war, and news of major events, from even just a short distance away, filtered through slowly.

Limitations on travel also translated into social restriction – people had little choice of spouse, since opportunities to meet potential marriage partners from even neighbouring towns were rare. Concepts of time, too, were different before the railways. Daily life was regulated by the sun, and towns just a few kilometres east or west of each other could operate on different schedules.

Then the railways arrived and changed everything. One of their first major impacts was to force countries to standardize their measurements of time, both nationally and internationally, since railway timetables would otherwise be too confusing. Greenwich Mean Time, the standard by which the world sets its clocks, was created partly as a result of the railways, and the US was divided into four time zones for the same reason. The Trans-Siberian, the longest railway in the world, still operates according to Moscow time, even though the line crosses seven time zones on its way to Vladivostok. Punctuality and time-keeping thus became vital, not just with regard to the railways, but in all spheres of life. The railways created the structured day, which, prior to their arrival, had been ten hours long, rather than today's norm of eight. In other words, they created the "nine-to-five" routine.

The railways overthrew all established concepts of distance and time, and social upheaval followed. The last vestiges of feudalism were swept away, since people were no longer tied to the land – indeed, they could now work far from home. People worked standard hours and expected to do so for a wage. Thus, the growth of capitalism went hand in hand with the expansion of the iron road. As people no longer had to find employment near their homes, towns and cities could become far larger than would previously have been possible. Suburban sprawl, often thought of as a product of the automobile age, is, in fact, the result of the development of commuter lines.

Access to long-distance travel, in relative comfort at fairly low cost, changed people's horizons and opened up their imaginations. What had previously been impossible became routine – such as going to the seaside or visiting an exhibition. On a social level, the scope for potential marriage partners suddenly broadened, being no longer confined to the immediate vicinity. The exchange of ideas took off as national conferences could now be convened, and the inventions of the Industrial Revolution spread – first across Britain, then across the world. Professional sport became feasible as clubs and their supporters could travel long distances to play other teams, and league size was limited only by how far a team could travel in a day.

Warfare, too, was revolutionized by the railways. Armies had traditionally sustained themselves by foraging and pillaging – an unreliable practice that made it impossible to keep troops in the same place for long, since supplies, especially for the animals, inevitably ran out. These logistical restrictions meant that battles took place over days rather than weeks or months. With the rise of railways, armies no longer needed to be constantly on the move, since they could be supplied with food and munitions from the nearest railhead. They were also invaluable in transporting troops quickly to quell domestic riots or launch wars against neighbours.

Nation states became more cohesive as country-wide railway systems developed. The railways, often state-owned, were the glue that bound a country together, linking disparate regions and enabling governments to expand their influence in remote, previously lawless areas. The railways also stimulated large movements of people: Siberia and the American West were both populated after major lines were built. Settlements everywhere congregated around the tracks; indeed, in the US, several towns that were bypassed by the iron road simply moved to be closer to it. Stations became hubs, attracting development and commerce.

As the railways expanded they brought change in their wake. Railway companies were often the largest organizations in their respective countries and, due to their size, required new

STEAM AND SPEED
Built in 1938, the *Mallard* was the fastest steam engine of all time, and came to symbolize the technological triumphs of the golden age of the railways.

types of business management and even accounting methods. The very engines of capitalism – bank loans, stock markets, information on investment – suddenly became possible. Railway companies needed banks to fund their expansion and, in turn, banks found railway companies to be their best clients, since they were the biggest and most ambitious. It was no coincidence that banks and railway companies were the driving force of mid- and late-19th century capitalism.

Moreover, since the railway companies employed more workers than any other, it was inevitable that, as the trade union movement was born and developed, the railways became the industry in which they flourished. Indeed, they were the site of many of the fiercest disputes between capital and labour.

The story of the railways is not just one of trains and technology, and this richer history, set in a wider social context, is the one this book aims to tell. Despite a strong challenge from the automobile, the railways remain a brilliant technological feat and a great way to travel – but they are, in fact, much more than that, as every page will show.

The First Tracks

LIMMAT
STEAM, 1847

Today's railways are a combination of inventions that were made over millennia, starting with the wheel around 8000 BCE and culminating in the steam engine in the late 18th century. By the early 1800s, steam engines — which began as huge, cumbersome machines — were small enough to be put on wheels, and so the self-propelling "steam locomotive" was born. The next stage was simply to hitch the locomotive to a train — consisting either of wagons carrying freight, or of coaches bearing passengers.

There were many who argued that train travel would never be popular, or that horses should provide the power, but once the world's first major railway, the Liverpool and Manchester line, opened in England in 1830, there was no stopping the spread of the iron road. The United States quickly followed, and the invention spread throughout Europe — tentatively at first, but then quite rapidly. Lines were opened to enormous fanfare, and people flocked to the new stations — many to begin routines of journeying to work by rail, many just to enjoy the new technology.

There were some initial set-backs, however. Every aspect of the railways, from tracklaying and signalling to training staff and building stations, had to be learnt from scratch. This was the birth of a completely new industry and teething problems were inevitable. There were accidents and fires, and investors fell prey to fraudsters and confidence tricksters. Indeed, locomotives were prone to blow up or break down, and a prominent politician, William Huskisson, was killed at the opening of the first railway when he failed to respond quickly enough to warnings of a passing train. Nevertheless, all these difficulties were overcome, and within a couple of decades trains were travelling at twice the speed of a galloping horse and covering huge distances. The railway age had begun.

From Wagonways
to Railways

THE WORLD'S FIRST RAILWAY, the Liverpool and Manchester line, opened in England in 1830, at the end of the Industrial Revolution. It was the culmination of decades of experimentation with tracks, wagons, and engines, and proved beyond doubt that the railway was the future of land transport. But it was also an ancient technology. The wheel had been invented more than 7,000 years earlier, and had soon been given a track. By the time of the Ancient Greeks (600 BCE–600 CE), the wheels of carts and coaches were running in specially dug out channels that prevented them from sliding off the road in wet weather, and similar tracks have been found in the ruins of Pompeii and Sicily. Myth has it that Oedipus slew his father when the two came across each other on one such road and argued over who had the right of way.

The earliest image of wooden tracks being used for transport dates back to 1350 and can be seen in a church in Freiburg im Breisgau, Germany. Within a couple of centuries, numerous wagonways (or paths made of such tracks) had been built in Germany and Britain to haul heavily loaded wagons out of mines. The first of these appeared in Saxony, which had become a major tin and silver mining region by the 14th century. Activity in the Saxon mines peaked in the 16th century, thanks to the development of the *Leitnagel Hund* – a four-wheeled mining truck that was far more efficient than its predecessors. It had an iron bar that projected from its underside into a groove between a pair of wooden tracks, to keep it from veering off course. Operating the truck demanded great skill, and there were inevitably accidents, but it soon revolutionized the German mining industry, making it possible to transport much larger quantities of ore to the surface for smelting. At first, this system was entirely dependent on manpower, but soon horses replaced men, enabling even heavier loads to be moved.

The next development was the introduction of rails for the trucks to travel on. The earliest of these, found in Germany and known as *Karrenbahnen*, were made of wood, and by the early 18th century, in the coal region of the Ruhr, they had a lip – an L-shaped flange that kept the wagons on the tracks. On some wagonways, the flange was fitted to the wheels of the trucks rather than the tracks, an arrangement that later became standard on the railways.

By the time the flange had been introduced, Britain had also developed a system of wagonways. It was based on the German system, but soon became more extensive than its precursor. Britain was the cradle of the Industrial Revolution, and her wagonways connected an ever-expanding network of mines to an increasing number of factories, and to waterways that enabled coal and minerals to be shipped even further afield. This transport system had a huge economic impact on Britain, and both the industrial and domestic consumption of coal increased tenfold between 1700 and the early 1800s. The network that emerged in the northeast of England in the 17th century was so busy with traffic that it became known as the Newcastle Roads. By 1660, there were nine wagonways on Tyneside alone, and several others in the Midlands to the south. In 1726, a

THE FIRST TRACKS
Misrah Ghar il-Kbir in Malta is the site of limestone cart tracks dating to around 2000 BCE. In places the ruts cross each other and form junctions, giving the appearance of tracks at a railway switching yard.

group of coal mine owners called the Grand Allies went a step further by linking their collieries to a shared wagonway. They even created a "main line", the Tanfield Wagonway, much of which had two tracks, permitting a continuous flow of inbound and outbound vehicles. The route linked several pits with the River Tyne, crossing the Causey Arch — a bridge with a 32-m (105-ft) span over a rocky ravine — en route. Costing £12,000 (around £1.5 million or US$2.4 million in today's money), the arch was built by stonemason Ralph Wood and still stands today. At the time it was the longest single-span bridge in Britain, and it is perhaps the oldest railway bridge in the world. It accommodated two tracks — the "main way" to take coal to the river, and the "bye way" for returning empty wagons — and at its peak, over 900 horse-drawn wagons crossed the arch each day. There were several such wagonways in Britain and the rest of Europe, but cooperative ventures were rare — many pit owners deliberately built wagonways that prevented rivals from reaching the waterways.

It was not until the late eighteenth century that iron rails were first used, notably by mining engineer Friedrichs zu Klausthal near Hanover, Germany. Soon afterwards, iron rails were laid to move trucks around the ironworks at the key industrial site of Coalbrookdale in the Midlands, England. The initial idea was to cover existing wooden rails with an iron cap so that they would last longer (they had previously been replaced every year), but advances in smelting technology soon made it possible to construct the entire rails from iron. It was around this time that the words "railroad" and "railway" were adopted for the wagonways of the Midlands, which now carried lime, ore, and pig iron as well as coal. Throughout this period, railway wagons also became larger and were able to carry loads of more than 2.5 tonnes (2½ tons), and the gauge of the tracks (the distance between them) was

TOP SPEEDS THEN AND NOW

Nicholas Cugnot's locomotive, 18th century

4KPH
(2½MPH)

Train à Grande Vitesse (TGV), 21st century

574KPH
(357MPH)

largely standardised at 1.5m (5ft). This width best suited the horses that hauled the wagons (any wider and they were too heavy to pull), and it was close to the gauge that eventually prevailed across much of the world – 1,435mm (4ft 8½in), or today's "standard" gauge.

These iron railways flourished for about 40 years. At their peak, thousands of miles of iron tracks stretched across Britain, as opposed to the mere hundreds of miles of wooden equivalents that preceded them, and they reached far beyond the coalfields, linking mines and quarries with ports, rivers, and canals. Their main purpose was to transport minerals to the nearest waterway, but a few carried passengers on a casual basis — usually workers hopping on for a ride to or from a mine or a quarry. Some lines, such as the Swansea and Mumbles line in South Wales, provided carriages for people, but the main business was freight.

A few canny mine owners devised more sophisticated railway systems, involving cables and the use of gravity. Ralph Allen, the owner of a quarry above Bath Spa, designed a wagonway on which the loaded wagons descending the hill into the city pulled the unloaded ones back up the incline behind them. Such "gravity railways" became common in the 18th century. The simplest ones used gravity to roll the wagons downhill, and horses to pull the empty ones back up. An entirely frivolous example was the *Roulette*, built for Louis XIV of France in the gardens of Marly, near Paris. The Sun King liked to entertain his guests by giving them a ride on the *Roulette*. Although technically a gravity railway, this was really more like a rollercoaster built into a hill. The carved, gilded carriage thundered down a 250-m (820-ft) wooden track into a valley and then shot up the other side. The passengers boarded from a small, classical building that could lay claim to being the world's first railway station, then three bewigged valets pushed the coach to the top of the incline, from where gravity took over, giving the aristocrats a novel thrill.

For all their variety, the early railways still required horses or humans to pull them along. What they needed was an engine to drive them, and just such a device was being developed. This was the steam engine, which began life as a stationary machine that generated power to drive water pumps, but was soon adapted to provide rotary power to drive wheels. It was a small leap to connect the engine to the wheels it was driving, thus creating a self-propelling, steam-powered vehicle.

THE CAUSEY ARCH
Shown here in a watercolour by Joseph Atkinson, the Causey Arch, built 1725–26, is thought to be the oldest surviving single-arch railway bridge in the world. The line has long since closed, but the bridge still serves as a footpath.

The idea of steam power goes back to Classical times — Archimedes recognized it, and Hero of Alexandria experimented with it — but it was only in the late 17th century that Frenchman Denis Papin harnessed it with his "steam digester", a crude pressure cooker that he adapted to make an "atmospheric engine" — essentially a cylinder containing a piston that could oscillate under the pressure of steam expanding and condensing. Applying the principles that Papin had documented, Thomas Newcomen, an ironmaster from Devon working in the early 18th century, developed the idea of producing steam engines to pump water from mines, and made 60 of them. After Newcomen died and the patents ran out, engineers copied his ideas and his engines were built in many countries, including the US, the German states, and the Austrian Empire, where one was used to power the fountains for Prinz von Schwarzenberg's palace in Vienna. However, it was Scottish engineer James Watt who first made steam power commercially viable, by making a series of technical improvements to Newcomen's designs so that they could be adapted to carry out a wide variety of tasks. He formed a partnership with English manufacturer Matthew Boulton, and soon their engines were powering looms, mills, and ships across the world.

Nicholas Cugnot, an artillery lieutenant from eastern France, made the first attempt to put a steam engine on wheels around 1672, when he designed what he hoped would be a motorized gun platform. On a test run in Paris, his engine propelled itself slowly forwards, but then it veered off course and overturned, prompting the city authorities to ban it as a public danger. There were various other attempts, both in Britain and the US, to build steam-powered road vehicles, but they were so heavy they destroyed the roads — a problem that was solved by Cornishman Richard Trevithick, who first put the

FRENCH STEAM PIONEER
Denis Papin invented the "steam digester", a type of pressure cooker that was designed to soften bones. It was the first device to use the power of steam, and led Papin to create the first steam-driven engine.

THE "STEAM TROLLEY", 1672
Nicholas Cugnot's steam-powered
engine on wheels is thought to
have been the first self-propelled
vehicle in the world.

engine on rails. Trevithick had a setback in 1801, when his "road carriage" caught fire, but three years later he produced a locomotive that travelled at 8kph (5mph) at Pen-y-Darren, an ironworks in Wales. Later still, he demonstrated his invention on a circular track near the present site of Euston station, London, playfully calling it *Catch Me Who Can*. Like Louis XIV's *Roulette*, however, it was more of a funfair ride than a serious commercial enterprise, and Trevithick went off to develop stationary steam engines for the gold and silver mines of Peru.

By the time Trevithick left England, all the technology needed for a modern railway was in place. Like railway tracks, the steam locomotive was slow to develop – indeed, it seemed for a while that horses would power the railways. It took time for new methods to replace the old, and for many years the railways were a patchwork of iron and wooden tracks, with steam locomotives being trialled while horse-drawn lines were being built. What the railways needed was a genius to bring these disparate elements together. That genius was civil engineer George Stephenson – a great synthesizer of ideas, who was soon dubbed the "father of railways".

The Father of Railways

HUNDREDS OF INVENTORS, at different times, contributed to the creation of the railways, but one individual stands out, not because he was the cleverest or the most innovative, but because he was the best at exploiting the ideas of others and turning them into workable concepts – George Stephenson. Born in Wylam, near Newcastle-upon-Tyne, England, he was a barely literate, self-educated man who did not suffer fools gladly, but who deserves the title of "father of railways", even though he made no significant inventions of his own. He played an important role in the development of two important lines: the Stockton and Darlington, completed in 1825, which was really the last and most sophisticated of the wagonways (see pp.14–21); and the Liverpool and Manchester, whose opening five years later heralded the real start of the railway age. He continued to play a vital role in the spread of the railways, both in Britain and abroad, until his death in 1848.

Stephenson started out as a pit boy, but he soon realized that in order to progress he needed engineering skills, and he learned these initially with the help of a local schoolmaster. Before long, he found work as an engine wright and was put in charge of all the stationary engines at Killingworth, a large coal mine in Northumberland. He quickly realised that the key to making better use of steam technology was to enable the engines to run on rails and haul loads directly, rather than using the cable system, whereby stationary engines reeled in cables attached to wagons (see p.71), and he persuaded the colliery

GEORGE STEPHENSON
A self-taught engineer, Stephenson pioneered a steam locomotive that ran on rails, and built the world's first fully fledged steam railway, the Liverpool and Manchester line, which opened in 1830.

LIVERPOOL AND MANCHESTER TRAIN TICKET, c.1830
Passenger train carriages on the Liverpool and Manchester were originally divided into first, second, and third class. Despite the basic conditions in third, the railways represented a new era of mobility for ordinary people.

owners to give him the means to build a "travelling machine" – his name for the locomotive. The result was unveiled in 1814 – a steam engine somewhat oddly named *Blücher* after Gebhard Leberecht von Blücher, a Prussian general who led his army to several victories against Napoleon, the common enemy of Britain and Prussia at the time. Incorporating features from Trevithick's engines (see pp.20–21), *Blücher* was built in the colliery workshop and proved to be more powerful than any of its predecessors, as it could haul 30.5 tonnes (30 tons) of coal up an incline at 6.5kph (4mph).

The success of *Blücher* spurred Stephenson to build another 16 locomotives over the next 10 years, most of which were commissioned by local collieries. One went to the Kilmarnock and Troon Railway in 1817, but was withdrawn because it damaged the line's cast-iron rails. The same fate befell a second engine that was sent to the railway at Scott's Pit at Llansamlet, near Swansea, in 1819. These failures demonstrated the great difficulty in developing engines that were light enough not to break the primitive tracks, but powerful enough to haul a reasonable load. Showing his versatility as an engineer, Stephenson initially solved this problem by using steam pressure to create a "steam spring" to cushion the weight of the load. He then simply increased the number of wheels to distribute the weight. In 1820, Stephenson was hired to build a 13-km (8-mile) railway at Hetton colliery. The result was a train that relied on gravity on the downward slopes and steam locomotion on the level or uphill sections. It was the first railway that used no animal power whatsoever.

However, Stephenson's engines continued to have difficulties, and he did not have the resources to solve them. In the early 1820s, he became quite despondent, but then developments in the coal town of Darlington lifted his spirits. A group of prosperous Quaker colliery owners, led by Edward Pease and his son Joseph, wanted to create a

GEORGE STEPHENSON'S RAILWAY GAUGE OF

1,435MM

(4FT 8½IN)

BECAME THE WORLD STANDARD

railway that would connect Darlington to Stockton at the mouth of the River Tees, where coastal shipping from London docked. They wanted to reduce the price of coal by making it cheaper to transport, and to counter an alternative plan that was being mooted to build a canal. Stephenson was the obvious man to prepare such a route and build the Stockton and Darlington railway, and was summoned to the Peases' home to discuss their plan. He was duly appointed surveyor and engineer on the project, and, since he had formed a company in 1823 with his son, Robert, to build locomotives at a works in Newcastle, he could use his own engines on the railway. Nevertheless, when Stephenson surveyed the area to be crossed, he encountered considerable opposition from local landowners and had to map out a route that would avoid their fox-hunting grounds.

The scheme was far more ambitious than any of the former wagonways. Nearly 60km (37 miles) of track had to be laid, and there were major physical obstacles too, notably the Myers Flat swamp and the Skerne River at Darlington. Stephenson eventually created a firm base in the swamp by filling it with tons of hand-hewn rock, and called on a local architect to help him design a stone bridge to cross the river. Despite its length and logistical difficulties, the line took only three years to construct, but even as it opened debate raged over what form of traction to use. Stephenson and his son produced the steam engine *Locomotion No. 1*, which, on the opening day of 27 June 1825, pulled a train of 34 wagons carrying 600 passengers and a variety of goods through the countryside. However, this was not enough to convince the Peases. The truth was that Stephenson's locomotives were unreliable – they often ran out of steam and frequently needed repairs – so most of those early trains were hauled by horses; at one point, the Peases even considered turning the whole line over to horse-driven trains. Eventually, however, a much better engine designed by an engineer at Stephenson's works, Timothy Hackworth, saved the day, and it was the horses that were phased out.

The completed Stockton and Darlington Railway was recognized as a major technical advance over its predecessors, but, given the use of horses, it was still effectively a superior type of wagonway. It was also flawed. It had few passing loops – which allow trains travelling in opposite directions to pass each other – so arguments and even fights between drivers were common. The owners also made the mistake of allowing anyone who was prepared to pay a fee to use their vehicles on the line, which meant that all kinds of conveyances, rickety and unstable, were used, resulting in frequent breakdowns. Nevertheless, the railway attracted a lot of traffic, and, although it took time to become profitable, it established an important precedent – Stephenson had decided on a gauge of 1,435mm (4ft 8½in), which became standard across much of the world's railway network.

The heavy traffic on the Stockton and Darlington line encouraged entrepreneurs across Britain to promote local railway schemes. Many of these were never built, but the most important became Stephenson's next big project – the Liverpool and Manchester line, which was conceived on a much larger scale than the Stockton and Darlington and would become the world's first modern railway. A group of wealthy industrialists in the northwest of England, annoyed at paying local canal owners' extortionate rates to transport their goods, sought to link the two towns with a railway. The 50-km (31-mile) line was much more ambitious than the Stockton and Darlington, and although originally conceived as a

LOCOMOTION NO. 1
This is a model of the locomotive built by Robert Stephenson and Company in 1825, which opened the Stockton and Darlington Railway, hauling passenger and goods wagons.

freight railway, it would also carry passengers, as it linked two very important towns that had a combined population of 350,000. To ensure reliability, the trains would be run directly by the company, which set the pattern for nearly all the lines of the future.

Stephenson was invited by the directors to determine the route. Again, there was a major area of swampy peat bog, Chat Moss, as well as a series of streams and rivers that needed fording, requiring no fewer than 64 bridges, including a nine-arch viaduct over the River Sankey. Nothing on this scale had ever been attempted before. Stephenson was again both surveyor and engineer, and personally studied the terrain. Local landowners violently opposed the line, and there was a false start when the initial Parliamentary Bill (which needed to be passed for the line to be built) was thrown out at the behest of the rival canal owners – partly a result of an embarrassing performance by Stephenson, who proved to be somewhat inarticulate in the intimidating atmosphere of Parliament. For a time, Stephenson was replaced, but he was soon reinstated, and work began in 1827. Stephenson personally oversaw construction all along the line, often riding long distances on horseback to check on progress. His solution to the Chat Moss problem was to float the railway embankment on a bed of brushwood and heather. He also excavated a 3.2-km (2-mile) cutting through Olive Mount at the entrance to Liverpool, and built the Sankey Viaduct with sandstone blasted out of the cutting.

The form of traction to be used remained an issue throughout the line's construction. The directors of the railway favoured locomotives, but were unsure whether the existing engines were up to the task, so they launched a competition, the Rainhill Trials, to decide who should design the engines for the railway. Five entrants took part in the trials, which were held on a completed section of track on

SANKEY VIADUCT
The viaduct over the River Sankey was one of the trickiest engineering challenges that George Stephenson faced in constructing the Liverpool and Manchester Railway.

6 October 1829, in front of 15,000 spectators. The technical requirements were strict, particularly regarding weight, which was fixed at a maximum of 6 tonnes (6 tons), and the engines had to complete twenty 4-km (2-mile) trips at an average speed exceeding 16kph (10mph).

One of the entrants, *Cycloped*, turned out to be a prank (the engine was in fact a horse on a treadmill), so *Rocket*, the entry of George Stephenson's son, Robert, faced only three rivals: John Braithwaite and John Ericsson's *Novelty*, Timothy Hackworth's *Sans Pareil*, and Timothy Burstall's *Perseverance*. In the event, the trial was easily won. *Perseverance* never managed more than 10kph (6mph), and the other two failed to finish the course. Meanwhile, *Rocket* thundered up and down the track, ensuring that the Stephensons won the £500 prize to help develop their engines.

Since the line carried freight in both directions – the raw materials from the port at Liverpool, and the goods being brought back – as well as passengers, it was double-tracked from the outset, which greatly increased capacity. The opening day on 15 September 1830 was an epoch-making event, attracting people from around the

CYCLOPED
In the 1829 Rainhill Trials to find the best locomotive, *Cycloped* was proposed as an alternative to the steam engine. Powered by four horses on a treadmill, it was disqualified from the trials, which were won by Stephenson's *Rocket*.

"George Stephenson told me as a young man that railways will supersede almost all other methods of conveyance"

JOHN DIXON, QUOTED IN *LIFE OF GEORGE STEPHENSON*, 1875

world, several of whom would return home to inspire the building of railways in their own country. The celebrations, however, were marred by tragedy – an accident that resulted in the death of William Huskisson, a prominent politician. Huskisson crossed the tracks to greet the Prime Minister, the Duke of Wellington, when the ceremonial trains stopped at Parkside, halfway down the line. Panic set in when another train, *Rocket*, approached. Huskisson failed to climb onto the Duke's carriage in time, and fell under the oncoming train. His leg was shattered and, although Stephenson took him to Manchester for help – reaching an amazing speed of 56kph (35mph) en route – Huskisson died that evening.

Despite this tragedy, the completion of the Liverpool and Manchester marked the peak of Stephenson's career, but it was by no means its end. He went on to build numerous railways and his son, Robert, who concentrated mainly on improving the locomotives produced by Robert Stephenson and Company, constructed a far longer railway, the 180-km (112-mile) London and Birmingham line, which is now part of the West Coast Main Line. The locomotive works thrived and eventually produced more than 3,000 engines before being absorbed by a larger company in 1937. George Stephenson also advised early American rail promoters (see pp.34–35), and assisted in the construction of lines in Belgium (see pp.43–44) and Spain. The Stephensons certainly left their mark on the railways. When the line celebrated its 150th anniversary in 1980, the then-chairman of British Rail observed: "The world is a branch line of the Liverpool and Manchester".

Powering the Engine

Steam was recognized as a potential energy source as early as the 1st century CE, when steam-powered devices appeared in the writings of Hero of Alexandria. But it was not until the late 18th century that steam power was put to practical use in the form of stationary engines. The principles behind these engines were refined simultaneously by Owen Evans in the US and Richard Trevithick in England. Trevithick developed the idea of using high-pressure steam, which allowed the engine to be small enough to be mounted on wheels. This meant that, for the first time, steam could be used for propulsion. His engine *Puffing Devil* – the world's first steam locomotive – made its first journey on Christmas Eve 1801.

How steam is created

One of the key innovations pioneered by George Stephenson in his 1829 *Rocket* was the fire-tube boiler, which became a fundamental feature of all steam locomotives. Earlier engines had used a single fire tube to heat the water in the boiler, but Stephenson used 25 copper fire tubes to greatly increase the heat transfer between the firebox and the boiler, meaning that steam could be created much more efficiently. Later engines used superheater elements in place of the fire tubes.

Main steam pipe
Superheater element pipes
Steam pipe
Chimney
Blastpipe
Regulator valve
Safety valve
Water
Firebox
Valve rod
Valve
Boiler
Piston rod
Air flow
Cylinders

KEY
■ Steam exhaust
■ Superheated steam
■ Saturated steam
■ Hot gases

FROM WATER TO MOTION
In a typical steam engine, forward motion is achieved by burning coal to heat water, creating steam that is passed at high pressure to the cylinders in order to turn the locomotive's running gear.

FUELLING THE ENGINE

A fireman shovels coal into the firebox of a steam engine, ensuring that the fire tubes are hot enough to superheat the steam in the element pipes.

Steam propulsion

Steam from the boiler is superheated to over 100°C (212°F) and transferred to the cylinders at high pressure, pushing the pistons which turn the driving wheels via a series of pivots and rods, converting linear motion to rotation.

High-pressure steam in

Slide valve

Cylinder   Piston

PHASE 1: OUTWARD STROKE

High-pressure steam is fed via a sliding valve into the front of the cylinder where it expands and pushes the piston, which rotates the wheels by a half-turn.

Low-pressure steam exits

Valve rod

Piston rod

PHASE 2: EXHAUST

The wheel is connected to the sliding valve via a series of rods. These open the valve to allow the steam, which has now lost pressure, to escape.

High-pressure steam in

Piston

PHASE 3: RETURN STROKE

The movement of the valve also allows high-pressure steam to enter the back of the cylinder, allowing the return phase of the stroke to begin.

Steam exits via exhaust

Piston

PHASE 4: EXHAUST

Once the wheels have made another half turn, the sliding valve allows spent steam to escape and fresh steam to enter, and the cycle begins again.

The First American Railroads

IN 1828, THE 90-YEAR-OLD CHARLES CARROLL STEPPED UP to make the inaugural speech at the breaking ground ceremony for the new Baltimore and Ohio railway. Carroll had witnessed the birth of the United States firsthand — he was the only surviving signatory of the American Declaration of Independence. Half a century later, as he commemorated the launch of this ambitious project that aimed to reach into the heartland of the continent, his words proved to be remarkably prescient: "I consider this among the most important acts of my life, second only to my signing the Declaration of Independence, if even it be second to that".

The United States, which had only recently freed itself from the shackles of colonialism, was far behind Great Britain, its former colonial master, in terms of technological development. Its earliest railways — it soon adopted the name "railroads" — were dependent on British imports, as were its river-boats, factories, and mining operations, all of which ran on British steam engines. To catch up, American industrialists kept a close eye on British railway developments, and often travelled across the Atlantic to pick up the latest information. The size of the US, and the ambition of its people, made it fertile ground for the iron road, and it was perhaps inevitable that the new nation would soon boast more miles of track than the rest of the world put together. In fact, the US would end up, at the peak of the railway boom in 1916, with more than 400,000km (250,000 miles) of line, by far the biggest rail network the world has ever seen.

COLONEL JOHN STEVENS
Inventor and lawyer John Stevens saw the early commercial potential of the railroads over the waterways of the US.

NORTH AMERICAN RAILWAYS TO 1860

Until the advent of the railroads, transport in the US had been difficult and slow. There were a few canals, but these iced up in winter. The roads were very poor, owned by turnpike trusts that were unable to maintain them properly as the tolls that were collected were insufficient. Steamboats were the best form of transport, but they only gave access to certain parts of the country. The first American railroad pioneer was Colonel John Stevens, a successful steamboat designer and operator who was obviously rather taken with the railways since he wrote a pamphlet entitled *Documents Tending to prove the Superior Advantages of Rail-ways and Steam-Carriages over Canal Navigation*. As early as 1815, he obtained the first railroad charter for permission to construct a line linking the Delaware river near Trenton with the Raritan river in New Jersey, though in the event it was never built – no investors came forward to finance the scheme, which was far ahead of its time. Undeterred, in 1825 Stevens designed and built a steam locomotive, which ran on a circular track on a narrow-gauge line at his estate.

Stevens and his two sons were involved in a number of other early projects, notably the Philadelphia and Columbia line, which was built to link the port of Philadelphia with Columbia on the Susquehanna river to give merchants in Philadelphia access to Harrisburg and Western Pennsylvania. They also founded the Camden and Amboy Railroad, which ran from Camden, across the Delaware river from Philadelphia, to Amboy, on the New Jersey shore opposite New York. Initially, all these lines were horse-drawn, but inevitably, given the distances involved, locomotive traction was considered – and for that, British technology was needed. John Stevens' son Robert travelled to Britain and brought back a locomotive, *John Bull*, which was built in the Stephenson Works. It arrived in parts and was assembled by Isaac Dripps, an engineer who fitted pilot wheels at the front to help guide the locomotive around the sharper bends on the American railway, and who was also credited with inventing the "cowcatcher" – in reality a cow killer that pushed away cattle or deer that had roamed onto the line, invariably fatally.

Building lines in the US in the early 19th century was by no means easy. First, the promoters had to obtain a charter from the state government, then they had to persuade investors, who were often local people, to support the scheme, and finally they had to find sufficient workers to build the line as there was often a shortage of labour. There was one key advantage compared with other countries. Once a charter was obtained, the railway company had "eminent domain" – the right to take over any land required for the line's construction. Sometimes, though, the law was difficult to apply in

"The introduction of so powerful an agent as steam to a carriage on wheels will make a great change in the situation of man"

THOMAS JEFFERSON, 1802

AN EARLY SUCCESS
The pioneering *John Bull* locomotive served for
over 30 years. It is the oldest working self-
propelled vehicle in the world.

practice. When the Erie Railroad was being constructed across upstate
New York, it was planned to cross Native American land. The local
tribe demanded US$10,000 (in modern terms, around US$300,000, or
£185,000) for the right of way. Appalled, the railroad works manager
blustered that the land was no good for anything else apart from
growing corn or potatoes. The local chief responded: "It pretty good
for railroad", and got the money.

Most of the early railway development was stimulated by
competition between the great cities of the eastern US, such as
Baltimore, Philadelphia, New York, and Boston. Each wanted to obtain
cheap access to the Midwest, where towns were growing rapidly,
creating an important market for produce. Baltimore proved to be the
most adventurous in promoting a railway stretching deep into the
hinterland. The Baltimore and Ohio was the most significant of these
early schemes, being the first attempt to build a rail link between an
Atlantic port and the Ohio River, and so reaching the Midwest.

As with so many of these early lines, the promoters of the Baltimore
and Ohio were unsure about whether to use horses or steam
locomotives to haul the trains. Given that they wanted the line to
reach the town of Wheeling, nearly 650km (400 miles) from Baltimore,
it is extraordinary that they even considered using equine power, but
they arranged a competition between the hay eater and the coal
burner. A locomotive builder, Peter Cooper, had built a little engine
nicknamed *Tom Thumb* for the line, and it proceeded to impress the
promoters with a test run on the initial 21km (13 miles) of track that

had been completed, reaching an exhilarating 29kph (18mph). On the run back towards Baltimore, Cooper foolishly agreed to race his locomotive against a powerful grey horse. The animal soon took the lead, thanks to its faster acceleration, but was then overtaken by the steady little engine when Cooper opened the safety valve to provide extra power. However, he overreached himself: after the locomotive had gained a significant lead, the belt that drove its pulley snapped, and the engine eased to a halt. The equine victory proved Pyrrhic, however, as Cooper had done enough to persuade the promoters that steam haulage, rather than horsepower, was the only way to make the line viable. Although work started in 1828, and trains started operating on part of the line two years later, it was not until 1853 that the tracks reached Wheeling on the Ohio River owing to legal, financial, and technical difficulties.

THE RACE BETWEEN OLD AND NEW
The *Tom Thumb*'s race against a horse became the stuff of railway legend. The locomotive was the first American steam engine to run on a commercial railway.

Further south, there was a far longer pioneering line, which was completed much more quickly and used American technology. The Charleston and Hamburg was an attempt to revive Charleston's foreign exports, which had gone into decline, and its local merchants hoped to secure the trade of the rich cotton-growing area in the region. They chose steam power from the outset, and the first engine, the *Best Friend of Charleston*, built at the West Point Foundry in New York, pulled its first train in December 1830. Unfortunately, a couple of months later, the pioneering locomotive suffered an untimely demise when an inexperienced fireman, annoyed at the sound made by the escape of steam from its safety valve, sat on the offending piece of machinery – which caused the boiler to explode, killing the fireman and scalding the driver. Despite this mishap, the line was complete by 1833, and at 219km (136 miles), it was, for a time, the longest in the world.

American railways differed from their European counterparts in several respects. The key difference was one of scale, not just in the extent of their reach, as they gradually extended further and further

RAILROAD COACH
This replica of one of the earliest Baltimore and Ohio Railroad coaches shows how they were little more than stage-coach carriages placed on railroad bogies.

FRONT   BACK

B&O CENTENARY MEDAL, 1827-1927
This medal was issued to commemorate 100 years
of the history of one of America's oldest railways,
the Baltimore and Ohio. It depicts the famous early
locomotive *Tom Thumb*.

west, but also in the size of the trains and locomotives themselves.
Their characteristically huge, bulbous chimneys – needed to contain
the sparks that might otherwise set fire to the countryside – were far
taller than their European equivalents, for the American lines had
few bridges or tunnels. Consequently, even today American trains
are almost 1m (3ft) taller than those in Europe, enabling them to
carry much greater loads. Overall, US railroads were bigger in every
sense than those across the Atlantic. They covered greater distances,
and were longer and heavier because they used stronger and larger
locomotives, all of which gave them a distinctive style (see pp.40–41).

The efforts to cut the costs of the new lines were successful, and
US railways were far cheaper to build than their European equivalents,
but as a result, they were also less reliable and slower. Some aspects of
the railroads were, however, better from the start. Locomotives, for
example, were fitted with cabs for the crew, a "luxury" that was
necessitated by the rigours of the US climate, but which did not
become universal elsewhere until much later. Right from the start,
too, passengers travelled in carriages that were open plan, rather than
in individual compartments like those in Europe. These were necessary
because travelling longer distances meant that travellers required
ready access to conveniences, a facility that was not available on most

European trains until well into the second half of the 19th century. These early lines were successful and mostly profitable, which attracted a wave of investment into the new industry. By 1837, at least 200 railroads were being promoted. Many of these were unrealistic or promoted by crooks intent on cheating potential investors, but many schemes were still completed, and by the end of the decade 4,425km (2,750 miles) of railway were in operation – a remarkable rate of progress. The spur for most of these lines was freight, particularly coal and minerals, but increasing numbers of passengers also flocked to the trains. Soon, the short lines were followed by long trunk railways such as the Erie and the Pennsylvania lines, linking the Eastern Seaboard with the Midwest. Later, in the second half of the 19th century, the transcontinentals brought the railways to the West. Before long, every town wanted to be connected to the railroad network as it was considered vital for their prosperity. Prominent local citizens would band together and form a company to obtain a charter, often investing their own money. A mere 20 years later, at the outbreak of the Civil War (see pp.60–65), there were nearly 48,280km (30,000 miles) of railway in the US.

The railways, in fact, grew symbiotically with the US economy, transforming the nation from a predominantly agricultural country into the industrial powerhouse of the world, all within a few decades. It is impossible to know whether the tracks spread so quickly because of the rapid growth in wealth, or whether it was the other way round, but there is no doubt that the US thrived because of the growing railway system and that the railroads welded this vast nation together (see also pp.120–27).

The Early Years of American Steam

Starting with the Baltimore and Ohio Railroad in 1828, the growth of the American railway network enabled the Industrial Revolution to take hold in the northeastern US, and opened up the west coast to exploration and colonization. US locomotive engineers produced some innovative designs, including geared locomotives and the first rack railway (see pp.108–109).

BALTIMORE AND OHIO GRASSHOPPER NO.2: *ATLANTIC* (1832)
Named because its long connecting rods and vertical cylinders gave it an insect-like appearance when moving, the Grasshopper *Atlantic* was the first US-designed locomotive to see commercial service on American soil.

BALTIMORE AND OHIO GRASSHOPPER NO.8: *JOHN HANCOCK* (1836)
The *John Hancock* was an improved model of the Grasshopper class, featuring a covered cab and dual-powered axles. It was used continuously on the Baltimore and Ohio Railroad from 1836 until 1892.

Engine weighs 41,140kg (90,700lb)

Engine delivers 4694kg (10,350lb) of tractive effort

152cm- (60in-) diameter drivers

BALTIMORE AND OHIO NO.57: *MEMNON* (1848)
One of the oldest surviving freight trains in the US, the *Memnon* was designed to transport coal. Its hauling power was aided by eight driving wheels, the central pair of which are "blind" (lacking flanges) to enable the train to better negotiate curves in the line.

CUMBERLAND VALLEY RAILROAD NO.13: *PIONEER* (1851)

The *Pioneer* was a lightweight locomotive with only one pair of driving wheels. It was used to haul up to three passenger carriages, and is pictured here in the livery of its retirement in 1901.

SHAY NO.1: *LEETONIA* (1906)

The *Leetonia*, one of engineer Ephraim Shay's geared locomotives, used toothed driveshafts driven by three vertical cylinders to power all 12 of its wheels, making it ideal for hauling timber at low speeds on steep grades and tight curves.

MOORE-KEPPEL AND COMPANY CLIMAX NO.4 (1913)

Similar to the Shays, the Climax-class geared engines were used by lumber companies. A cylinder on either side of the boiler powered eight wheels via a centrally mounted transmission.

READING COMPANY NO.1251 (1918)

Built using parts from older locomotives, No.1251 was a shunting engine with six driving wheels. Its "saddletank" design meant that no tender was required – water was carried in a tank on top of the boiler.

Conical smokestack

Boiler runs at a pressure of 75psi

Front driver was originally flangeless

BALTIMORE AND OHIO NO.147: *THATCHER PERKINS* (1863)

Named after its designer, the company's Master of Machinery, *Thatcher Perkins* was rushed into service to meet the demands of the American Civil War. Its six driving wheels and four leading wheels were designed to cope with the steep tracks in the Appalachian Mountains.

48 × 66cm (19 × 26in) cylinders

Europe Takes to the Rails

A S BRITAIN WAS PIONEERING THE RAILWAYS, the cafés of Paris were abuzz with news of the recent developments – but not everyone was enthusiastic. Just as railway opponents in Britain had warned that it might be impossible to breathe when travelling at more than around 50kph (30mph), or that cows would stop producing milk because of the noise of the railway, in France and the rest of Europe, too, there were eminent doubters of this new technology. Indeed, the French habit of philosophizing over major issues meant that Parisian intellectuals discussed the pros and cons of the new railways in great detail – the writer Edmond de Goncourt warned that when travelling on the railway, "one was so jolted about that it was quite impossible to collect one's thoughts".

However, despite the naysayers, the major European countries – particularly France, Belgium, and the German Confederation – were now scrambling to construct their own lines. The economic advantages of doing so were obvious, but there were political reasons too – railways were not only vital assets in war, they could help bind nations together. At first, Europe was dependent on Britain both for technology and drivers, but many countries soon became independent, notably France, whose early efforts were close behind Britain's. In 1823, during a brief revival of the French monarchy, Louis XVIII signed an Act that permitted the construction of France's first railway. The 23-km (14-mile) track ran between St-Étienne and Andrézieux in the Massif Central and was built to carry coal from the mines to the Loire for shipment to

MARC SEGUIN
French inventor Marc Seguin (1786–1875) pioneered the multi-tube boiler for steam engines. He also developed the first suspension bridge in Europe.

the rest of the country. The line opened in 1827 and, although horse-drawn, it was an instant success. As a result, extensions were added, and by 1832 the line, which now used locomotives and carried passengers, stretched to the major city of Lyon. The elaborate French coaches were an improvement on the rather more austere British trains and were divided into compartments, an arrangement that soon became standard across Europe.

France's equivalent of George Stephenson (see pp.22–29) was Marc Seguin, a scientist and inventor who had in fact advised Stephenson on how to improve the boilers of his locomotives. He produced two locomotives for the extended St-Étienne–Lyon railway, each featuring a multi-tube boiler (see pp.30–31) and a mechanical fan to deliver oxygen to the fire. Later, in another case of Anglo-French cooperation, Robert Stephenson built locomotives designed by Seguin. The lengthy debate over the advantages and disadvantages of railway construction slowed the pace of development in France, so there were only 560km (350 miles) of track by 1840, compared with 3,200km (2,000 miles) in Britain.

The cause of the railway promoters was not helped when the world's first major rail disaster occurred between Versailles and Paris, in May 1842. The train, returning from Versailles, was so heavily laden with holidaymakers who had been watching the celebrations for the king's fête that it required two locomotives to haul it. The leading engine suffered a broken axle – a relatively commonplace event in the early days of railways – and then derailed, along with three carriages, which quickly burst into flames. The death toll was at least 50, and may have been as many as 200; people couldn't escape because they were locked in and many bodies were consumed by the inferno. As a result, the French authorities stopped locking passengers into their carriages, although the practice continued elsewhere, contributing to the high death toll of the 1889 Armagh disaster, the worst in Irish history (see pp.139).

Many other countries around Europe joined the Railway Age in the 1830s, and the state was usually much more directly involved than in Britain, where the government had remained aloof. Nowhere was this more true than in Belgium, a new country carved out of the Netherlands in 1830 and anxious to demonstrate its independence. The railways were an ideal way of doing so, since building a railway system was thought to stimulate a sense of national identity. Consequently, the country's first king, Leopold I, approved the design of a whole network, and in 1834 building started on the first line. This crossed the entire country from Antwerp in the north to Mons in the west, and into Prussia via Aachen in the east – a total of 248km (154 miles), a very ambitious scheme at that time. Together with an Ostend–Liege line forming an east–west axis, Belgium quickly created a fully planned national railway system – the first of its kind in the world. Inevitably, George Stephenson was involved, his company providing the first three locomotives and he himself travelling incognito in 1835 on the first train carrying the royal party. When the train broke down, Stephenson went to the engine to help fix the problem, and was knighted by the king for his pains. The support of the government gave Belgium a lead in railway development, and by 1843 most of the heart of Belgium's railway network – which forms a "cross" shape centred on Brussels – had been built, giving the heavily industrialized country the densest network in the world.

Germany's first railway also opened in 1835, doing so in Bavaria, where King Ludwig approved a steam-hauled line that ran the 6.5km (4 miles) between Nuremberg and Fürth. Unlike most of the inaugural lines, this was built mainly for passengers, as it relieved traffic on the busiest highway in Bavaria between the two towns. The congestion was the result of peculiar local circumstances. For centuries, the Nuremberg authorities had forbidden labourers and foreigners to live in the town, so they had to commute from Fürth, which had become a dormitory town, presaging a use for the railway that remains commonplace today. Saxony, another important German state, followed Bavaria's lead, building Germany's first major railway, linking Leipzig with Dresden. Saxony was the industrial heartland of Germany, similar in character to the northwest of England, where the pioneering Liverpool and Manchester line had been built (see pp.25–29). More than 200 factories had sprung up in the region, and local

NUMBER OF LOCOMOTIVES IN GERMANY BY 1880

9,400

THE FIRST GERMAN RAILWAY
This contemporary painting shows the departure
of the locomotive *Adler* from Nuremberg in 1835.
The *Adler* was the first commercial locomotive in
use in Germany and was in service until the 1850s.

industrialists, realising that a railway was essential to carry the
minerals and ore needed by the factories, quickly raised the money to
build the 105-km (65-mile) line, which was built remarkably swiftly
thanks to the use of British technology and personnel.

The railways were particularly important for Germany as a
means of uniting the country. As early as 1817, economist and
visionary thinker Frederick List had understood the importance of
the railways for Germany. He argued that a nation could prosper only
through trade and industry, and that a fast, efficient rail network
could carry food and industrial products throughout the country.
His theory was borne out. Customs duties between states were
soon scrapped as impractical, and within a generation of the first rail
line being completed, Germany's railway system had helped it
become a powerful unified state.

Like the Nuremberg–Fürth line, the first line in Holland, another
relatively early starter, was also built for passengers rather than
freight. The Holland Iron Railway between Amsterdam and

Haarlem opened in 1839 and reached Rotterdam eight years later. It was extremely successful, killing off the competing coach and barge traffic that had previously dominated the route between the country's two main cities. Holland, though, did not have the centrally planned scheme of its Belgian neighbour and so never developed such an intensive network.

The Belgian, German, and Dutch railways were all steam-hauled, but the idea that railways could be operated successfully by horses still lingered. In Austria, remarkably, the early network was entirely horse-drawn, and grew to an extensive size. It included the world's longest horse-drawn railway – a 145-km (90-mile) line linking Linz in Upper Austria with Budweis in Bohemia (home of the world-renowned beer, now in the Czech Republic). The horse-drawn system was later extended further to the salt works at the Upper Austrian health resort of Gmunden, and by 1836 it had reached an impressive 274km (170 miles). Only then did the Austrians replace horses with steam engines.

The railways of both Italy and Russia began as royal initiatives, albeit for the private purposes of connecting royal palaces. In Italy, the King of the Two Sicilies, the portly Ferdinand II, fancied connecting his main palace in Naples to his other residence on the bay of Naples at Portici with an 8-km (5-mile) railway line, which was completed in October 1839. The idea had been recommended to him by a Frenchman, Armand Bayard de la Vingtrie, who was keen to make money from railway schemes. The first section of the line was built quickly and proved to be immensely popular, carrying up to 1,000 people per day. Oddly, the king himself eschewed travelling on the inaugural journey, perhaps because he was aware of the risks of train travel.

In Russia, Tsar Nicholas I built the first railway line between his main residence in St Petersburg and Tsarskoe Selo, the enormous royal residence favoured by Catherine the Great. He was advised by

THE RAILWAYS COME TO ITALY
This 1839 painting by Salvatore Fergola depicts the inaugural train leaving Portici station in Naples, Italy. The line was Italy's first railway, and today forms part of the Naples–Salerno line.

an Austrian engineer, Franz Anton von Gerstner, who was keen to bring Russia into the railway fold, and had sought to build a far more ambitious line between St Petersburg and Moscow. Initially, however, only the Tsarskoe Selo line was commissioned, and opened in 1837 with the first train, carrying eight full coaches, taking a mere 28 minutes to reach Tsarskoe Selo — an impressive average speed of almost 50kph (30mph). The following year, the line was extended by 26km (16 miles) to Pavlosk, a small holiday resort complete with buffets, concerts, and a ballroom to entertain the St Petersburg crowds on their day trips. To attract the crowds, the railway subsidised the public entertainment at Pavlovsk, which is described in Dostoevsky's *The Idiot* as "one of the fashionable summer resorts near St Petersburg". At first, the line was hauled by horses and various locomotives imported from Britain and Belgium, but before long the animals, exhausted from pulling the heavy trains, were put out to grass and steam locomotives were introduced. The line was a great success, with people flocking to the railway both out of curiosity and the desire to sample the attractions. More than 725,000 people travelled on the line in its first year, an average of 2,000 per day. The 640-km

THE LEGACY OF TSAR NICHOLAS I
The St Petersburg–Moscow line was Russia's first major railway. Wary officials warned the tsar – wrongly, as it turned out – that allowing people to travel on the line would result in an uprising.

"Railway! A magical aura already surrounds the word; it is a synonym for civilization, progress and fraternity"

PIERRE LAROUSSE, 1867

(400-mile) long St Petersburg–Moscow line was completed in 1851, becoming one of the longest and most impressive trunk routes in the world at the time.

Most countries in Europe adopted the 1,435-mm (4ft 8½-in) gauge devised by Stephenson (see p.25), and this proved vitally important in ensuring that a continental network was created, with trains passing through borders relatively easily – although customs and technical factors relating to signalling and driver training usually meant delays at the frontier. Russia and Spain were exceptions – both used a 1½-m (5-ft) gauge for fear of invasion from hostile neighbours, reckoning that making trains change gauge would prove a useful defensive barrier.

Travelling on these early lines was not always made easy, either by the regimes of the day or the railway companies. Governments were suspicious of their citizens' desire to travel, and the companies were diligent in collecting fares. On the Leipzig–Dresden line, for example, there were no advance ticket sales and access to the station was allowed only a quarter of an hour before the train left – a practice that persists in remote parts of Europe even today. Passengers were required to purchase a return ticket and children under 12 were banned. In Russia, there was also an extraordinary amount of bureaucracy involved in taking a train. Passengers had to obtain an internal passport before travelling, and then go to their local police station to obtain permission for the journey. Even today, Russians have to show their internal passport before buying a ticket for a long-distance journey. Nevertheless, despite the bureaucracy and the technical problems incurred on many pioneering lines, all these early railways proved popular and successful, spurring the rapid spread of rail travel throughout Europe and to many other parts of the world.

Western European Railways

In the mid-1830s, railway technology spread from its birthplace in Britain to continental Europe. Belgium enthusiastically adopted steam locomotion as a means to cement its fledgling nationhood. France stifled the iron road with bureaucracy (see box, opposite), while the German states used the railways to further the case for national unification. The lines spread in the ensuing decades until Europe was criss-crossed with a vast web of railways. Spain and Portugal, however, chose to use different gauges from the rest of the continent. This map shows modern Europe's main lines.

SWEDE

NORWAY

OSLO

STOCKHOLM

GLASGOW EDINBURGH

DENMARK

EIRE
DUBLIN

UNITED
KINGDOM

COPENHAG

LONDON AMSTERDAM HAMBURG

ATLANTIC
OCEAN

BRUSSELS
BELGIUM GERMANY BERLIN
PARIS FRANKFURT POLAI
LUXEMBURG
PRAGUE

FRANCE VIENNA
AUSTRIA

BAY OF
BISCAY

SWITZERLAND BUDAPES
LYON MILAN HUNG
SLOVENIA
TURIN ZARGREB
BOSNIA
SARAJEVO
PORTUGAL CROA

MARSEILLE

LISBON MADRID BARCELONA
SPAIN
ROME ITALY

MEDITERRANEAN
SEA

A SLOW START FOR FRANCE

Given its large landmass and ready supply of raw materials, it is perhaps surprising that France was one of Europe's laggards in the early days of railway construction (see pp.42–43). Legislation to permit the laying of rails in France was passed in 1842, but growth was hindered by a high degree of government intervention: tracks and infrastructure were built by the state, while only the locomotives and rolling stock were supplied by railway companies.

THE CONTINENT'S FIRST LINE

In 1835, the very first railway in continental Europe was built in Belgium. The line ran about 27km (16 miles) from Brussels to the city of Mechelen, which brought about the rise of metalworking industries in the town. Many new European lines used British expertise in their construction, seeing as Britain had a decade's head start on rivals.

KEY

○ Major city

—— Main line

—— National boundary

Railway Mania

THE SUCCESS OF THE FIRST RAILWAYS stimulated enormous interest from potential investors and promoters of new lines across the world. There was a tendency for people to try to jump on the bandwagon, creating periods of railway mania, which occurred in nearly every country that developed a network. Unfortunately, not all of these promoters were honest, and some had the sole intention of trying to make people part with their money.

Oddly, the first mania happened before a single line was completed. In 1824–25, during the run-up to the opening of the Stockton and Darlington Railway (see pp.24–25), entrepreneurs around Britain put forward ideas for other lines, and prospectuses for around 70 were published – a remarkable number, given that they were still an unproven technology. However, a downturn in the economy following a poor harvest in 1825 and a spate of banking failures soon soured the optimism, and almost all of these schemes were quietly forgotten. The success of the Liverpool and Manchester line (see pp.25–29) prompted another spate of railway promotion in the mid-1830s, but it was the huge surge in applications for new lines from 1844 onwards that led to the use of the term "railway mania". The phenomenon recalled previous promotional fevers such as the South Sea Bubble of 1719–20 and the canal mania of 1791–94, and foreshadowed more recent frenzies such as the dot-com boom of the 1990s.

In Britain, by the mid-1840s, railway construction was established as a legitimate and profitable business, and the healthy economic conditions were ripe for a major boom. The usual method for raising capital was to organise local public meetings at which investors would buy "scrip" – vouchers that could later be exchanged for future shares – for a small deposit in the proposed company. Having raised part of the capital, the promoters would then go to Parliament for approval of their proposal. There had been something of an economic slump in the early 1840s, but as the economy recovered there was an upsurge in railway promotion. Railways were seen as a method of getting rich quickly, and from 1844 to 1847, British parliamentary approval was obtained for more than 12,800km (8,000 miles) of line – nearly five times the amount that had already been laid, and a large proportion of Britain's current rail network of 15,750km

(9,790 miles). At the time, building a railway was a relatively simple task, provided the terrain was favourable – no more difficult than opening a local shop or erecting a row of houses. Once permission was obtained, it was a matter of creating a narrow permanent way, laying the track, and putting in the odd raised wooden platform at stations. There was none of the complexity of today's technically sophisticated railways.

The rapidity with which the mania took hold was astonishing. In 1843, only 160km (100 miles) of new line were approved by the British Parliament, but over the following three years the figures were respectively around 1,200km (800 miles), nearly 4,800km (3,000 miles) and an astonishing 7,200km (4,500 miles), as 272 acts were granted. The scale of this boom can be judged by the fact that it represented a theoretical amount of £700m worth of capital investment – ten times

"THE RAILWAY JUGGERNAUT OF 1845"
This cartoon depicts the ruthless business of railway mania with vultures circling overhead, crocodiles wearing lawyers' wigs, and the devil perched on a locomotive called *Speculation*.

Britain's annual exports at the time. However, the boom collapsed even faster than it grew. The economy slumped again in 1847, and as a result, only 27km (17 miles) of new line were approved by 1849, but an astonishing two thirds of the mileage approved thus far was eventually completed within a few years, and even some of the failed projects were revived in the smaller booms of 1852–53 and the 1860s.

Although most of the projects, even the failed ones, were genuine attempts at building a railway, some of them were blatantly fraudulent, while others were based on the belief that the expansion would last forever. This was the how the biggest fraudster of the period, George Hudson, created a massive empire, which inevitably collapsed when the bubble burst. A strange-looking fellow, who one biographer describes as having "a cannon-ball of a head set upon his bulky shoulders, the formality of a neck having been disposed of", Hudson was full of energy and had a fondness for the good life – perhaps the typical profile of a fraudster. He did, in fact, succeed in building several railways, including the core of the Midland Railway, which was one of the most extensive lines in Britain. He had some other good ideas, too, such as establishing a ticket clearing house through which railway companies reimbursed each other for running trains on each other's tracks. As he grew in confidence, however, he used the money he raised for new schemes to pay dividends on previous projects – what is now called a Ponzi scheme. His accounting practices had, in fact, been so dubious that on his demise it was impossible to find out where all the money had gone. He had become rich, as one wag put it, "by keeping everything but his accounts". His career, so glittering that he was elected Lord Mayor of York and later an MP, came to an abrupt end in 1849 when his dishonesty was exposed, after which he vanished into obscurity.

THE INFAMOUS GEORGE HUDSON
Railway promoter, entrepreneur, and fraudster George Hudson created a business empire that changed the face of railway development forever.

"This big swollen gambler… deserved a coalshaft from his brother mortals"

THOMAS CARLYLE, PHILOSOPHER AND WRITER, ON GEORGE HUDSON

Switzerland underwent a period of railway mania in the 1850s, helped by Alfred Escher, a powerful Swiss businessman and politician, and a keen supporter of the railways. He had observed the growth of railways in other countries, and feared that Switzerland was missing out on the economic prosperity offered by a rail network and would become "the sad face of Europe's backwater". In 1852, he helped push through a law allowing private companies to build and run railways. This launched a frenzy of construction by competing firms – joined by Escher himself, who founded Swiss Northeastern Railway and enjoyed great success. Over the following decades, the Swiss rail network extended across the country, including the ambitious Gotthard Railway in the 1870s (see pp.106–107).

In France, a law passed in 1865 to encourage railway construction in remote areas led to a period of rapid railway expansion. At the time, France's railways were controlled by six large companies, and the idea was to encourage new entrants on to the network to ensure better coverage of rural areas where the six were reluctant to go. The law allowed local authorities to sponsor these lines, and speculators piled in, seeing the possibility of making money out of the grants being offered, despite the fact that most of these lines would never be viable. Within ten years, nearly 4,800km (3,000 miles) of remote lines had been built, many with a narrow gauge to reduce costs. However, few of them made money and they soon had to be rescued by the state, forming the core of what later became the French nationalized railway system, SNCF.

In Italy, too, it was the government that stimulated a period of rapid expansion. Creating a national rail network was seen as essential after the unification of Italy in 1861, and the state sponsored a rapid expansion through a concession system. However, most of the companies that built the lines had insufficient capital and got into financial difficulties when the lines, which were poorly constructed, failed to attract enough passengers. The state inevitably took over and nationalized the railways, which resulted in many investors losing money.

Perhaps unsurprisingly, it was the US that suffered the biggest bout of "railway fever", as they called it. There were, in fact, sporadic boom periods of railway construction throughout the latter part of the 19th century, as humorously described by the historian Stewart H. Holbrook, who related the story of a fictional town called Brownsville:

> First some up and coming individual, or simply a fanatical dreamer, said forcibly that his home town Brownsville needed a steam railroad... the idea grew and blossomed and burgeoned and even soared meanwhile taking on all of the beautiful hues of the sky in the Land of Opportunity. It also dripped with gold, gold for all of Brownsville, soon to be a mighty metropolis, teeming with commerce.

... and so on, until an application was made to the state for permission to build the Brownsville Railroad. This type of scene was enacted many times over across the US during every bout of railroad fever.

The US has more than its share of crooks in its railway history. A group of "robber barons" emerged from the early railway companies, often using dishonest methods of speculation to gain control of profitable lines. It was a time of wild risks and gambles. In one famous incident – a takeover battle for the Erie Railroad – three railway barons, led by Jay Gould, holed up in a hotel in New Jersey with several million dollars in cash, protected by armed guards to evade the jurisdiction of the New York courts, which had found in favour of their rival, Cornelius Vanderbilt. (Gould and his associates did eventually win the battle for the Erie Railroad – see pp.241–42). Such events, while not commonplace, were part and parcel of the colourful period of railway speculation in the US.

The final bout of speculative building in the US was in the early 20th century, and involved a series of tramways called "electric interurbans". These were a hybrid of trains and trams that connected towns up to 80km (50 miles) apart with cheaply built single lines sited next to existing highways. There was a remarkable period of expansion of these lines from just 3,200km (2,000 miles) at the turn of the century – by 1906 there were 14,400km (9,000 miles), and by the outbreak of World War I, 24,000km (15,000 miles). By then, it was possible to travel all the way from Wisconsin to New York using a series of interurbans. It was a cheap ride, costing 10 cents for the journey, but it was slow, for the interurbans averaged around 32kph

"NORD 2-3-0"
A French locomotive leaves a depot in Boulogne.
France's national rail system, the SNCF, was founded to
rescue the struggling private railway lines following a
surge in development. It still operates today.

(20mph) at best. Sadly, according to one historian, "the interurbans
were a rare example of an industry that never enjoyed a prolonged
period of prosperity", and most investors lost all their money. The
demise of the interurbans was swift because they were inherently
unprofitable, serving sparsely populated areas and facing competition
from the growing use of motor vehicles. Already at the start of World
War I, systems were closing and they were all but wiped out by the
1930s, when their vehicles and tracks needed renewing and there was
no money for such investment.

All the manias across the world left their mark. Many investors
lost their shirts, but many of the lines were built and a good proportion
of those survive today. As with other industries, the manias had
their roots in genuine need, and many of today's lines worldwide
owe their existence to these excesses.

Wheels and Bogies

The wheels of a locomotive are mounted on a chassis known as a bogie (see box, below) and are designed to keep the engine aligned with the tracks. Each wheel tapers slightly from the inside outwards, which helps to steer the train around curves (see panel, opposite), and is fitted with a projecting rim or "flange" on the inside edge. Ordinarily this should not touch the track, and is a safety feature to prevent the train from derailing. Wheelsets — two wheels joined by an axle — are variously sized and perform subtly different functions: large driving wheels are powered by the pistons of the locomotive, while smaller, unpowered leading and trailing wheelsets support the weight of the engine and enable the train to pass through junctions and bends in the line.

Bogies

Each leading and trailing wheelset is mounted on a frame beneath the carriage. The strength and rigidity of the structure, or "bogie", enables the wheelsets to resist torsional forces when the train turns. Most bogies fix wheelsets in place in an inflexible frame, but "steerable" bogies allow the axles to rotate laterally around a pivot between the two wheelsets, increasing the stability of the train around bends. Modern bogies also house the train's braking and suspension systems.

Each wheelset consists of two wheels connected by an axle

Axles may rotate laterally for steering

GERMAN RAILWAY BOGIE, c. LATE 19TH CENTURY

THE IRON GIANT
A steam engine is lowered onto its bogie, with large driving wheels and smaller leading wheels visible. As well as being strong enough to carry heavy engines, train wheels and bogies were engineered to withstand immense rotational and torsional forces.

How it works

The flanged wheel was invented in 1789 by English engineer William Jessop. The raised rim on the inner wheel edge prevents derailment and does not touch the rail during normal running, unless the track is poorly maintained. The conical edges of the train wheels allow the wheelsets to slide across the heads (tops) of the rails, enabling the train to follow curves. Railway engineers observed that the characteristic side-to-side swaying action of a train in motion was due to its tapered wheelsets wobbling up and down the railheads in order to "hunt" for equilibrium. They termed this movement "hunting oscillation".

Conical wheel edges slide across railhead

Flanges do not touch the rails

Railhead

Wheelset

TOP VIEW

NEGOTIATING CURVES

On a curved track, the train's outer wheels have to travel slightly further. To compensate, the wheelset slides across the railhead, allowing the outer wheels to use the larger radius of their inner edge. The inside wheels meanwhile slide onto the smaller radius of their outer edge. This action allows the train to lean into the bend, much like a cyclist leaning into a corner.

Point of contact with rail during straight running

Wheelset tilts as train leans into the bend

Outside wheel slides up head onto larger radius

Inside wheel slides down head onto smaller radius

Railhead

SIDE VIEW

The American Civil War

BOTH GOVERNMENTS AND MILITARY commanders soon appreciated the potential of the railways for warfare. Shortly after its opening in 1830, the Liverpool and Manchester Railway (see p.25–29) was used to carry a regiment of troops from Manchester to the docks in Liverpool en route to quell a rebellion in Ireland. The 50-km (31-mile) journey took just over two hours, rather than the two days it would have taken by foot, and the troops arrived in a much fresher state. Around this time, revolutionary fervour was brewing in Europe, and by the late 1840s, rulers across the continent were using the railways to help crush these revolts. The first major movement of troops by rail took place in 1846, when a contingent of 14,500 Prussian soldiers was sent to put down the Krakow rebellion of Polish nationalists against their Austrian rulers. The Prussians rapidly suppressed the uprising, with considerable bloodshed, after covering the 340-km (200-mile) journey in just two days. Then, two years later, Tsar Nicholas I of Russia, the most reactionary of the mid-19th-century monarchs, sent 30,000 troops on the newly built Warsaw–Vienna railway to help his ally, Emperor Ferdinand I of Austria, to put down another nationalist rebellion – this time in Hungary. Again, the result was a defeat for the revolutionaries, with much loss of life.

After this, the scale of troop movements around Europe increased. In the winter of 1850, Austria used the railways to send a 75,000-strong army, along with 8,000 horses and untold equipment, from Vienna to Bohemia. Due to poor weather and the fact that trains travelled along a single line, the move took longer than expected – 26 days for a mere 240-km (150-mile) journey – demonstrating that an enormous amount of planning was still needed to use the railways effectively. Three years later, the French organized a massive movement of troops during the Crimean War, in what is now Ukraine. Most of the army of 400,000 men despatched to fight in the Crimea travelled to the Mediterranean seaports on the railway being built between Paris and Marseilles. Although the line was not finished, troops were able to use long sections of it, greatly improving their journey. In fact, it was during the Crimean War that the first railway line intended specifically for military purposes was built. This was the work of the British, who fought alongside the French, and who had struggled to bring men and supplies up to Sevastopol, which they were besieging, from the port of Balaklava 13km (8 miles) away. The hilly road was little more than a dirt track, and a bottleneck soon built up in the port. To relieve it, a group of navvies (see pp.84–89) was sent from Britain to build a line between the port and the camp outside Sevastopol. They were a wild bunch, causing mayhem on their journey by getting drunk and trying to catch apes in Gibraltar, but they were very effective builders. The Grand Crimean Central Railway — an overblown name for a short narrow-gauge railway powered partly by horses and partly by steam engines — was built remarkably fast (just seven weeks) in 1855. It proved to be of enormous value, enabling troops and provisions, including heavy guns, to be hauled up the hill to support the assault on Sevastopol. The railway made it possible to bring an unprecedented number of guns to bear on the town, which eventually succumbed under the barrage, effectively ending the war.

It was during the American Civil War, however, that railways came of age as strategic assets. The conflict had been brewing for a long time, and had its roots in the differences between the northern and southern states. The North was industrializing and developing its economy on the basis of manufacturing, but the South remained primarily agricultural (cotton was its principal export) and depended on slave labour. The trigger for the war was the inauguration of Abraham

WAR ON THE RAILS
This newspaper sketch shows the capture of a train near Gunpowder Ridge, on 11 July 1864, during the invasion of Maryland.

DERAILED CIVIL WAR LOCOMOTIVE
Soldiers survey the aftermath of an attack in 1864.
Both the deployment and destruction of railways
played a crucial role in the American Civil War.

Lincoln as president in 1861. Lincoln opposed the expansion of slavery to
new states; the southern states, fearing the complete abolition of slavery,
seceded from the Union in the spring of 1861, thus starting the war.

The Civil War was a bloody affair, claiming the lives of 620,000 soldiers.
The battles between the Southern Confederates and the Northern
Federal Army were fought on an unprecedented scale. Throughout
history, even wars that raged over long periods typically featured only a
handful of battles. However, during the four years of the war between
the states, a remarkable 10,000 military encounters took place, of which
nearly 400 were significant enough to be considered full-scale battles –
which means a battle was fought every four days. Moreover, the war was
fought over an area even bigger than Europe, a vast territory that was
only made accessible by the railways.

By the outbreak of the war, US railroads extended over more than
48,000km (30,000 miles). The lines covered most of the eastern states
and much of the Midwest, so both troops and matériel could be carried
rapidly around the country. Both sides understood the importance of
the railways, but the North made better use of them. Even before the
war started, Lincoln ensured that the key railways were taken under
government control and that military traffic was given priority. The

outcome of the first major land battle of the war – at Bull Run, Virginia, a small river just 32km (20 miles) south of Washington, DC – was determined by the clever use of the railways by the Confederates. The battle started as an attempt by the Federal Army to bring the war to a rapid close by capturing Richmond, the Confederate capital. The Federal Army attacked the enemy alongside Bull Run, and initially gained the upper hand. However, they found themselves defeated by a counter-attack, made possible by the quick arrival of Confederate reinforcements via rail from the Shenandoah Valley in the west. This was an important lesson for both sides, and from then on most of the war's major battles took place at or near railway junctions or stations.

The Federal Army launched the Peninsular Campaign – another effort to capture Richmond – in March the following year, and brought "the war's wizard of railroading" into action. This was Herman Haupt, a brilliant engineer whose background made him the ideal man to harness the railways for wartime use: he had graduated from West Point, the US Army training college, but then became a professor of mathematics and engineering, and had been appointed superintendent of the Pennsylvania Railroad, one of America's most important lines.

Haupt established two main principles regarding the use of railways in war. Firstly, the military should not interfere with the operation of services, since it was vital to keep to reliable railway timetables. Secondly, it was crucial to ensure that empty freight cars were returned to their place of origin and not used as warehouses (or even offices by senior personnel), because running out of wagons in wartime could mean the difference between success or failure in battle.

Haupt's first task in the Peninsular Campaign was to repair the Richmond, Fredericksburg, and Potomac Railroad, a 24-km (15-mile) vital artery that connected the two capitals, Richmond, Virginia, and Washington, DC. The Confederates had wrecked the line in order to damage the Federal Army's capability, and they had done a particularly thorough job, twisting the rails so that they could not be used again and

THE WESTERN AND ATLANTIC RAILROAD DELIVERED AN ARMY OF

100,000

MEN TO GENERAL SHERMAN'S FORCES AT ATLANTA

"Haupt has built a bridge… and there is nothing in it but cornstalks and beanpoles"

ABRAHAM LINCOLN, 28 MAY 1862

burning down bridges. Several kilometres of track had been put out of commission, but in response, Haupt performed what seemed to be a miracle. He rebuilt the railway within two weeks, making it possible for a full complement of up to 20 trains per day to run on the line. His greatest achievement was to erect a 120-m (400-ft) trestle bridge high over the Potomac Creek in just nine days, even though he had only unskilled workers and poor, unseasoned wood at his disposal. This spectacular achievement was lauded by Lincoln when he visited the site: "I have seen the most remarkable structure that human eyes ever rested upon". Perhaps unsurprisingly, however, the president only viewed the bridge from the embankment and did not venture over it.

Haupt's talents also included devising methods to destroy the enemy's railways, a task that proved to be just as important as repairing existing lines and building new ones. Thanks to Haupt's principles, troop movements by rail were carried out without any major mishaps. The greatest movement of the war was when 23,000 men were needed to defend Tennessee after the defeat of the Federal Army at the Battle of Chickamauga in Georgia. The defeated army had retreated to Chattanooga, a rail hub in neighbouring Tennessee, and needed reinforcements. In an extraordinary operation, involving seven railways and two ferry trips, the reserve troops travelled 1,950km (1,200 miles) in just two weeks to relieve the siege of Chattanooga. The town then became a crucial stage for the Federal Army's invasion of the South, which ended the war. That final push was also dependent on the railways. When General Sherman left Chattanooga on his march towards Atlanta, which signalled the end of the conflict, he relied on the railways for supplies. As he wrote after the war, with military precision:

That single stem of railroad [The Western and Atlantic] supplied an army of 100,000 men and 32,000 horses for the period of 196 days from May 1 to November 19 1864. To have delivered that amount of

THE GENERAL
Buster Keaton heroically lifts a railway sleeper out
of the path of his engine in hot pursuit of hijacked
locomotive *The General* in the film of the same name.

forage and food by ordinary wagons would have required 36,800 wagons,
of six mules each... a simple impossibility in such roads as existed
in that region.

The most famous episode of the war – immortalized in *The General*, a
1926 Buster Keaton film – occurred on the railways. A group of 21 Federal
soldiers led by James Andrews penetrated enemy lines at Marietta, a
town near Atlanta, Georgia, and stole a train hauled by a locomotive
called *The General*, with the intention of wrecking the Western and Atlantic
Railroad. A Southern conductor, William Fuller, furious at the hijacking
of his train, pursued the hijackers, first on foot, and then on a gandy
dancers' handcart (a device used for track maintenance). He eventually
commandeered a locomotive and, evading the obstacles placed on the
line by Andrews, caught up with *The General* when it ran out of fuel. The
raiders fled into the countryside, but seven, including Andrews, were
caught and hanged, while the rest escaped to the North. This, however,
was a side-show. The lesson of the war was clear. Railways were now
invaluable military assets, and so they remained for 100 years or more.

Signals in the Steam Age

In the earliest days of the railways, trains ran up and down single tracks and signalling was not a necessity. As rail traffic and speeds increased, however, train safety grew to be a major concern and signalling became essential to prevent collisions. Hand and arm signals were soon replaced by flags and lanterns, and in 1832 the first elevated wayside signalling was introduced. By the 1860s, mechanical signals were in general use, but no single system was agreed upon. Semaphore signals were widely adopted in Britain, but were not standardized until 1923, while ball signals were common in the US. Colour light signals came into use from the 1950s.

HAND AND ARM SIGNALS
The earliest form of signalling – hand and arm signs – was still in use in the 1930s. Here a signalman for the Southern Pacific Railroad uses hand signals to direct a slow-moving freight train in 1937.

Signalling tokens

One of the main safety mechanisms in train signalling is the block system, which allows only one train to enter each "block" of a railway at a time. In the 19th century, tokens provided evidence that a block was free. In the original "staff and ticket" system, the signalman gave the train driver a token or "staff" to allow entry to a block. At the other end, the staff was given up, allowing a train to proceed in the opposite direction. If a second train followed the first along the same "block", both carried written permission or a "ticket". Later systems were operated by means of tokens inserted in a trackside machine.

BALL TOKENS, INDIA

Early signal systems

As railway networks became more complex, the companies that ran them largely relied on timetabling to maintain train distances and prevent accidents. However, signals indicating if a line or "block" (section of the line) was clear were crucial in case of timetable alteration or train breakdown.

BALL SIGNAL (1837)
The most common signal on the early US railways, it gave rise to the term "highball": when the ball was raised, it was safe to proceed, although this was later reversed.

SEMAPHORE (1840)
Widespread after the 1850s, and still in use today, it signalled "danger" in the horizontal position and "all clear" when angled either up or down.

WOOD'S CROSSBAR SIGNAL (1840)
Crossbar signals, in use from the 1830s, indicated on/off (stop/go) with a revolving wooden board. When the crossbar was swung parallel to the line it signalled clear.

REVOLVING DISC SIGNAL (1840)
The disc revolved vertically to signal stop and go, much like semaphore signals. In keeping with most signals of the time, the disc was made of wood and painted red.

DOUBLE DISC SIGNAL (1846)
Like the crossbar, the double disc rotated on a wooden or steel signal post. Both were shortlived, however, as the "clear" signal was hard for train drivers to see.

Heroic Failures

THE RAILWAYS AS WE KNOW THEM were not the only form of rail transport that was considered in the latter half of the 19th century. Indeed, before the current system became standard, tracks, wagons, and engines were combined in all kinds of ways that may seem eccentric today. Some of these ideas might have been successful had they received the proper attention, but others were patently ill-considered and bound to fail.

Perhaps the most spectacular failure was the "atmospheric railway" – a brainchild of British engineer Isambard Kingdom Brunel, the otherwise unimpeachable builder of the Great Western Railway, the SS *Great Britain* (the first propeller-driven iron ship), and the Royal Albert Bridge. His contention was that locomotives were uneconomical because they had to haul themselves as well as their trains (which made uphill travel even harder), and his solution was to remove the engine altogether, creating a train that was propelled by a series of stationary steam engines located along

BRUNEL'S FOLLY
A section of Brunel's atmospheric railway lies reconstructed in the town of Didcot, Oxfordshire. The vacuum tube in the centre contained a piston that hauled the trains.

the track. At the time, locomotives were far from popular — people were afraid of suffocating in tunnels and of sparks setting fire to farmland — so alternatives were welcomed, and in 1844 an Act of Parliament sanctioned Brunel's idea. It was to be tested on the South Devon Railway, a broad-gauge line that Brunel would build from Exeter to Plymouth.

The atmospheric system worked by means of a tube that ran down the centre of the track. This functioned like the cylinder of a steam engine (see pp.30–31), having a piston inside it that was connected to the first carriage of the train (the "piston carriage"). The connecting arm of the piston travelled through a slit in the top of the tube, which was kept airtight with a long strip of leather and metal components that opened and closed as the piston passed through it. A steam engine at the side of the track created a vacuum inside the tube, which forced the piston forwards, hauling the train along with it. The train then travelled some 5km (3 miles) until it reached a second engine, which created a new vacuum and propelled the train to the next engine, and so on. A total of 11 engine houses were completed for the line, which took it as far as Newton, about 42km (26 miles) short of the planned terminus at Plymouth — the final series of engine houses was never built.

The railway opened in September 1847 on the 18-km (11-mile) stretch of line between Exeter and Teignmouth, and at first it seemed to work well. According to Brunel's biographer:

> the new method of traction was universally approved of. The motion of the train, relieved of the impulsive action of the locomotive, as singularly smooth and agreeable; and passengers were freed from the annoyance of coke dust and the sulphurous smell from the engine chimney.

It was also fast, with a top speed of 109kph (68mph) and an average of around half that, which were both remarkable speeds for trains of the period.

There were, however, difficulties from the outset. Setting off from a station proved to be a problem, as the train often needed a helping tow from horses or an extra engine attached to a tow rope. The system was also inflexible, as the pipework prevented the trains from being routed from one track to another. The biggest problem, however, was maintaining the vacuum itself. The leather flaps that sealed the pipe failed to be airtight, and there were rumours that they were gnawed by rats. Likewise the metallic parts of the seal were corroded by salt from sea-spray. Consequently, the atmospheric system was abandoned after a mere eight months, and the equipment replaced by conventional steam locomotives.

It was an expensive failure. The shareholders of the South Devon Railway were almost £400,000 (in modern terms, around £35 million, or US$55 million) poorer as a result, which was a huge sum at the time. Much of the money had been spent on the elaborate engine houses, which Brunel had constructed in an Italianate style, their large chimneys disguised as campaniles. Each house cost several times the price of a conventional locomotive, and they were so elegant that one, at Starcross, was later used as a chapel. Also, installing atmospheric traction had been nine times more expensive than the original estimate, and the static engines burned far more coal than expected, costing twice that of conventional traction.

Brunel's failure was particularly painful since it happened in public, on a commercial railway, but there were plenty of other disasters that happened in relative privacy. In 1824, for example, British inventor W.F. Snowden designed a train that eschewed the use of steam power altogether. It had a single line of wheels that ran in a U-shaped rail flanked by a pair of flat rails that kept the carriages upright. To propel the train, "industrious labourers" in the leading carriage literally cranked a wheel that was connected to a gear that engaged with the toothed edge of one of the rails – thus providing human traction, and requiring superhuman stamina on the part of the labourers. Not surprisingly, the idea was never taken up, despite a pamphlet published in 1834 extolling its virtues. However, Snowden's system did highlight a problem that is common to all railways – that wheels

"He had so much faith in his being able to improve it that he shut his eyes to the consequences of failure"

DANIEL GOOCH, BRUNEL'S COLLEAGUE, ON THE ATMOSPHERIC RAILWAY slip in damp conditions and on inclines – a problem Snowden solved by keeping the gear locked in the track. A related idea was to have a rack and pinion (see pp.108–109) in the centre of the railway to aid traction, and such devices are still used on mountain lines today.

Rope or cable railways were another attempt at solving the problem of how to haul trains. Again, as with atmospheric railways, the idea was to have stationary engines placed along the track, but this time for hauling cables attached to the trains. On the Canterbury and Whitstable line in Britain, which opened in May 1830, trains were hauled by rope for 6.5km (4 miles) out of Canterbury and then by locomotive for the remaining two miles. Several other lines used cables to deal with inclines. Nearly two miles of the Düsseldorf–Elberfield line in Germany was cable-hauled, as was part of the Brussels–Liège line in Belgium, and the Denniston Incline on the South Island of New Zealand. The Liverpool and Manchester (see pp.25–29) had cables for the first part of the line out of Liverpool station, as did the London and Birmingham for the incline between Euston station and Camden Town. One of London's first railways, the London and Blackwall, was cable-drawn for its entire 6-km (3½-mile) length. Cables were complicated to operate, however, and as locomotives became more powerful, most of these systems were phased out (although the German one remained in operation until 1927). A cable system was even proposed for the first deep tube line built on the London Underground – the City and South London line, completed in 1890 – but given its length of nearly 8km (5 miles), planners decided to use the new technology of electric power instead.

Monorails were another great hope of the railway pioneers, and although a few were constructed – and indeed some still operate – they have never overcome the basic problems of being expensive to build, and being inflexible due to the structural requirements of their rails. The first patent for a vehicle designed to run on a single rail was granted in November 1821 to British civil engineer Henry Robinson Palmer, who described it as "a single line of rail, supported at such height from the ground as to allow the centre of gravity of the carriages to be below the upper surface of the rail". The vehicles straddled the rail, rather like pannier baskets on a mule, and were horse-drawn. The idea was to make it easier to transport goods across worksites, and the first monorail was built in the Deptford Dockyard, London, in 1824. The following year, another line, the horse-drawn Cheshunt Railway, was built at a brickworks in London. At its opening it carried passengers – an historic moment, as it predated the world's first passenger railway, the Stockton and Darlington (see pp.24–25), by three months. Monorails have since resurfaced from time to time, but never with much success. A steam-driven monorail was first demonstrated at the United States Centennial Exposition in Philadelphia in 1876, and although a couple of versions were built, neither lasted very long. The oldest monorail in the world is the Wuppertal Suspension Railway in Germany, which opened in 1901 and still operates today, carrying 25 million passengers a year. In the later 20th century, a number of monorails were built in urban areas in Asia, including Tokyo in Japan and Kuala Lumpur in Malaysia.

ROPE AND STEAM
Propelled both by cables powered by stationary steam engines, and moving steam locomotives, the Canterbury and Whitstable Railway was known locally as the "Crab and Winkle" line.

Fanciful ideas for new transport systems continued into the 20th century. Perhaps the strangest of all was the balloon railway constructed near Salzburg in Austria in the early 1900s. This consisted of a large balloon tethered to a slide running on a single rail up a mountainside. The hydrogen balloon hovered some 10m (33ft) above the car, which could carry up to ten passengers. Once loaded, the balloon was freed, pulling up the car beneath it. To descend, the car's tanks were filled with water. Its inventor, Herr Balderauer, believed that his system would replace the costlier funiculars that were being built across the Alps (see pp.102–107), but perhaps unsurprisingly, it failed to attract investors.

AN UNUSUAL SUCCESS
The German suspended railway, the Wuppertal Suspension Railway, photographed in 1912. It has run for over a century and continues to operate today.

India: Dalhousie's Colonial Imperative

INDIA WAS THE JEWEL IN BRITAIN'S CROWN during the 19th century, and its colonial rulers were eager to impose their dominion over the subcontinent. The railways were vital to this process and were brought to India by the British East India Company – effectively a commercial arm of the British government. The first Indian railway, which ran from the company settlement of Bombay, was commercial in aim, prompted by events on the other side of the world: the American cotton harvest had failed in 1846, and this spurred the cloth manufacturers of Manchester to use India as an alternative source of cotton. However, in order to ensure the steady supply needed to keep their factories running, transport to the port at Bombay needed improving, and so the cotton magnates pressed the British government to build a railway.

Due to bureaucratic delays – it took months to receive a reply to a letter sent from India to Britain – and indecision on the part of the British rulers, work on the 34-km (21-mile) line between Bombay and Thane, or Tana, did not start until 1850. It was an experiment to see if it was possible to build railways in the harsh climate of the Indian subcontinent. The Thane line was not easy to construct. Now part of Bombay's busy suburban network, it originally went through difficult territory, including a hill that had to be cut through and a marsh. Nevertheless, it was completed in three years.

The opening of the line in April 1853 was a momentous affair, not least because it was the first railway in Asia. Unlike northwest England, where railways had originated, India was still a rural, unindustrialized nation, and the sight of powerful locomotives belching fire and steam impressed and frightened the local populace in equal measure. People lined the tracks in their millions to watch the 14-carriage train bearing a rich assortment of VIPs on its inaugural journey, and many spilled onto the tracks, slowing the progress of the train, which nevertheless managed the journey at an average speed of 32kph (20mph) – a very creditable effort.

Another, more ambitious, project started simultaneously in Bengal, in the northeast of India. This was a 195-km (121-mile) line stretching from Howrah, on the western side of the Hooghly river, via nearby

Calcutta to the small town of Raniganj in the coalfields of Burdwan, from which it had previously taken two seasons to cart the coal down to a river for transport to the rest of the country. Work on the line started in 1851, but a couple of shipping mishaps delayed progress. First, the coaches intended for the line were lost when the ship carrying them sank at Sandheads on the Bengal coast, and then, astonishingly, the locomotives for the line were sent to Australia instead of Calcutta as a result of one of the most expensive clerical errors in history. The locomotives eventually arrived in Calcutta – a year late – but, despite these setbacks, the line, nearly six times longer than the Bombay–Thane railway, opened in February 1855.

The success of these two lines led to a rapid expansion of the railway system. Unlike in Britain, where the process was unplanned and haphazard, the development of the rail network in India followed a clear plan laid out by the colonial administration. In 1853, Lord Dalhousie, the governor-general, set out a programme for the development of India's trunk lines in a 216-page handwritten memorandum. Dalhousie was a hard-working, capable administrator who later claimed to have given India all the necessary "engines of social improvement... Railways, uniform postage, and the Electric Telegraph". His "minute", as he called the memorandum, set out the justifications and guidelines for the railways of India, whose territory then included what is now Bangladesh and Pakistan.

Dalhousie emphasised the economic benefits that the railways would bring. They would increase trade between India and the mother country – Britain importing cotton and India receiving manufactured goods in return. Railways would encourage enterprise, increase production, facilitate the

LORD DALHOUSIE
Governor-General of India from 1847 to 1856, Lord Dalhousie set out a visionary scheme of railway building in India that aimed to rival the wonders of the ancient world.

THE EAST INDIAN RAILWAY COMPANY WAS ESTABLISHED IN 1845 WITH A CAPITAL OF

£4,000,000

25,000

LABOURERS DIED BUILDING THE WESTERN GHATS RAILWAY

discovery of natural resources such as coal and minerals, and encourage overall economic development as they were doing in Europe and the United States, which were now both three decades into the railway age. However, the core of Dalhousie's argument was not commercial but political. The British administrators and soldiers who ruled the country were thinly spread, and railways would enable them to travel rapidly to maintain control – an advantage that was worth almost any price.

For his part, Dalhousie was nothing if not a visionary. In his minute, he wrote enthusiastically:

the complete permeation of these climes of the sun by a magnificent system of railway communication would present a series of public movements vastly surpassing in real grandeur the aqueducts of Rome, the pyramids of Egypt, the Great Wall of China, the temples, palaces and mausoleums of the great Moghul monuments.

An exaggeration, perhaps, but it gives an idea of the enormity of the scheme. Dalhousie's blueprint was given urgency by a mutiny of the army's Indian soldiers that began in May 1857 and threatened colonial rule. The mutiny – which began with soldiers refusing to bite on musket cartridges covered with tallow made from either beef fat (offensive to Hindus) or pork fat (offensive to Muslims) – had broken out in remote parts of the country. The military realized that rather than bringing vast numbers of British troops over to manage the Indian regiments, it was cheaper to build railway lines to ensure that troops could be despatched at speed to deal with insurrections wherever they happened. Although the mutiny halted work on railway projects across India, work recommenced at a faster pace when peace was restored in June 1858.

The railways, in other words, were a nakedly colonial project that paid scant regard to the needs of the native population. The British decided on the location of the lines and when they would be built. They were designed to serve British interests and would later be seen by nationalists such as Mahatma Gandhi as agents of imperialism. The British government accepted Dalhousie's plan and the railways were constructed to the pattern he had devised. Major trunk routes radiated from the port cities and centres of colonial administration, such as Calcutta, Bombay, and Madras, and further lines connected other large towns and cities. It was, as one writer suggests, a period of great "romance and excitement", but it was also a time of hardship, particularly for innumerable Indian workers, thousands of whom died constructing the railways. The country's diverse and rugged landscape also posed formidable challenges. Bridges, for example, had to withstand far greater pressures than those of Europe, because the monsoon rains made rivers swell to enormous, and destructive, proportions.

COLONIAL RAIL
This plate taken from the *Illustrated London News* shows the arrival of a railway locomotive in India in 1875. By 1880, India had around 14,500km (9,000 miles) of track.

The Western Ghats, a chain of mountains that run down much of the western side of the subcontinent, proved to be an almost insuperable barrier. Although not immensely high – a mere 2,695m (8,840ft) – they rise sharply and ruggedly beyond the narrow coastal lowlands, presenting what at the time was the most difficult section of railway terrain in the world. It took engineer James Berkley several years just to survey the route, although the line was only 24km (15 miles) long. When it was finished, the line featured two major inclines (see pp.204–205) – the Bhore and the Thul Ghats – as well as numerous tunnels. Berkley devised an ingenious way of overcoming the steep gradient. Instead of building a continuous track, he carved out a reversing section at a bend near the summit, obviating the need for a stationary engine to haul the trains uphill. It was a cheaper and neater solution than a conventional route, and was imitated on several other mountain lines, notably in Brazil and the Andes. The system involved driving a train along a narrow line towards a precipice, so it required nerves of steel on the part of the driver, and indeed the passengers.

BHORE GHAT REVERSING INCLINE
The railway reversing station (see pp.204–205) on the Bhore Ghat incline in the Western Ghats, seen here in 1880, was an ingenious way of negotiating the Indian hills, although it involved a hair-raising reverse towards a precipice.

"If we did not rush about from place to place by railway, much confusion would be obviated"

MAHATMA GANDHI, *THE ESSENTIAL WRITINGS*

To create the track bed for the Ghat line, whole sections of the mountain had to be blasted and workers let down on ropes to drill into the face – a perilous process. On numerous occasions, the ropes failed or slipped, sending workers down into a ravine from which their bodies were never recovered. Illness, however, was the biggest killer. Numerous killer diseases, including typhoid, malaria, smallpox, cholera, and blackwater fever, took a high toll on the overworked and undernourished workers, who died by the tens of thousands. The lives of the Indian workers, or "coolies", as they were known, were considered cheap in Colonial India. As one government report tellingly reads:

> The fine season of eight months [work except in tunnels halted during the monsoon] is favourable for Indian railway operations, but on the other hand, fatal epidemics, such as cholera and fever, often break out and the labourers are generally of such feeble constitution, and so badly provided with shelter and clothing, that they speedily succumb to those diseases and the benefits of the fine weather are, thereby, temporarily lost.

As Anthony Burton, the author of a book on railways and the British Empire, observes: "the notion that lives – and the inconvenient loss of working time – could be saved by providing proper shelter and decent conditions does not seem to have been considered".

The spread of the railway in India came at a high cost, but it remained a remarkable achievement, and Dalhousie's plan was adhered to long after his departure and death. His belief that the project would be bigger than the construction of the pyramids was borne out. Within 25 years of the opening of the Thane line, India had an extensive network of trunk lines. By the turn of the century, there was a remarkable 40,000km (25,000 miles) of track – a network that has survived to this day with few closures, and which remains a key part of the infrastructure of a nation in which a motorway network was only developed late in the 20th century. The Indian railways have become synonymous with India itself.

Early Indian Railways

Railway construction took place at a rapid pace on
the Indian subcontinent from the 1850s onwards.
Following Dalhousie's recommendation of a series
of arterial "trunk" routes to connect India's major
cities, the first lines were built inland from the
regional hubs of Bombay on the west coast, Madras
in the south, and Calcutta in the east. Smaller
regional lines – built in an alarming variety of
gauges – fanned out from these main lines, and
by the early 20th century India boasted more than
40,000km (25,000 miles) of track. This map shows
the main rail network planned by Dalhousie and
built in the colonial era.

Jamnagar
Rajk

*ARABIAN
SEA*

*INDIAN
OCEAN*

KEY

- Major city
- City/town
- ——— Main line
- ——— National boundary

CROSSING THE RIVER
A steam locomotive is
floated across the River
Jumna on a pontoon at
Kalpi, northern India, in
the late 1800s. The river
was later bridged, but
before and during this
contruction, workers had to
use improvised measures
such as this to transport
locomotives over the river.

The Navvies: Digging, Drinking, and Fighting

THE MEN WHO BUILT THE RAILWAYS were a tough bunch — and they needed to be, as they had an arduous job, carried out in remote areas and often in harsh conditions. They were also at the cutting edge of technology, working in a new industry that had developed its own machinery and working methods. It was a learning process for all concerned, from the contractors and engineers to the men who laid out the embankments and dug the tunnels. Astonishingly, the tracks used by modern, high-speed trains would be quite recognizable to the engineers who built the first lines. After a few early experiments with granite sleepers and wooden rails, the basic design was adopted almost everywhere in the world — iron (later steel) rails laid on wooden sleepers, resting on stone aggregate or ballast (see pp.90–91).

For much of the 19th century, laying the tracks was very labour-intensive. A surveyor drew an approximate line on a map after walking the site, then thousands of workers were hired by a contractor. The workers were called "navvies" because they were thought to have the same skills as the navigators who built the canal system a generation earlier. These navvies were proud of their name, but by no means all the workers on the railways qualified for it. According to Terry Coleman, author of *The Railway Navvies*, the key book on the history of the navvies, they "must never be confused with the rabble of steady, common labourers whom they out-worked, out-drank, out-rioted and despised". The labourers came and went, many returning to the farms at harvest time. If they stayed, however, it took a year for labourers to qualify as navvies, who were considered an elite class of worker. To be navvies, they had to work on all the hard tasks, such as tunnelling, excavating, and blasting, and not simply shovelling earth; they had to live with the other navvies in camps and follow the railway as worksites moved along; and they had to match the eating and drinking habits of their fellows — consuming nearly 1kg (2lb) of beef and 4.5l (9½ pints, or over a gallon) of beer a day. The navvies came from all over Britain and adopted their own particular dress code. According to Coleman, they favoured "moleskin trousers, double-canvas shirts, velveteen square-tailed coats, hobnail boots,

NAVVIES USING A BRICKMAKING MACHINE
Although their reputation as volatile, hard-drinking fighters was often deserved, the navvies also carried out long hours of hard labour, and had to put up with poor working and living conditions.

gaudy handkerchiefs and white felt hats with the brims turned up". It was not really suitable garb for such hard, manual work, but it demonstrated style. They were known by nicknames that ranged from the eclectic "Bellerophon" or "Fisherman" to the more common "Gipsy Joe" or "Fighting Jack".

To some extent, the skills needed to build the railways were tried and tested. There were similarities with building canals and digging out mines, but in terms of scale, perhaps only cathedral-building compared – although cathedrals took centuries to complete, while railways took only a few years. The scale and extent of the earthworks alone was unprecedented. The most visible features of the navvies' trade were bridges and tunnels, but the vast majority of their work consisted of moving enormous quantities of earth. Railways require relatively straight routes and gentle gradients, so the land has to be adapted before the track can be laid. Peter Lecount, an assistant engineer on the London & Birmingham, calculated that building it involved lifting 708 million cu m (25,000 million cu feet) of earth – a greater task than the building of the Great Pyramid at Giza. Occasionally, new techniques were deployed, such as laying embankments through marshy land, or crossing large rivers with bridges. Worksites commonly had hundreds of men attacking the earth with their primitive tools and hauling the dirt away in wheelbarrows, or by horse and cart on the flatter sections. As railway historian R.S. Joby recounts:

rough-looking gangers drive their butty gangs to ever greater feats of
earth-moving by threats, promises, and, at times, a well-timed kick for
the pay of the gang depends on the efforts of the team as a whole.

A great deal of gunpowder was used, the fuse-setters and navvies
crouching behind any available cover to shield themselves before
returning to prepare the next blast. Safety precautions were minimal
and risk-taking was considered manly. Not surprisingly, navvies often
died young. In the Kilsby Tunnel on the London & Birmingham,
three men were killed as they tried to jump, one after the other, over
the mouth of a shaft in a game of "follow my leader". On the Great
Western, a man was told to stop cutting under a large overhang of
earth, but he ignored the warnings and was buried alive within

INTO THE DARK
Tunnelling under Blackfriars Bridge, London, in the
1860s. In a life filled with risk and tough conditions,
working in tunnels was the epitome of both for the
navvies. Accidents were frequent.

minutes. Those who survived the numerous accidents — ranging from unexpectedly large explosions to simple falls and collisions — were soon worn out by the hard work and the excessive lifestyle. The forty-year-olds looked fifty, and the rare sixty-year-olds looked eighty. The sheer numbers of workers involved in railway-building was also colossal — far greater than in any previous industry. In spring 1847, for example, 169,838 men were working on the railways in England and Wales, out of a total population of 16 million. Initially, the firms employing these men were small, local concerns, but large contractors soon emerged, employing thousands of navvies. These contractors were powerful men such as Samuel Peto and Thomas Brassey, who built railways all over the world.

Not surprisingly, navvies were rarely welcome in the towns where they were working. They caused a great deal of disruption, and shopkeepers took advantage of the surge in demand to raise food prices. As accommodation was scarce in the remote places where lines were being built, the navvies slept in huts in filthy conditions, sometimes sharing their quarters with pigs and attracting vermin. They often shared beds — one man sleeping while the other worked — and they were accompanied by a retinue of "many women but few wives", as one writer put it. As a result, disease was rife. Riots were not uncommon, particularly on payday, or, as sometimes happened, when the navvies had *not* been paid. In 1866, the village of Wiveliscombe in Somerset, England, was terrorized by 70 navvies demanding beer and bread after the local railway company went bust. A local resident of a Devon village described the chaos when the navvies found themselves without work after the railway was finished:

> More than a hundred discharged on Monday, and a pretty row there was: drunk altogether and fighting altogether, except one couple fought in the meadow for an hour... the same night the villains stole all poor old xxx's fowls [and] there is not an egg to be got hereabouts.

Similar scenes were played out in other countries. The navvies may have been wild, but they got the job done, so much so that British men found work on many European railways. In 1843, Thomas Brassey, a contractor, was commissioned to build the line between Rouen and Le Havre in northern France, and a local newspaperman sent to observe construction was greatly impressed:

I think as fine a spectacle as any man could witness, who is accustomed to look at work, is to see a cutting in full operation with about twenty wagons being filled, every man at his post, and every man with his shirt open, working in the heat of the day, the gangers looking about, and everything going like clockwork. Such an exhibition of physical power attracted many French gentlemen who came on to the cuttings at Paris and Rouen, and looking at these English [actually many were Scottish and Irish] gentlemen with astonishment said '*Mon Dieu! Les Anglais, comme ils travaillent!*' [My God! The English, how they work!]... It was a fine sight to see the Englishmen that were there, with their muscular arms and hands hairy and brown.

There were often labour shortages in the US, and men had to be brought in from other countries to build the railways. The construction of the Erie Railroad in the late 1830s and early 1840s coincided with a large influx of men from Ireland who were fleeing the famine at home and were eager to work on the railway. Unfortunately, the men were from two different parts of Ireland – Fardown and Cork – and the former took against the latter in a dispute over lower wages. In the ensuing conflict, the Fardowners set upon the Corkonians in a series of battles that lasted several days. This culminated with the Fardowners cutting down the rickety structures in which the Corkonians lived, bringing the roofs down on top of them. It is a wonder that they found enough time to build the railway at all, but construction was unaffected.

In the 1860s, the Central Pacific company was building the line eastwards from California on the first transcontinental (see pp.120–27). However, the construction was desperately undermanned, due to both a lack of immigrants and the competition from the lucrative mining industry. One of the line's promoters named Charles Crocker hit upon the idea of taking on Chinese workers, but had to overcome resistance from his worksite managers who thought that these "tiny rice-eaters" could not handle such work. They were proved wrong, however: the Chinese were extremely good labourers and

TYPICAL AMOUNT OF
EARTH MOVED BY ONE
NAVVY IN A DAY

2,000 KG
(4,400 LB)

RAILWAYS ON THE STEPPES
Convicts build the Ussuri section of the
Trans-Siberian railway in the far east of
Russia in the early 1900s.

accepted lower pay than their white counterparts, prompting Crocker
to organise the recruitment of thousands of men from China. Chinese
labourers also worked on the legendary South American railways,
accompanied by the fearsome local workforce, the *rotos* (see pp.202–203).

In Russia, the construction of the Trans-Siberian Railway in the
1890s (see pp.180–87) also meant that a lot of men had to be brought
in from afar. The line, which is still the longest in the world, required
huge numbers of workers and had 80,000 enrolled at its peak. The
local people, mostly tribesmen, were unwilling or unable to work,
and as the line progressed further east into the almost deserted steppe
the shortage of labour was acute. Convicts were drafted in, with
13,500 prisoners and exiles working on the line at the peak of its
construction. Labourers also had to be brought in not only from
European Russia, but from as far afield as Turkey, Persia, and Italy.

This conscription of workers continued throughout the 19th century,
after which mechanization reduced the need to mobilize such vast
labour forces. Until then, however, the railways were the work of strong
men wielding primitive tools. Their legacy can still be seen, not only in
railways that have since been modernized, but in the embankments and
cuttings that remain where lines have been closed. All over the world,
the landscape was transformed by their herculean labours.

The Permanent Way

The rails, sleepers, and ballast of a finished railway line have come to be termed the "permanent way". This dates back to the early days of railway construction when a temporary track was laid first in order to rapidly transport materials to site. After the substructure was largely completed, the track was replaced by the permanent "way". The substructure of a track is called the "formation". Since a consistent "grade" (gradient) is required in order for trains to run smoothly, the ground is first prepared to form the "subgrade". The subgrade might also be covered by a layer of sand or stone called a "blanket" before overlaying it with ballast. The "gauge" (distance apart) and alignment of the rails are monitored to ensure that they remain constant throughout straight sections and curves in the line.

LAYING THE TRACKS
Workers follow a track-renewal train as it places rails on newly laid sleepers. Before the mid-1900s, navvies (see pp.84–89) carried out the process by hand. These "bullhead" rails had the same profile on the head (top) and foot (underside), allowing them to be inverted and reused when the head wore out.

Track materials

Wooden rails were used for the pony-drawn wagonways of the 17th century, but a more lasting material was required to support the steam engines of the 19th century. The cast-iron rails of the first railways were succeeded by sturdier wrought-iron rails in the 1820s, while steel – which was stronger still – came into use in the 1850s. Crushed-stone ballast is still the most common foundation material, but concrete slabs, which are more stable and durable, are increasingly used.

TRACK STRUCTURE
Most railway tracks consist of flat-bottom steel rails fixed to timber or concrete sleepers. The layer of ballast beneath has the benefit of reducing noise from rail traffic, but requires maintenance due to displacement from the weight of passing trains.

Rails
Sleeper
Permanent way
Shoulder
cess
BALLAST/SUB-BALLAST
Track
foundation
BLANKET (SAND, OPTIONAL)
Formation
SUBGRADE (LOCAL MATERIALS
SUCH AS TOPSOIL)
GROUND LEVEL

Track gauges

The "gauge" of a track is the horizontal distance between the inside faces of the two rails, and determines the axle width of trains that can run upon it. While a range of gauges was used when the railways were built in the 19th century, standardization became necessary as individual lines were connected to form national and international networks. As such, "standard" or "international" gauge (1,435mm or 4ft 8½in) is used for around 60 per cent of the world's railways.

COMMON GAUGES
- 1,435mm (4ft 8½in)
- 1,520mm (4ft 11⅘in)
- 1,000mm (3ft 3⅜in)
- 1,067mm (3ft 6in)
- 1,676mm (5ft 6in)
- 1,668mm (5ft 5⅔in)
- 1,600mm (5ft 3in)
- 950mm (3ft 1⅖in)
- Other gauges

Cuban Sugar Railways

FEW NATIONS REMAINED UNTOUCHED by the railway boom of the 19th century, and many were affected in remarkably different ways. Cuba was the first country in Latin America to build railways, but their purpose was very different from those of the US and Europe. Their chief role was to transport sugar – a crop that was grown in vast plantations to satisfy the sweet teeth of the developed world – and so they did little to help the general population. Cuba had become a sugar economy somewhat by accident, after an increase in the price of sugar in the late 18th century made its cultivation highly profitable. Relying heavily on slave labour, the industry grew rapidly in the early 19th century, but transporting the cane to the mills was expensive because of the island's poor roads. Indeed, in the rainy season, from May to November, the tracks became muddy and rivers flooded, making movement almost impossible. What was needed was a railway to shift the cane swiftly and cheaply – from the plantations to the mills for processing, and then on to the coast where it could be shipped abroad.

CUBAN SUGAR RAILWAY
Constructing the first Cuban railway, between Havana and Bejucal, involved a massive workforce of slaves from the plantations and Irish immigrant labourers.

150 YEARS OF CUBAN RAIL
These commemorative stamps
were isued in 1987 to mark the
150th anniversary of the opening
of the first Cuban railway line,
one of the earliest in the world.

Such a line was duly built, and the crop that was brought to Cuba by
Christopher Columbus in 1493 found its way back to Europe in
unprecedented amounts, making fortunes for Cuba's sugar barons.

Throughout the 19th century, Cuba was a Spanish colony, but its
railway opened long before that of its imperial master. Indeed, although
Cuba was undeveloped and wretchedly poor at the time, it was one of
the first countries in the world to build a railway – by the time its first
line opened in 1837, only six other countries had railways. In 1830, just
as the Liverpool and Manchester line was being completed in Britain
(see pp.25–29), leading plantation owners in Cuba set up a commission
to consider building a railway network. In 1834, once a route had
been established and sufficient funds raised, work started on a 74-km
(46-mile) line between the capital, Havana, on the coast, and Güines,
inland on the Mayabeque River.

It was a grand and sophisticated operation. The first part of the
26-km (16-mile) route, from Havana to Bejucal, climbed to 98m
(320ft) above sea level, a very steep gradient for a railway at the time.
The line also had several bridges, the longest of which, across the
Almendares River, needed 200 supporting pillars. Moreover, unlike
many other early lines, the Cuban railway was designed to have two
tracks right from the start. To supplement the thousands of slaves
owned by the railway company, workers were brought in from
abroad to help construct the line. These were largely Irish immigrants
who had only recently reached the US, and men from the Canary
Islands, which was also under Spanish rule. The new arrivals did not
thrive. The Irish in particular suffered, being unused to the tropical
climate, which was at its worst during the rainy season. Badly fed
and poorly sheltered, large numbers of workers succumbed to the
effects of tropical diseases. Many of them also turned out to be
drunks and quickly found themselves in the filthy colonial jails,

where they soon perished. The survivors found that when their contracts ended the railway companies did not fulfil their promise of returning them to the US, and they were left to wander the streets of Havana, penniless and destitute. The Canary Islands immigrants fared little better, even though they spoke Spanish. Their employers considered them more likely to try to escape, so they were treated like prisoners on the work sites. Forced to work up to 16 hours per day, many of them died of exhaustion.

The project ran out of money, but new investors stepped in and the first section of the Bejucal line was completed by 1837, just three years after work had begun. The locomotives and drivers were imported from England, and when the section to Güines opened the following year, the railway boomed. Although it was primarily intended for freight, passengers flocked to the railway too, generating as much revenue as the sugar in the early years. There were two trains a day in each direction – a 30-wagon freight train, and a seven-car passenger train.

The success of the line prompted further railway construction. The first section of a second line – built to bring sugar, molasses, and rum to the port of Cárdenas – was completed in 1840, after which the system expanded rapidly. A decade after the first line opened, the area around Havana was criss-crossed with lines connecting all the neighbouring districts, and the sugar industry boomed as a result. In 1846, Havana alone had 169 sugar mills producing more than 40,000 tons of sugar and 45,000 barrels of molasses each year. The railways serving these mills were highly profitable, but they were geared so specifically towards the sugar industry that they provided little support to other industries, or indeed to passengers. They were built purely to help sugar merchants export their produce, and so were not treated as commercial enterprises. Unlike in Europe and the US, where every railway junction soon became a bustling town, the railways did not stimulate urban development in Cuba.

APPROXIMATE NUMBER OF AFRICAN SLAVES TRANSPORTED TO CUBA

800,000

By 1852, nine companies had built a total of 565km (350 miles) of track, although the pace of

THE CUBAN SUGAR RAILWAYS

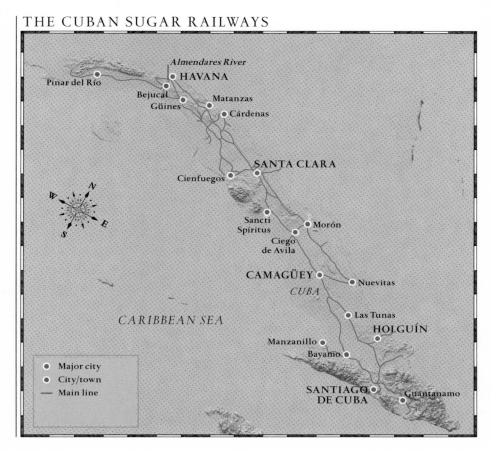

growth slowed down due to a slump in world sugar prices and a clampdown on slavery. However, sugar prices recovered, stimulating a second boom in railway construction. The Crimean War of 1854–56 raised prices even higher – sugar was already a global commodity, and the war diverted British shipping from carrying sugar from Asia, creating a surge in demand. The sugar barons found themselves with enormous amounts of cash, which they used to invest in more and more railways. Consequently, the amount of track laid reached 1,288km (800 miles) in 1868, providing this impoverished island in the Caribbean with one of the densest railway networks in the world. It was bettered only by a few major European nations, and in fact had more miles of track per inhabitant than any other country in the world – more, even, than England, the mother of the railway.

CUBAN SUGAR MILL
An American locomotive waits outside a
sugar boiling house in Cuba in 1857. Such
locomotives took sugar from the mills
to the ports for export.

By the late 19th century, the Cuban railways had reached a remarkable 8,000km (5,000 miles) of track, half of which were standard-gauge lines designed to shift sugar out of the plantations and sugar products from the mills. The rest were mainly narrow-gauge tracks, often crudely laid, for hauling cane on the plantations themselves. Unfortunately, however, not only did the railways fail to serve passengers, they failed to stimulate the economy, for they remained dependent on British and US technology: no Cuban supply industries were ever established. If anything, the railways had a rather damaging effect on the wider economy – they exacerbated the differences between the rich areas, which benefited greatly from their construction, and those that were poor, which became even more neglected. They were also concentrated in the affluent western half of the island. Only a handful of lines were built in the east, where there were few plantations. Crucially, the east–west line connecting the two halves of the island was not built until the 20th century, because it required a government subsidy, which was not forthcoming. As the

BEGGING IN HAVANA
At the height of its success as a sugar economy, Cuba was awash with foreign labourers, many of whom never returned home, and ended up begging on the streets of Havana.

GREGG COMPANY RAILWAY CAR
Like most of Cuba's railway technology, this freight car, used
for transporting sugar cane, was imported from the US. Cuba
never developed its own train manufacturing industry.

authors of a study of the Cuban railways argue: "the railroad
development of the first decades lacked the long-term perspective
that would permit the growth of a national grid". In fact, the economic
effect of the railways was quite perverse. By making the plantation
owners so rich, they helped perpetuate the slave system that might
otherwise have collapsed.

The railways' dependence on the sugar trade was ultimately their
undoing. They were profitable as long as sugar boomed, because there
was no other form of transport. In the late 19th century, however,
another collapse in sugar prices rocked Cuba's economy, leading to
the takeover of the railways by British investors. Few lines were found
to be viable, so much of the network was shut down. By the early 20th
century, the remainder of Cuba's railways were entirely owned by
British and US companies. These monopolized the western and
eastern networks respectively, but the stagnation of Cuba's sugar
industry drove the railways into crisis. The spread of the motor car
and improvements in Cuba's roads only deepened the railways'
problems, which would only be solved when the network was
nationalized in the late 1950s.

The Spread of the Railways

TAHAO, NO.20
V&T RAILROAD
STEAM, 1875

As train travel increased and the benefits of rail links became evident, it seemed that nothing could stop the spread of the iron road. There was no obstacle – financial, geographic, or social – that could not be overcome by the railways. Soon mountains were being crossed or tunnelled under in territories as far apart as the Austro-Hungarian Empire and India. Rivers were forded and houses demolished to make way for stations in town centres. Even disease-infested jungles were conquered, such as the swamps on the Panamanian isthmus, although only at a terrible human cost. The United States, with its vast western deserts, soon boasted not just one transcontinental railway, but four – and Canada laid three of its own. Urban transport, too, was revolutionized. London's Metropolitan Railway, the world's first underground line, opened in 1863, and became the blueprint for many such systems across the world.

Although trains were becoming commonplace, there was little improvement in the quality of services – largely because the majority of travellers had no other means of transport, so their custom was taken for granted. There were exceptions, of course – prestige services such as those developed by George Pullman, who provided not only far better meals, but comfortable overnight sleeper carriages – but by and large rail transport offered few comforts. Nor was it entirely safe. At first, trains were so few and so slow that collisions were unlikely, but as the tracks filled up and trains travelled faster, accidents became inevitable.

The railway companies soon became the dominant industry of the day. They were larger than any other business, and by their very nature operated across vast areas. Perhaps most enduringly, they liked to demonstrate their importance by building huge stations that became the cathedrals of the age – a source of pride to both the railway companies and the communities they served.

Crossing the Alps

MANY OF THE FIRST EUROPEAN RAILWAYS ran from cities to ports, so that goods could be transferred onto ships. As the network developed, however, it hit a major hurdle in the heart of the continent – the Alps. From the earliest days, the governments promoting the railways realized that this was an obstacle that would have to be surmounted, but it posed the hardest challenge yet encountered by railway builders. Engineers had to develop new skills and techniques, excavating tunnels far longer than any previously cut and erecting bridges over deep, inaccessible ravines.

The first railway to cross the Alps was the Semmering. It was built over the Semmering Pass by the Austrian Empire to connect the imperial capital, Vienna, with the Empire's only seaport, Trieste (now in Italy). A circuitous route via the Hungarian plains had been considered, but the transalpine railway's main backer, Archduke John of Austria, was determined to find a way over the mountains. This was a remarkable challenge and it took a remarkable man to design and build it: Carl von Ghega, an engineer with mountain-road-building experience who had engineered the Emperor Ferdinand Northern Railway from Brno to Breclav (both now in the Czech Republic). In 1842, Ghega was put in charge of the entire Austrian railway-building programme. Believing that an essential part of this programme was a link between Austria and the Adriatic, he travelled to the United States to learn about railway construction methods, and how they might be applied to finding a way over the mountains. He returned convinced that a railway over the Semmering was feasible.

The Semmering was a mountain pass that had been used by travellers on foot and on horseback since the Middle Ages. Although it was the lowest of the Alpine crossings, and so remained open longer than others in winter, the pass still rose to more than 900m

CARL RITTER VON GHEGA
Born Carlo Ghega to Albanian parents in Venice, the engineer was granted the title of Ritter ("knight") in 1851 for the astonishing feat of building the Semmering railway, which many had thought impossible.

THE FIRST RAILWAY ACROSS THE ALPS, 1857

(2,955ft) above sea level, and building a railway across the range required extraordinary ingenuity and innovation. The Austrian Government backed the project because the revolutions that swept across Europe in 1848 convinced the new Emperor Franz Joseph of its necessity – not only to unite the ends of his disparate Empire as they sought to fragment and affirm their national identities, but also to create employment at a time of economic depression. Establishing a connection from Vienna to the sea became both politically and economically essential.

Ghega chose a route through the Alps that started at Gloggnitz in Lower Austria and ran to Mürzzuschlag in Styria. As the crow flies, these two towns are 21km (13 miles) apart, but the railway covered twice that distance with its curves and switchbacks, the track running across curved viaducts that arched their way over broad valleys before entering long tunnels. In all, the route required 14 tunnels, the longest of which was 1,400m (4,595ft); 16 viaducts, several with two levels; and more than 100 curved stone bridges. Avalanche sheds were built to protect the line from falling rock and snow on its perilous path along the mountainside. Even with all these structures, the ascent still rose by gradients of up to

1 in 40 (2.5 per cent), very steep for the locomotives of the time; the curves, too, were sharper than those on other lines. To overcome these difficulties, Ghega also worked to develop engines that could handle them. In 1851, he initiated a competition, similar to the Rainhill Trials 22 years earlier (see pp.27–28), to find the best locomotive. An engine called *Bavaria* won, but when the line opened, it proved unable to haul heavy loads up the steep inclines. A new engine, designed by Wilhelm Freiherr von Engerth, a professor of engineering at Graz University, took its place.

All the construction work was carried out by hand, with the help of gunpowder (the only explosive available at the time). The workforce, which was made up of Germans, Czechs, and Italians, as well as Austrians, was enormous – 20,000 people at its peak. Perhaps inevitably, accidents occurred during construction. In the worst single incident – a rock fall in October 1850 – 14 men lost their lives, and in all, around 700 men died, many from diseases such as typhus and cholera. In one astonishing near miss, the building of the railway almost changed the course of history. The young Otto von Bismarck,

THE SEMMERING RAILWAY
Traversing 41km (26 miles) of sheer drops and
previously impassable moutains, the Semmering
railway represents an incredible feat of engineering.

who later unified Germany and became known as its Iron Chancellor, represented his country at an inspection of the line. He was nearly killed when a gangway over a ravine broke beneath him – he only survived by clinging, cartoon-style, onto a ledge as he fell.

The first freight train travelled over the pass in October 1853 and passenger traffic began the following July. By 1857, the all-important connection between Vienna and Trieste was complete. While the line cost four times its original estimate, it proved its worth as a vital trade link for the Austrian Empire in what turned out to be its declining years. Moreover, the railway blended so well into the landscape that it has today been designated a UNESCO World Heritage Site, with the double-layered viaducts singled out as a particularly distinctive feature.

NUMBER OF WORKERS THAT BUILT THE

SEMMERING RAILWAY

20,000

NUMBER OF WORKERS NOW BUILDING THE

GOTTHARD BASE TUNNEL

2,000

After the success of the Semmering, other routes were soon being planned through the Alps. A route under the western Alps was proposed in 1848, but the revolutions of that year and the Italian Wars of Unification delayed its progress. Once Italy was unified in 1861, interest revived and a plan was laid to build a line under Mont Cenis, connecting Bardonecchia on the Italian side with Modane in Savoy, which had been annexed to France in 1860 and, more widely, linking Milan and Turin in Italy with Grenoble and Lyon in France.

Going over the Mont Cenis pass was considered out of the question given that it reached a height of 2,081m (6,827ft). However, a temporary rack railway (see pp.108–109) capable of climbing steep gradients, the Mont Cenis Pass Railway, was opened alongside the pass road in 1868. The 80-km (50-mile) line was used to speed up the carriage of mail between Britain and India via the Italian port of Bari. Worked by British engine drivers, it was the first ever rack railway based on the fell mountain railway system, which used a toothed third rail to propel the locomotive up steep hills. However, it proved short-lived and was dismantled in 1871, when the more efficient Fréjus Tunnel replaced it.

The 13.6-km (8½-mile) Fréjus Tunnel, built at a height of 1,200m (3,940ft), was at the time of its construction the longest in the world. Initially, tunnelling techniques were still primitive: they involved drilling a hole and placing explosive charges in it. Progress was slow at first. Five years after work had started in 1857, less than 2km (1 mile) had been completed. Then the engineer, Germain Sommeiller, invented a pneumatic rock-boring machine, the pace increased and, with teams working from both ends, the tunnel broke through on 26 December 1870. Thanks to a new method of determining the route known as indirect triangulation, which involved teams of surveyors taking bearings on many points on the mountain, the two ends of the tunnel were only half a metre (less than 2ft) out of direct alignment when they met up. The Mont Cenis Railway – the first international railway linked by a tunnel at the frontier – opened for traffic in October 1871.

The second major tunnel under the Alps was the Gotthard Tunnel, which was also immensely difficult to construct due to the geology of the region. It took from 1871 to 1881 to build and, at 15km (9½ miles), was slightly longer than the Fréjus Tunnel. Work was faster thanks to the use of dynamite, invented by Alfred Nobel in 1867, but it still took an outstanding man, the Swiss engineer Louis Favre, to work out a way of getting through the mountain. Favre devised an innovative way to reach the tunnel mouth, at an elevation of more than 1,100m (3,610ft). He created tunnels that circled around at a gentle gradient through the rock, so that the route spirals up the mountain to reach a point above itself. At Wassen, for example, passengers heading south can see a church spire from below then, a few minutes later, they find themselves viewing it from above. These loops add considerably to the journey time – the line between Lucerne and Chiasso on the Swiss-Italian border is 225km (140 miles) long, and around a fifth of the route is made up of loops.

Sadly, Favre did not live to see his creation completed. In 1879, he suffered a heart attack – very likely brought on by the strain of the project – during a tour of inspection of the tunnel, and died at the age of 54. He was not the only one to die: more than 200 tunnel-builders died in accidents – many drowned when drilling hit underwater streams, others were killed by rock falls and collisions with the wagons used to take out the stone.

After the Gotthard Tunnel opened in 1882, other rail routes were soon carved through the Alps via tunnels including the Simplon, which at 19km (12 miles) became the world's longest when completed

CHAMONIX-MONTENVERS RAILWAY
Following the success of the first mountain railways, Alpine trains became popular for tourism. The Montenvers rack railway, which opened in 1908, took tourists up to France's largest glacier, the Mer de Glace.

in 1906, and the Lötschberg, which opened just before the start of World War I. The Swiss developed electric locomotives to pull trains through these tunnels, which would otherwise have filled dangerously with smoke from steam engines (see pp.224–29).

Today, Switzerland is constructing a series of ambitious railway tunnels through the Alps in order to reduce road traffic over the mountains. The aim is to bypass the old Gotthard Tunnel's slow, winding route, which is already operating at full capacity. To achieve this, the massive AlpTransit project aims to increase rail capacity through these huge new tunnels. The longest – indeed, it will be the longest in the world, surpassing the 23-km (14½-mile) Seikan Tunnel in Japan – will be the Gotthard Base Tunnel. Due to open in 2016, it will have two tunnels, each 57km (35½ miles) long. The new Gotthard rail link, consisting of the Zimmerberg Base Tunnel (for which no completion date has been given) and the Ceneri Base Tunnel (due to open in 2019), along with the Gotthard Base Tunnel, will mean trains can cross the Alps by rail at just 550m (1,805ft) above sea level. This lower elevation will make it possible to create a high-speed link for passenger trains as well as for freight, reducing the travel time between Zurich and Milan from the current 4 hours to 2½ hours. The AlpTransit project also includes the 35-km (22-mile) Lötschberg Base Tunnel between the cantons of Bern and Valais in Switzerland, which opened in June 2007.

All these routes through the Alps represent one of the heroic achievements of the railway builders. Moreover, they have proved remarkably safe since completion, with accidents a rarity despite the harsh conditions in which the trains operate, especially in winter.

Climbing Mountains

The technology that enables locomotives to ascend steep grades of track was invented in the early days of the railways. John Blenkinsop's 1811 patent for a steam railway at the Middleton colliery, Britain, used an engine with a geared cogwheel, or "pinion", that engaged with a line of teeth, or "rack", located between the rails. However, it was not until the 1860s that the system was used on a mountain railway. Rack-and-pinion tracks maintain traction on grades of up to 48 per cent, whereas the steepest incline that conventional ("adhesion") trains can climb is around 10 per cent, even with assistance from extra locomotives. These specialized tracks also provide essential braking power to ensure that steep slopes can be safely descended.

The Riggenbach and Locher systems

Various rack-and-pinion systems have been developed and adopted since Blenkinsop's first design.

RIGGENBACH SYSTEM (1863)

The Riggenbach system was the first of the rack-and-pinion systems to be used widely, but its welded "ladder" arrangement proved expensive to maintain.

Slot for pinion cog

RACK PROFILE   RACK TOP VIEW

LOCHER SYSTEM (1889)

The Locher system was first used in 1889 and used a horizontal pinion on either side of the rack, enabling trains to climb much steeper grades. It was very stable and allowed carriages to withstand crosswinds.

Rack teeth   Horizontal pinion

PROFILE   VIEW FROM ABOVE   Rack tooth

PEAK-SCALING PIONEER
The 4.8-km (3-mile) Mount Washington Cog Railway in New Hampshire, US, is the oldest rack-and-pinion railway in the world. It opened in 1868 and climbs almost 1,100m (over 3,500ft) to the summit of Mount Washington, the highest peak in the northeastern US. The line still uses the ladderlike rack created by its founder, Sylvester Marsh, while the engine's tilted boiler is designed to stay level on the steep grades of the track.

How it works

Rack-and-pinion steam engines have one or more pinions, which are powered by the cylinders via connecting rods. Some designs place the pinion centrally on the axle, between the train's wheels, while others mount them on separate axles. Most rack-and-pinion trains have flanged running wheels, and so are capable of running on standard rails. Steam-powered trains pushed their carriages uphill, then reversed back down the slope in order to maximize braking power. Today, most rack-and-pinion trains are powered by electric or diesel engines.

THE ABT SYSTEM (1885)

Designed by Swiss engineer Roman Abt and considered an improvement over the Riggenbach system (see below left), the Abt system has a rack with two or three rows of teeth – each row offset from its neighbour – to ensure that the pinion is constantly in contact with the rack.

Pinion

Axle

Pinion teeth engage with rack, driving the train uphill

Rack

RACK AND PINION SIDE VIEW   RACK AND PINION END VIEW

The Panama Railroad:
A Deadly Rush for Gold

ALTHOUGH THE PANAMA RAILROAD was less than 80km (50 miles) long, its construction was deadly: as many as 12,000 men may have died building it, from a fatal mix of harsh working conditions and tropical diseases. The railway created a crucial link between the Atlantic and Pacific coasts of America, however, making it an essential element in the creation of the United States. It was also hugely profitable for its owners and shareholders.

On 24 January 1848, demand for transport across the Panama isthmus became pressing. On that day, James W. Marshall found gold at Sutter's Mill in California, triggering the first Gold Rush. But reaching California from the east coast of America was a huge challenge. The gold prospectors had three options: to sail 24,000km (15,000 miles) around Cape Horn at the southernmost tip of America, a voyage that took at least 85 days across notoriously storm-ridden seas; to travel 3,200km (2,000 miles) overland across the US on wagon trails, a route that took at least six months and was also fraught with perils; or to sail to the mouth of the Chagres River in what is today Panama and cross the narrow isthmus by dugout canoe up the river and on mules over the hills, to Panama City and the Pacific, an 80-km (50-mile) journey that took up to eight days. By 1848, various canal and rail routes across the isthmus had already been proposed – and abandoned – by Gran Colombia, the US, and France respectively; indeed, the Spanish had

1849 GOLD RUSH
This guide to the "Wonderful Gold Regions" of California, published in 1849, includes information on the different routes to the goldfields.

THE 1855 PANAMA RAILROAD

first considered building a canal in the 1520s, before settling for the Camino Real, the overland mule track that was still in use when the first gold-diggers arrived. In 1846, The US Government concluded a new treaty with the Republic of New Granada (Colombia and Panama), which guaranteed the republic's sovereignty in exchange for US transit rights across the isthmus. This paved the way for a transcontinental route. A year later, the US Congress subsidized a mail and passenger steamship service up and down the Atlantic and Pacific coasts from New York to the Chagres River and from Panama City to Oregon, enabling people and goods to reach Panama easily.

New York entrepreneur William H. Aspinwall had won the bid to build and operate the Pacific mail steamships, and, with the onset of the Gold Rush, he set out to build a railway across the Panamanian isthmus too. To assess the possibilities, Aspinwall travelled to Panama and Colombia with John L. Stephens, a lawyer and writer who had travelled in Central America. They established the Panama Railroad Company, which was granted an exclusive 49-year concession to build a railway, highway, or canal across the isthmus, as well as 250,000 acres of public land. On the back of this, Aspinwall raised US$1 million by selling stock in the company. An astute businessman, he also persuaded the US Congress to pay an annual fee of US$250,000 (around £55,000) to transport mail over the isthmus. Meanwhile, the demand for a passenger train had become evident: by the end of May 1849, 55 ships had landed more than 4,000 passengers at Chagres, all eager to reach California.

The route was first surveyed by US Army colonel George W. Hughes, who was misleadingly optimistic about the railway's construction. His survey indicated that the terrain would not be hard to traverse: it did not mention the deep swamps, thick jungle, and dangerous hills the route would have to cross. Aspinwall believed the railway would need to be just 32km (20 miles) long, from the furthest navigable point on the Chagres River to the Pacific Ocean. He contracted experienced American civil engineers George Totten and John Trautwine to build the railway, but they soon realized the disastrous errors of the survey – for a start, Hughes had overestimated the length of the navigable passage on the Chagres – and withdrew from the contract. However, both were eventually rehired as employees of the company, and the reserved 41-year-old Totten ultimately proved to be the hero of the venture.

Totten and Trautwine were all set to begin work on a route starting from the estuary of the Chagres River, when they found that George Law, the entrepreneur who had won the contract to convey the US mail along the east coast, had bought all the suitable land. They were forced to move the terminus, and found a new site further north at Manzanillo Island. This meant they had to start construction by building a causeway to the mainland, and then build on land known ominously as the Black Swamp. To lay rails over the swamp entailed shipping tons of limestone rock from an abandoned quarry at Bohio, way up the Chagres River, to build a solid base for the tracks. Once on firm land, at the aptly named Mount Hope, they were able to use their first rolling stock – a locomotive and string of wagons. However, less than 2km (1 mile) up the river they encountered further seemingly bottomless swamps and had to sink yet more tons of rocks. Another problem soon emerged: it was pointless building bridges from wood as they decayed within a few months in the tropical climate.

The railway builders were also unprepared for the weather. Annual rainfall was around 3.5m (11ft), and it rained constantly from June to December. The Chagres River could rise 15m (50ft) in a couple of hours. Not only was this hazardous for men working semi-submerged in the water, it resulted in a climate teeming with tropical diseases

THE VIEW ON ARRIVAL
Passengers eager to cross the Panamanian isthmus arrived
by steamship at the mouth of the Chagres River, shown here,
where they would travel on by dugout canoe, mule — or train.

and insect life. Tarantulas, scorpions, centipedes, wood ticks, and
insects such as ants — white, red, and black — could be deadly, and
malaria-carrying mosquitoes posed a permanent threat. The swamps
were also infested with alligators.

The workers were a veritable foreign legion, turning up from all over
the world and often known only by nicknames or numbers on a payroll.
Few records were kept and it is not known exactly how many men died.
However, it has been reckoned that at one point, one in five of the
workers was dying every month. Another estimate suggests that one

man died for every railway sleeper along the route – around 74,000 men, although this number is implausibly high. Whatever the actual mortality rate, the railway's doctor, J.A. Totten (George's brother), found it difficult to dispose of the bodies. His solution, wrote historian Joseph L. Schott in his book *Rails across Panama*, was to

> pickle the bodies in large barrels, keep them for a decent interval to be claimed and then sell them in wholesale lots to medical schools all over the world… the bodies brought high prices, and the profits from the sale of the cadavers made the railway hospital self-sustaining during the construction years.

Relations among the international workforce were often fraught. One day, a gang of French labourers stopped work, hoisted the Tricolore, sang the Marseillaise, and refused to discuss their grievances except in their native tongue, which foxed their Irish foreman. The company chairman, who spoke French, refused to negotiate except in English. He resolved the stalemate by cutting off their rations: the men went back to work, their grievances unknown to this day.

IN ITS FIRST 12 YEARS OF OPERATION, THE PANAMA RAILROAD CARRIED MORE THAN

US$750 MILLION IN GOLD

Moreover, the whole region was lawless and subject to banditry at the hands of the Derienni, land pirates who stole the gold transported from California and ruthlessly killed their victims. To combat the Derienni, Askinwall hired Randolph (Ran) Runnels, a famous Ranger who had hung up his guns after a religious conversion, but seen in a prophecy that he would be called upon to take up a mission in a "strange land… with a great river full of demons and monsters". Panama fitted the description, and Runnels set up a mule express business as a front for a vigilante force, called the Isthmus Guard, capable of taking on the bandits. In early 1852, the Guard struck the Derienni while they were relaxing, dancing, and gambling, and hanged 37 of them by the seashore.

THE DERIENNI
"Graphic Histories" such as this one, published in 1853, fuelled tales of the "Robberies, Assassinations, and Horrid Deeds" perpetrated by "Cool Blooded Miscreants" on the trails across Panama.

As if terrible conditions, disease, a restive workforce, and lawlessness were not trouble enough, the company ran out of funds when only 13km (8 miles) of track had been laid; its stock value fell, and construction ground to a halt. Meanwhile, shipping magnate Cornelius Vanderbilt had started work on a rival route through Nicaragua. Fortunately for the Panama Railroad Company, this route was as plagued by problems as their own.

The great turnaround in the railway's fortunes came in December 1851, when two steamships arrived at the mouth of the Chagres River carrying a thousand passengers desperate to reach California. Hearing the toot of the whistles on Totten's locomotives, they demanded carriage over the existing section – anything to avoid the ghastly mule ride. To deter them, Totten asked an exorbitant fee of 50 cents per mile and US$3 for each 45kg (100lb) of baggage. To his surprise, they accepted. Soon, so many people were queuing up to use the railway that the income from fares enabled Totten and engineer James Baldwin to push rapidly ahead to a limestone quarry, enabling them to transport stone by rail to strengthen the line. The company was able to raise another US$4 million in stock on the strength of the demand.

It was not all plain sailing even then, however. In the summer of 1852, many of the workers and their bosses died in a mysterious epidemic. At the same time, renewed banditry forced Runnels to carry out more mass hangings. Then Totten's request to use iron instead of wood for the bridge over the Chagres triggered a row with a new company director in New York (Stephens' death had deprived Totten of his major supporter). Totten was sacked and the remaining 34km (21 miles) of the railway entrusted to an engineer named Minor C. Story. Regarded as a boy wonder in the railway construction business, Story had no idea of the conditions in Panama. He employed

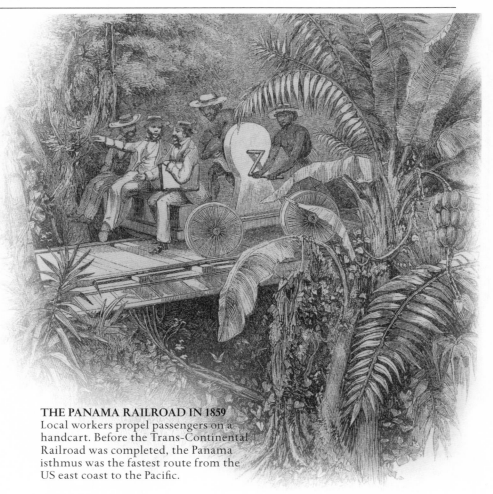

THE PANAMA RAILROAD IN 1859
Local workers propel passengers on a
handcart. Before the Trans-Continental
Railroad was completed, the Panama
isthmus was the fastest route from the
US east coast to the Pacific.

the materials he had used successfully in New England, but his wooden
bridges collapsed in the tropical climate and he fled, in Schott's words,
"bankrupt financially, tarnished in reputation, and broken in spirit".
After a year, Totten was recalled and recruited more workers, from
Europe, India, and China. Further disasters befell the project, among
them a train hitting a bull on the tracks and toppling into a ravine.
Nevertheless, by the end of 1853 Totten had completed the crucial iron
bridge and the way was almost clear for the run to Panama City.

Around this time, a tragic episode took place among a group of
Chinese labourers, who had proved hard and reliable workers, cleaner
and more sober than the Irish, who mocked them for taking a daily
bath. However, the Chinese relied on a regular supply of opium to
maintain their morale. When an accountant in New York cut off the

supply for being too expensive – and criminal – more than a hundred of the desperate Chinese committed suicide, hanging themselves from trees, walking into the water weighed down with stones, or asking Malay labourers to slay them with machetes.

By now the railway, although still incomplete, was profitable. In 1854, its 50km (31 miles) received over US$1 million in fares from more than 30,000 passengers, and on 27 January 1855, the two gangs working from opposite ends of the line joined hands. For 15 years, the Panama Railroad's monopoly of transit across the isthmus – and from the east to west coast of America – made it prodigiously profitable. It paid for its construction within four years on receipts boosted by a scale of charges set up by a group of tipsy clerks: once the railway was complete, it charged US$25 in gold for a first-class fare, making it by far the most expensive railway journey in the world at the time, mile for mile. In its first 12 years, it transported over US$700 million in Californian gold and more than 500,000 bags of mail without loss, although the cost of maintenance – including the replacement of rotting pine railway sleepers with hardwood lignum vitae – dented profits. The Panama Railroad Company's glory days continued until 1869, when the completion of the first transcontinental railroad across the US (see pp.120–27) took business away from it, but 10 years later, the shareholders made a handsome profit when the directors of a French group with plans to dig a canal across the isthmus paid US$20 million for the stock.

Totten stayed on as the railway's chief engineer until 1875, overseeing improvements and maintenance. Immediately after the railway's completion he had devised a scheme for a canal with locks across the isthmus. When Ferdinand de Lesseps, the man behind the Suez Canal, embarked upon his project for such a canal, Totten was appointed chief engineer. Totten also found time to build a daunting mountain railway in Venezuela. Yet his achievement is recognized only by a modest plaque at the station in Panama City. As Schott writes, "the brief obituary in the *New York Times* stated that he was a retired engineer. It failed to say that he was the man directly responsible for building the first transcontinental railroad the world had ever seen".

TRAIN AT COLON STATION, 1885
A locomotive on the Panama Railroad at the station in Colon, the town that sprung up around the railway workers' original shanty town on Manzanillo Island.

Crossing America

THEODORE JUDAH WAS A DRIVEN MAN, determined to realize his dream: he believed that the United States needed a railway running across its vast landmass to connect east and west. The restless, dark-haired son of a clergyman, Judah played the organ as a hobby and came across as rather earnest. Nicknamed "Crazy Judah" in his day, "he was never considered an entirely normal man", according to Oscar Lewis in *The Big Four*. Judah was, however, an experienced railway engineer who had laid out the route for the spectacular Niagara Gorge Railroad in the State of New York and the Sacramento Valley Railroad, the first in California.

Judah was not the only dreamer: building a transcontinental US railway had been the ambition of various railway promoters ever since the first train had chugged down the Baltimore and Ohio Railroad in 1830 (see pp.32–39). Such a railway was seen not only as economically beneficial but also as a way of bringing together the different regions of the US, which stretched across a landmass of nearly 5,000sq km (3,000sq miles); without the railway, it is possible that the US might not even have remained united.

It was Judah, however, who almost singlehandedly persuaded Congress to pass a law creating a railway that would link the existing tracks in the east with California, 3,000km (1,800 miles) away. In 1862, Abraham Lincoln signed the Pacific Railroad Act – an act all the more remarkable given that the Civil War was in full swing and Washington in a state of war. The legislation came with a generous bonus: to ensure the railway was built, the

THEODORE JUDAH, 1848
Even by his friends, Judah was regarded as a "fanatic"on the subject of the railroads that he dreamed of and built, but he was also resourceful, industrious, and hardworking.

companies that built it would receive government subsidies of between US$16,000 and US$48,000 for every 1.6km (1 mile) completed, depending on the difficulty of the terrain. Moreover, they would be granted all the land extending 16km (10 miles) to one side of the track.

Once he had seen the legislation passed, Judah travelled to California to survey a possible route through the Sierra Nevada, a rugged mountain range that reaches 4,420m (14,500ft) above sea level. Many doubters argued it would be impossible to traverse the range. Moreover, despite the government funding, Judah still needed more money to finance to project. His breakthrough came at a meeting in the upstairs room of a modest grocery store in Sacramento, where Judah had organized an event to attract potential investors. A group of four enterprising and ultimately very lucky men – Leland Stanford, Charles Crocker, Mark Hopkins, and Collis P. Huntington, all small-town merchants with ambition – decided to back his crazy endeavour. The Big Four, as they became known, founded the Central Pacific Railroad company, which won the contract to build the line heading eastwards from California.

Sadly, like many railway pioneers, Judah did not live to see the fruits of his labours. He fell out with the Big Four over their efforts to extract as much money as they could from the scheme by fraudulent activity, and headed back to New York. At the time, the only route back to the east coast was via Panama (see pp.110–119), where Judah unfortunately contracted yellow fever and died at the age of 37.

Meanwhile, the Central Pacific encountered difficulties, from winter snow to a lack of funds caused by the corrupt activities of the Big Four. Few local people were willing to work for the company because mining and gold-digging were more lucrative, so thousands of Chinese labourers were shipped across the Pacific to provide manpower. Progress was slow at first, but by 1867, the railway over the Sierra Nevada at the Donner Pass (2,160m/7,085ft) was completed. This was the toughest engineering challenge of the railway, and

"I am going to California to be the pioneering railroad engineer of the Pacific Coast"

THEODORE JUDAH

subsequent progress on the plains was far easier. When the Civil War ended, in 1865, the Union Pacific Railroad, which had the contract for the other end of the track starting in Council Bluffs, Iowa, began to make good progress. Boosting the Union Pacific's construction, many ex-Civil War soldiers joined the teams of railway-builders, providing a disciplined workforce supplemented by freed slaves.

Like the Central Pacific, the Union Pacific was deeply corrupt and became a vehicle to enrich its backers, notably Thomas C. Durant, the company's vice-president, and his cronies. Both companies came up with a simple scheme to purloin the public purse: they created separate construction companies, which were given contracts to construct the line at inflated prices, creating vast profits for these companies, which in turn paid out generous dividends to their proprietors – who just happened to be the owners of the railway companies. In this way, all the main railway backers became multimillionaires at the government's expense.

Building a railway in the sparsely populated west of the US required a remarkable level of organization, and as many as 10,000 workers at its peak. The railway was constructed in stages: first, an advance party surveyed the route; then graders smoothed out the route, shifting huge amounts of rock and earth, laying the embankments and building the bridges; these were followed by the tracklayers, who put down the sleepers and rails.

The workers lived in camps that moved forwards with the railway. These virtual towns became known as "hells on wheels". They were infamous for their spartan accommodation and saloons – the original of those later portrayed in so many Westerns. Fights were frequent, both with fists and with guns, and the danger of shoot-outs in these townships was constant. The workers also risked attack from Native Americans justifiably incensed at the land grab. The railwaymen responded with force to the raids and massacred countless Sioux and Cheyenne people, including women and children, in reprisals, although they established a better relationship with the Pawnee, allowing them free rides on the railway and establishing an alliance with them against the Sioux.

Groups of workers fought among themselves too. The government contracts had been set up in such a way that the two companies were competing to build the most track, as no meeting point had been specified. At one stage, the two lines passed each other on a mountainside: the Irish labourers of the Union Pacific were blasting rock, which tumbled down on the Chinese workers of the Central Pacific below. Enraged, the Asians started a fight that was only ended by negotiations between the companies. The Central and Union negotiated a truce over where their respective tracks should meet. This was at Promontory Summit in Utah, where, on 10 May 1869, Stanford and Durant took turns to bang in a golden spike. A momentous occasion, it was marked by celebrations across the US as the news spread rapidly by telegraph. In Chicago, an 11-km (7-mile) parade jammed the streets, while in New York, the event was marked by a 100-gun salute. In Sacramento, 30 locomotives that had been assembled for the occasion tooted their whistles in a tuneless concert. Despite the corruption and construction problems, it had taken only six years for the line to be

THE MEETING AT PROMONTORY SUMMIT, 1869
Samuel S. Montague of Central Pacific Railroad (centre left)
shakes hands with Grenville M. Dodge of Union Pacific
Railroad (centre right). The workers' celebratory liquor
bottles were removed from some versions of the picture.

GOLDEN SPIKE
The golden spike that
marked the "railway wedding" at
Promontory Summit, Utah, in 1869
– regarded as the day that the eastern and
western states of America were united.

completed, rather than the expected ten years – although, in
fact, the tracks were not quite continuous across the US until
the bridge over the Missouri between Council Bluffs and Omaha
was completed in 1872.

The "railway wedding" at Promontory Summit is still celebrated
today in US history as the day on which the country was united. The
importance of the achievement cannot be overestimated. A journey
that would have taken six months on precarious wagons through a
harsh climate – baking in the summer, freezing in winter – could
now be achieved in a few days. It triggered the settlement of the
West, and immigrants flowed westwards.

Soon, other transcontinental railways were under construction,
both in the US and in Canada. The next two lines opened in 1883
– the Southern Pacific (the name of the ocean was used by nearly all
the companies), which ran to Los Angeles in California, and the
Northern Pacific, which terminated at the other end of the western
seaboard in Seattle, Washington. Generous government grants of
land stimulated this intense bout of railway construction, as well as
a conviction that the lines would bring profits through the
anticipated influx of immigrants.

A fourth line was built without any government support, thanks
to the tenacity of a remarkable one-eyed frontiersman, James J. Hill.
Known as the "Empire Builder", he was probably the greatest North
American railway-builder. Hill was a strange-looking fellow, lithe
and short with a huge nose, a small mouth, and deep-set eyes, one of
which he had lost in his youth in an archery accident. He was also a
remarkable wheeler-dealer, who for 30 years pursued his vision of
building a line that would open up the vast prairies of Montana to
settlers and made it possible to export grain to the Far East. Moreover,
his line the Great Northern Railway – which in 1893 linked St Paul,
Minnesota, to Seattle, Washington – was built to a higher standard
than those of his rivals, with gentler gradients and without the tight
curves that make trains slow down.

To complete the "set" in the US, the Atchison, Topeka, and Santa Fe Railway crept quietly westwards, funded by real estate offices that sold the land that had been granted to it by the government. The railway, which linked up with existing California lines in 1884, became the most successful of the transcontinental lines by carrying freight through to the port at Los Angeles. Indeed, freight was the mainstay of most of these lines. However, the flow of immigrants proved profitable too, and the lines competed to attract them to the areas served by their routes. The railways promoted themselves to potential settlers, even opening offices in Europe to attract new migrants so that they could cash in on their vast land holdings. All kinds of dubious claims about the fertility of the land and the mildness of the climate were made to entice desperate people seeking a better life – many of whom gave up after their first winter of heavy snowfall or summer of drought.

Canada, then a British colony, was determined to build a transcontinental line too. This was for commercial reasons, but also to unify the disparate parts of the country – notably British Columbia, which had threatened secession. If anything, the achievements of the builders of the first Canadian line, the Canadian Pacific Railway, were greater than those of their rivals south of the border. As ever, the man in charge, William Cornelius Van Horne, was a remarkable character who took a hands-on approach. He travelled from site to site and was not averse to walking over rickety trestle bridges to show his workers that they must be equally fearless.

It was 4,300km (2,700 miles) from the developed regions of Ontario to the Pacific Ocean, half as far again as the distance covered by the first US transcontinental, and the terrain was certainly no easier. The route of the Canadian Pacific ran to the north of the Great Lakes and, although the initial sections were relatively flat, the granite shelf of the Canadian Shield required considerable blasting through hard rock. There were also two mountain ranges, the Rockies and the

"If he'd of lived, he'd of been a great man. A man like James J. Hill"

F. SCOTT FITZGERALD, *THE GREAT GATSBY*

Selkirks. The line was initially built at a very steep gradient of 1 in 22 (4.5 per cent) to reach the mountain heights, but these steep stretches were later replaced by spiral tunnels. The tough conditions took a high toll on the 15,000 workers, half of whom were Chinese, and at least 800 men died through want of basic safety measures. It took 13 years to complete the line, which opened without fanfare, on Van Horne's instructions, in 1885.

It was another 30 years before the opening of the next Canadian transcontinental, the Canadian Northern Railway, which took a more northerly route through the mountains. It was built gradually, in sections, with the aim of attracting settlers to the vast prairies of western Canada. The rivalry between the first two lines then prompted the decision to build a third, the Grand Trunk Pacific/ National Transcontinental Railway, built in two sections east and west from Winnipeg. This was the hardest of the three to build, and was in many ways unnecessary, since for hundreds of miles it ran parallel to the first Canadian transcontinental.

As a result of all this frenzied construction, there were no fewer than five transcontinental routes across the US by the end of the 19th century, and the three Canadian transcontinental railways were all completed by the end of World War I. However, Canada had overreached itself, given its sparse population, and its second two railways were declared bankrupt soon after their completion – a fate also suffered by several of the American transcontinentals. Nonetheless, these lines continued to operate, providing vital links within their respective countries, and were instrumental in stimulating population growth and economic development: the railways had conquered the West. Most of the tracks still survive today, playing a vital role in transporting freight.

CANADIAN PACIFIC RAILWAY
A freight train crosses Surprise Creek Bridge in the Glacier National Park, British Columbia. The original bridge, one of several over deep chasms on the line, was wooden. It was replaced by a steel bridge in 1894.

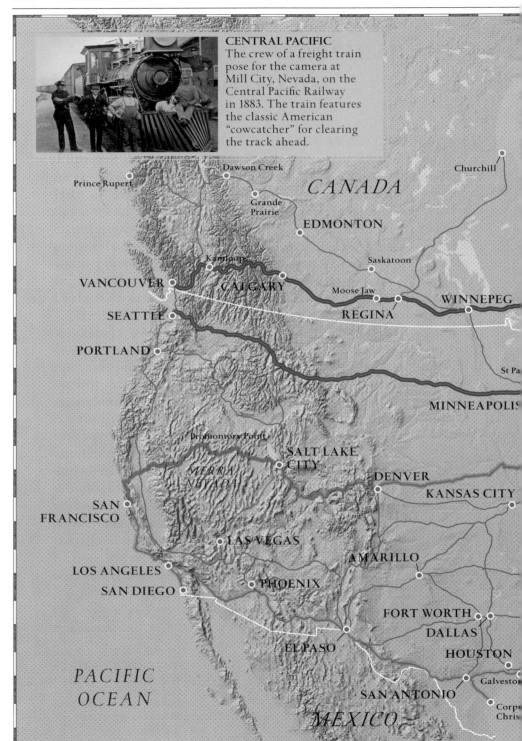

CENTRAL PACIFIC
The crew of a freight train pose for the camera at Mill City, Nevada, on the Central Pacific Railway in 1883. The train features the classic American "cowcatcher" for clearing the track ahead.

Prince Rupert

Dawson Creek

Churchill

CANADA

Grande Prairie

EDMONTON

Kamloops

Saskatoon

VANCOUVER   **CALGARY**

Moose Jaw

WINNEPEG

SEATTLE   **REGINA**

PORTLAND

St Pa

MINNEAPOLIS

Promontory Point

SALT LAKE CITY

SIERRA NEVADA

DENVER

KANSAS CITY

SAN FRANCISCO

LAS VEGAS

AMARILLO

LOS ANGELES

PHOENIX

SAN DIEGO

FORT WORTH

DALLAS

EL PASO

HOUSTON

PACIFIC OCEAN

Galveston

SAN ANTONIO

Corp Chris

MEXICO

North American Transcontinentals

The first railway to cross North America was the Pacific Railroad – a combination of the Union and Central Pacific lines that linked Chicago and California. The fledgling United States of America was unified for the first time, opening up the country to further settlement and exploitation. The success of the first route spawned a profusion of alternatives – as well as three lines across Canada – which have together helped the US rail network to become the most extensive in the world.

IDSON BAY

Moosonee

Bathurst   Amherst

QUEBEC

MONTREAL

Lake Superior

Sault Ste Marie

Ottawa

Lake Huron

luth

Lake Ontario

Lake Michigan   TORONTO

Buffalo

Milwaukee

DETROIT   Lake Erie

CHICAGO

BOSTON
Providence
New Haven

NEW YORK

PHILADELPHIA

PITTSBURGH   Baltimore

DIANAPOLIS

WASHINGTON D.C.

ST LOUIS   Cincinnati   Newport News

ATLANTA

RMINGHAM   Savannah

Baton Rouge   Mobile   JACKSONVILLE

NEW ORLEANS   Tampa

GULF OF MEXICO   MIAMI

ATLANTIC OCEAN

KEY

- ○ City
- ○ Town
- ———— National boundary
- ———— Main line

HISTORIC ROUTES:

- ———— Southern Pacific
- ———— Union Pacific
- ———— Great Northern
- ———— Central Pacific
- ———— Canadian Pacific

Going Underground

B UILDING A RAILWAY UNDERGROUND was a radical idea, and it took a visionary man to dream up the scheme. That man was Charles Pearson, solicitor to the City of London, who realized in the 1840s that something had to be done about the congestion and chaos of the city's streets. The world's first metropolis, London was booming thanks to the Industrial Revolution. In the first half of the 19th century, its population had grown from 1 million to 2.5 million. As it had grown, its traffic problems had become unmanageable, with pedestrians, hackney carriages, and horse-drawn buses all competing for space on the roads.

Pearson realized that central London was crowded with terrible slum housing, but people could not live far from the centre as walking was the only way to get to work. The solution, he decided, was to build railway lines that extended beyond the city boundary; the central section of the railways, however, would have to be built beneath the city streets, so that houses would not have to be demolished. Pearson hoped these railways would allow people to move out to far better conditions than existed in the inner city "rookeries", with gardens and fresh air.

A serial campaigner, who fought for universal suffrage, civic rights for Jews, and penal reform, Pearson is best remembered for his ground-breaking achievement as pioneer of what became known as the Underground. He first set out his idea in 1845, in a pamphlet proposing a glass-roofed railway down the Fleet valley between King's Cross and Farringdon. Various inventors came up with similar ideas at the time. One scheme was to drain the Regent's Canal, which encircled central London, and convert it into a railway. Another proposal was for an overhead railway on arches, like those later constructed in New York and Chicago. A third, the most stylish, was for a "crystal railway" around London: a line either above or below street level, combined with a boulevard or walkway lined with shops and houses, and all covered by a glass arcade.

The 1840s were a period of intense railway construction. A central station for the whole capital was proposed at Farringdon, on the edge of the City of London, but in 1846, a commission ruled this out because of the destruction it would cause in the City. Instead, the mainline stations were located on the edge of the central area. Ironically, this aggravated congestion as passengers pouring off the trains tried to get around the centre of the city. Pearson's vision of an underground railway to link the stations was the obvious solution. He pushed through his

NUMBER OF NAVVIES WHO BUILT THE FIRST UNDERGROUND LINE BY HAND OVER TWO YEARS

2,000

plan, obtaining funds from the City of London as well as investment from existing railway companies, and the scheme received parliamentary approval in 1853. Unusually among railway pioneers, Pearson did not seek any financial gain from the project.

The Metropolitan Railway Company was founded in 1854, but it was not until early in 1860 that work started on a line to link three of the mainline stations – Paddington, Euston, and King's Cross – with the City, using a new method known as "cut and cover", which involved digging a cutting, laying the railway, and covering it with a tunnel. This technique was disruptive at ground level and meant that the railway usually had to follow the line of existing streets. Interestingly, one house that had to be demolished on the route of the line, at 23 Leinster Gardens, was recreated as a façade in order not to ruin an elegant terrace, the open track behind the façade serving as a vent for the steam trains. It became a running joke among postboys to send novices to that address to deliver telegrams.

Although the building of such a line was unprecedented, there was only one major mishap, when the Fleet River burst its banks and flooded the works to a depth of 3m (10ft) in June 1862. Despite this, the 7.5-km (5-mile) line opened in January 1863, only a few months behind schedule, at a cost of £1 million (around £50 million in today's money). Sadly, Pearson had died the previous September and missed the sumptuous banquet held at Farringdon station to celebrate its opening.

There had been doubts as to whether people would venture onto this new type of railway. Not only were the stations gas-lit and dark, but the trains were also hauled by steam engines that belched out smoke and steam, despite being equipped with special condensing equipment. The doubters, however, were proved wrong. Londoners

"CUT AND COVER" CONSTRUCTION
Navvies build a section of the Metropolitan
District Railway to link London's mainline
stations in the 1860s. This "cut and cover"
method caused significant disruption.

had few concerns about trying out this new invention – the world's first subterranean railway – and 30,000 braved what *The Times* had warned would be "dark, noisome tunnels" to travel on it on the first day, 10 January 1863. The Metropolitan Railway, which gave its name to underground systems all around the world, was an instant success. It provided cheap labourers' trains early in the morning, which proved hugely popular. After the workmen's trains came thousands of office clerks who worked in the City of London and could afford the more expensive fares charged later in the morning. Throughout the day, the trains attracted all types of traveller in three different classes.

The Metropolitan Railway sought to ban smoking at first, on the grounds that the locomotives already created a foul fug, but after a complaint in Parliament, the railway was forced to allow smokers on the trains. Indeed, the air was sometimes so filled with smoke that chemists near the stations enjoyed a roaring trade in Metropolitan Mixture (strong smelling salts), sold as a panacea for passengers overcome by the fumes. In general, though, one of the reasons people

UNDERGROUND INSPECTION
Chancellor of the Exchequer William Gladstone (front right) takes a tour of inspection of the Metropolitan Railway, with the company's directors and engineers, in 1862, a year before the line's opening.

"A journey from King Cross to Baker Street is a form of mild torture"

TIMES EDITORIAL, 1884

were attracted to the system was that it was safe. No severe accidents occurred during its crucial early days, and indeed very few have happened throughout its history. Within a dozen years of the opening of the first line, no fewer than 70 million people were travelling annually on what had soon become known as the Underground.

Flushed with success, the Metropolitan Railway began to expand almost immediately. It built two extra tracks between King's Cross and Farringdon, called the City Widened Lines, which were then extended further into the City. Other promoters were keen to get involved, and one was chosen to share the expansion of the network. This was the Metropolitan District Railway (later the District line), run by James Staats Forbes, a rival of the Metropolitan's chairman, Edward Watkin. The two were already in competition when they set out their respective schemes to expand the Underground: Forbes ran the London, Chatham, and Dover Railway, while Watkin was a director of its competitor in Kent, the South Eastern Railway.

For the next 30 years, the rival railways expanded the Underground system rapidly into north and west London. They had rather different conceptions, which is why the Metropolitan line extends far beyond central London into the Metroland developed in the 1920s and 1930s, while the District line only extends as far as the more central Wimbledon, Richmond, and Ealing. Nevertheless, thanks to the dynamism of this duo, the Underground network soon spread well beyond the existing city boundaries, and, wherever the lines were built, new housing soon sprang up.

Despite their achievements, the Metropolitan and District railways never reconciled their differences and remained in dispute over who should complete the Circle Line, which links nearly all of London's main-line terminals, until its completion in 1884. The two companies ended up running the line jointly, but remained in competition: the Metropolitan ran the clockwise trains and the District the anticlockwise ones. Hapless visitors to London had to choose between the two companies' ticket offices and could end up going the long way round the Circle if they unwittingly bought the wrong ticket.

In 1890, the first deep "tube" line, bored out of the London clay rather than being built by the cut and cover method, was completed. The City and South London Railway ran under the River Thames between Stockwell and the City. As there was inadequate ventilation in the tunnels deep underground, the trains were powered by electricity rather than steam. The line was dubbed the "tuppenny tube" as two pence was the fare for all journeys, and it too was an instant success – despite the fact that the trains operating the service had tiny windows and were universally known as sardine boxes. Other Tube railways soon followed. Both the Waterloo and City Line and the Central Line, the most successful of the early lines, had opened by 1900.

A series of pioneering promoters continued to develop the Underground. The next was Charles Yerkes, an American with a prison record who had once run Chicago's tramways, and turned out to be a transport visionary. He brought together several lines, both existing and proposed, under the auspices of the Underground Electric Railways Ltd (UERL); electrified the Metropolitan, District, and Circle lines; and, remarkably, built three deep Tube lines in the space of five years – the Piccadilly and Bakerloo lines, and the Hampstead section of the Northern line. By 1907, all the Tube lines through central London, except the Victoria Line (opened in 1968 and completed in 1972) and Jubilee Line (opened in 1979 and extended in 1999), had been built.

After Yerkes, progress was more in marketing than engineering. Frank Pick, who started working for the network in 1906 and ran it until 1940 alongside chairman Albert Stanley (later Lord Ashfield), created the public image of the Underground. Pick and Stanley were a successful partnership: Pick was an assiduous obsessive, while Stanley was more strategic. Their creation lives on today, a public organization whose achievements have been recognized around the world.

Pick instigated the design of both the famous red, blue, and white roundel that became the instantly recognizable Underground sign, and the innovative and much-imitated map devised by Harry Beck. An electrician employed by the company, Beck created the map, based on electrical diagrams, in his spare time. Pick also commissioned the Johnston Sans typeface for the organization, advertising posters

UNDERGROUND SIGN
Commissioned by Frank Pick, the
Underground logo first appeared as a
red disc in 1908. It was later adapted
into a bullseye by designer Edward
Johnston, and has evolved into the
distinctive roundel still in use today.

by artists both known and unknown, and cutting-edge architectural designs for new stations. For his part, Stanley persuaded the government to pay for suburban extensions of the system. Together, the pair built up the UERL into a vast organization encompassing almost all the Underground lines and London's buses, and ran the nationalized London Transport from its creation in 1933 until World War II, a period widely regarded as its heyday.

Although the system was neglected after the war and usage fell dramatically, it has revived since the 1970s and flourishes today. Built by people with vision, the London Underground is more than just a transport system; it is the mechanism that made it possible for London to grow in the way it did. The Underground allowed people to live further out, as Pearson wanted, but also enabled the centre of the city to remain compact and accessible. Today, the underground attracts record numbers of passengers. The network will soon benefit from the addition of Crossrail, running under London in an east–west direction and linking up with all the Underground lines, which will greatly relieve pressure on the system.

Uniquely, the London Underground has become the emblem of the city it serves. Thanks to Pearson and subsequent developers, London became the first city with a railway beneath its streets, and Britain was once again a pioneer. It was not until the end of the 19th century that other cities started building railways underground. Budapest, in Hungary, was the second city in the world to develop a metro system, which opened in 1896, more than 30 years after London's. Major cities such as Paris, New York, and Berlin followed in the early years of the 20th century. Now, most major cities boast an underground railway system and there are nearly 200 metro and subway networks around the world, from Yerevan in Armenia to Los Teques in Venezuela.

Death on the Rails

NOWADAYS, TRAVELLING BY RAIL is extremely safe, but this was not always the case. In fact, it took several generations to finally tame the "iron horse". Surrounding this strange and inherently dangerous beast, there were many other hazardous elements. In the words of an old-time railwayman: "Accidents don't happen by accident". Besides the trains themselves – especially their brakes – faulty signalling, defective tracks, human error, and organizational blunders were all culprits. Today, because of the knowledge that train travel is usually perfectly safe, any rail accident attracts an inordinate amount of attention from the media and public. However, no such attention was ever paid to the fate of the earliest railway workers, who put their lives on the line, literally. In Britain in the 1860s, 800 workers were killed every year, ten times the number of passengers who perished. The number of fatalities among both workers and passengers has declined steadily since then, but working on the railways, particularly on the track, remains a dangerous occupation.

The sheer metallic brutality of railway accidents often took more than a physical toll on those involved; they also caused mental anguish, which would now be identified as post-traumatic stress disorder. An early sufferer, British novelist Charles Dickens, described his feelings after he was involved in an accident at Staplehurst in Kent in 1865. At first, he behaved impeccably, nursing the sick and dying. He was, he said, "not in the least flustered at the time", but when he clambered back into his carriage he could not stop shaking. Recounting the incident later also provoked the same reaction: "In writing these words I feel the shake and am obliged to stop". Dickens never fully recovered from the trauma, remaining frightened of rail travel for the rest of his life, and dying – in a strange coincidence – on the fifth anniversary of the accident.

The only positive outcome of an accident is when it triggers improvement in safety measures or procedures, a process often ghoulishly dubbed "tombstone technology". This was evident as far back as 1842, after the first major disaster in France at Meudon on the line from Paris to Versailles (see p.43). Most of the deaths were caused not by the crash itself, but because the compartments were locked – to deter interlopers who had not paid for their tickets – so passengers were unable to escape from the wrecked train. Thereafter, compartments were left unlocked. Similarly, an appalling crash at Armagh in Northern Ireland in 1889 spurred on legislation that greatly increased the railway inspectorate's enforcement powers, and introduced better braking systems. Many of the fatalities in the Armagh crash were children, which heightened the tragedy and prompted such a strong legislative reaction. However, a famous contemporary wit, the Reverend Sydney Smith, suggested that it would take the death of a member of the nobility to really effect change: "We have up to this point been very careless of our railway regulations. The first person of rank who is killed [he suggested a bishop, a breed for whom he had a particular loathing] will put everything in order and produce a code of the most careful rules".

Even today, a safety inspector believes that "the railway gets safer and each incident enables us to improve still further". In the past few decades, installing powered doors, which passengers cannot open, has helped eliminate the problem of people jumping on or off moving trains – a form of idiocy that caused half the deaths and injuries at stations reported by British Rail in the 1980s. But tombstone technology has not

ARMAGH RAIL DISASTER
On 12 June 1889, a packed train with inadequate brakes slid backwards down a steep hill and collided with an oncoming train. It was Ireland's worst railway disaster – 89 people died, mostly children, and hundreds were injured.

always been applied. Wooden coaches had long been known to increase the risk of fire in the event of an accident, but as late as 1928, a crash near Bristol, England, involving these old-fashioned carriages resulted in 15 deaths when inflammable gas ignited. Even then, wood-framed coaches were not entirely abandoned in Britain until after 1945. Technological faults can also combine with other conditions to cause tragedy. In India, the deadly Bihar rail disaster of 1981 is thought to have been caused by flash flooding combined with a brake failure. The train derailed and plunged into a nearby river, taking all 800 of its passengers with it. This was one of the worst accidents in railway history, claiming the lives of an estimated 500 or more people.

Sometimes a train itself may be faultless, but other structural defects can spell doom. Using steel instead of iron has made rails stronger, but the "fishplate" joining rails can be weak. It was a faulty fishplate that caused an accident at Brétigny-sur-Orge near Paris, France, in the summer of 2013, killing seven people. Often, the rail tracks are only as safe as the structures that support them. Most famously, the first rail bridge over the River Tay in Scotland, built in 1878, was not designed to withstand really high winds. It collapsed a year after it was built, plunging a passenger train into the river below. As that memorably bad poet William McGonagall put it:

Beautiful bridge of the Silv'ry Tay!
Alas I am very sorry to say
That ninety lives have been taken away,
On the last Sabbath day of 1879
Which will be remembered for a very long time

2004 TSUNAMI RAIL DISASTER
An earthquake in the Indian Ocean on 26 December 2004 triggered massive tidal waves along the coast. A train in Sinigame on the southwestern coast of Sri Lanka was destroyed.

ON AVERAGE, ONE PERSON IS KILLED PER
5 BILLION KM
(3 BILLION MILES)
OF RAILWAY TRAVELLED

Some accidents are beyond human control. The deadly earthquake and tsunami of Boxing Day 2004 devastated the coast of South Asia. It also caused the world's worst rail disaster when 1,700 passengers were killed on a coastal railway in Sri Lanka. Other types of railway "accident" are all too human, and deliberate. Acts of railway sabotage have been common, not least in the repertoire of British Army Colonel T.E. Lawrence, also known as Lawrence of Arabia (see pp.288– 93). Many saboteurs, such as the French railwaymen who wrecked their own tracks in the latter stages of the German Occupation in World War II, are regarded as heroes. Others, such as members of the French Communist party responsible for a crash that killed 21 people in 1947 on the main line between Paris and Lille, are generally considered terrorists. More recently, attacks at stations and on trains as far apart as Madrid, London, and Mumbai demonstrate the vulnerability of railways to attack by those with evil intent.

Just as pilots are blamed for aircraft crashes, so engine drivers (confusingly called engineers in the US) are always in the spotlight. Fatigue, often after 12 or more hours at work, was the biggest problem before legal limits were introduced. This automatic fatigue syndrome affected not just drivers but other workers as well, such as the overworked signal repairmen who caused the Clapham disaster in London in 1988. Back in 1879, a time when the companies were fighting any attempt to limit working hours, a parliamentary enquiry reported the case of a guard who had been on duty for 19 hours and consequently failed to apply the brake on his train. And of course drivers are not immune to personal problems. Many people believe that the worst crash ever recorded on the London Underground, at Moorgate in 1975, which killed 43 people, was caused by a suicidal driver.

THE LEGEND OF CASEY JONES
In 1950, the US Post Office issued
a series of stamps honouring the
"Railroad Engineers of America".
Casey Jones was one of the drivers
immortalized in a stamp, and
described as "a railroader's hero".

The most frequent cause of railway accidents, killing thousands over the decades, is driving too fast. Nowadays, there are many more controls preventing drivers from speeding, and warning systems to notify them if they do. However, even on modern trains, speeding remains a problem, as seen in the appalling accident that killed 79 people in the summer of 2013 just outside Santiago de Compostela in northwest Spain. One driver who died while travelling too fast went on to become a cult figure in American folklore and folksong – Casey Jones. A crack engineer (driver) on the Chicago Fast Mail, Jones "took his farewell trip to the promised land" when he crashed into a stalled train in the fog in April 1900 while trying to make up lost time. Jones was killed on impact, but he saved the lives of all his passengers and crew by slowing the train at the last moment. As Wallace Saunders put it in his song *The Ballad of Casey Jones*:

> Casey smiled, said, 'I'm feelin' fine,
> Gonna ride that train to the end of the line.
> There's ridges and bridges, and hills to climb,
> Got a head of steam and ahead of time'.

Thankfully, train crashes are increasingly rare, especially in industrialized countries. In fact, it is car, rather than train, drivers, who remain the most likely cause of accidents on the railways, particularly at level crossings. In the US, this problem is much worse than elsewhere because there are about 200,000 level crossings across the country. They account for some 4,000 accidents and 500 deaths every year, nearly all of them car occupants, rather than rail passengers. In three-quarters of the cases, an official report attributed the disaster to "the impatience of the driver of the vehicle involved", a tendency that improvements in the design of level crossings and modernization of the warning signs can do little to improve. Train drivers have to sound their horn at every road crossing, however minor, which is why in the US trains are heard so frequently. Cumbersome lorries also pose a threat. On a line in rural France in 1997, a diesel train scythed a slow-moving petrol tanker in two, killing 31 people. It was the worst rail accident in France, a country proud of the safety of its trains.

Railway management has always been a legitimate target for blame, as one 19th-century American lawyer in a case involving a head-on collision remarked: "This is one helluva way to run a railroad". Operations were initially haphazard, because no one knew anything about railways. As writer-engineer L.T.C. Rolt put it: "When we consider operational methods in the early days of railways the remarkable thing is that there were not more serious accidents". But organizational danger has, if anything, grown over the past few decades, mainly due to the outsourcing of railwork and maintenance, and the increasing prioritization of performance, punctuality, and, of course, cost. These kind of institutional inadequacies led to the most serious accident of modern times in Europe. In June 1998, 101 passengers were killed after the locomotive on a German high-speed train separated from the carriages, which then derailed. At the time, the Germans were desperately trying to catch up with the French, who had taken the lead in Europe in high-speed rail travel, and had taken short cuts to achieve the right balance of suspension, wheel design, and track flexibility. Deutsche Bahn had been warned of the problem but chose to ignore it, perhaps due to a combination of pride and an unwillingness to delay the introduction of high-speed travel.

Arguably the worst systemic problems in modern railways – including several fatal accidents – were caused by the privatization of British Rail in the 1990s. It was replaced by 94 separate organizations, many run by inexperienced executives. Track maintenance was also outsourced to a variety of companies, and it was shortcomings in this area that led to a crash at Hatfield, north of London, in 2000. Four passengers were killed and 70 were injured. Investigations into the crash revealed that the cause was a fractured rail, which exposed the failings of the private maintenance companies. Train speeds throughout Britain were reduced to a mere 32kph (20mph) for more than a year, which had repercussions for passengers and train companies alike. As a result of the accident, track maintenance was partially re-nationalized in 2002.

In the 21st century, as in the 19th century, railways and passengers are vulnerable to both natural and unnatural disasters. However, thanks to modern technology, trains are statistically the safest and most eco-friendly way to travel.

Stopping the Train

In rail's infancy, a train's brakes were simple wooden blocks, applied to the wheels by turning hand controls at several points along the train's length. As speeds increased, however, a more effective way of braking was required to stop trains over a shorter distance, and various attempts were made to create a brake with one point of control, operated by the driver. In 1875, a competition was held in Britain to find the best solution. The clear winner of these Newark Trials was the Westinghouse automatic air brake, which was widely adopted in the US. Britain initially used the less successful vacuum brake, but air brakes have since come into standard usage worldwide.

Brake blocks

The first simple brake blocks were soon developed to become "continuous" brakes. In this system, brakes were located on every carriage and were controlled from the locomotive engine by ropes, chains, or pipes running the length of the train. The wooden block was suspended by a lever, or levers, between the brake cylinder and the wheel. As technology progressed, the block was more often made from cast iron, which is still used widely, although modern railways also use a wide variety of composite materials.

BRAKE BLOCK ON NORFOLK AND WESTERN NUMBER 521, 1958

A DANGEROUS JOB
Before brakes were controlled solely from the engine, many trains had brake vans, with hand-operated screw brakes manned by brakemen. The train driver coordinated the braking with signals from the engine whistle.

Air braking systems

During the 1870s "battle of the brakes", air brakes could bring a train travelling at 80kph (50mph) to a halt in half the time taken by vacuum brakes: the braking distance for Westinghouse's automatic air brake was 237m (777ft), compared to 450m (1,477ft) for a vacuum brake – a considerable safety advantage. Today, air or pneumatic brakes are the standard system used by railways around the world. These brakes use compressed air to apply a brake block to the wheel.

AIR BRAKE APPLICATION
A pump compresses air for use in the system. The driver controls the air with a triple valve. When this is applied, compressed air is released into the brake pipe and air pressure forces the piston to move against a spring in the brake cylinder, causing the block to be applied to the wheels.

AIR BRAKE RELEASE
When the driver releases the brake valve, air leaves the brake pipes. As air escapes from the exhaust, a spring in the brake cylinder pushes the piston back, causing the brake blocks to disengage from the wheels. The auxiliary air reservoir meanwhile refills.

The Railway Experience

TRAVELLING ON TRAINS was not comfortable in the early days. Across Europe, the coaches were primitive with no amenities, and were based on horse-drawn stagecoach designs. Compartments seated six people facing each other, with doors on both sides. Carriages were made up of what was effectively a room supported on two axles, with a basic suspension system. Originally, most of the superstructure was made of wood, which was a fire risk and provided scant protection in the event of an accident.

On the Liverpool and Manchester, and on other early lines, there were different ticket prices. Passengers willing, or able, to pay a little more could obtain a place in the mail carriage, which had only a couple of comfortable corner seats and offered more privacy. At the other extreme, there was the discount option of riding in a charabanc-style wagon with sides open to the elements. As passenger travel became more popular, a hierarchy developed. Cheap tickets were available for boxlike wagons, which had holes in the floor for drainage, but often no seats. They were used on many railways throughout Europe and gave people an awful experience of rail travel. Fortunately, these open wagons were considered too dangerous, as well as horribly uncomfortable, and were soon phased out. To replace them, compartment-style carriages were built for second- and third-class passengers, with less space for people's legs and much harder seats than first-class carriages.

Some of the Trans-Siberian Railway services (see pp.180–89) were billed as "luxury", with staff instructed to empty spittoons and keep carriage temperatures at a balmy 14°C (57°F). In practice, however, customer service was not a strong point. Delays were standard, and at stations peasants scrambled out to cook soup on the platforms, further delaying the train. For everyone else, the dining cars served meals by St Petersburg time, regardless of the line's seven time zones: towards the east, passengers had to eat breakfast at 2pm, while dinner was served at 3am sharp.

The truly affluent had the option of bringing their own conveyances. The aristocracy simply arrived at the station in their personal horse-drawn coach, which was then lifted on to a flat wagon and held down with chains, rather as motorists put their cars on some trains today. The upper classes could thus avoid soiling their petticoats or pantaloons

THIRD-CLASS SATIRE
A cartoon by the French illustrator Honoré Daumier
showed porters lifting third-class passengers, stiff as
frozen cod, out of a wagon.

by sitting on cushions used by the masses, though even they could not
escape the smoke and ashes that enveloped all early travellers. The
dilemma facing passengers when the weather was hot was whether to
open the window and risk wrecking their clothes from the cinders, or
keep it closed and swelter. An infuriated English social reformer and
abolitionist, Harriet Martineau, reported that sparks had burned no
fewer than 13 holes in her gown during a journey in the United States.

In the early days, the ride was bumpy whatever vehicle class
passengers were travelling in. The springs were weak, or non-existent,
and the primitive track, made up of short rails, was uneven. Worse, the
couplings between the coaches were not rigid, but involved an
arrangement with chains. Every time the train set off or slowed down,
passengers were thrown about. There was no brake mechanism to
prevent the carriages from bumping into one another and despite the
padded seats in the superior coaches, complaints from the more well-
to-do travellers about their uncomfortable journey were frequent and
sustained. Luckily, the slowness of the trains reduced the severity of

these rough rides, but it was not unknown for the chains to break, leaving some poor passengers stranded. This explains why the last coach of the train was soon fitted with a red light — its absence would warn signallers that the train was not complete.

The compartment system made it easy for passengers to get on and off, but its main disadvantage was that people could not move within the train, so had no access to toilet facilities or refreshments. When journeys grew longer, trains had to stop at intermediate stations for "comfort breaks" — not an expression used in the 19th century — and meals. That was already the case across the Atlantic, where the design of coaches was different from the outset. Interestingly, some of the first American carriages were based on canal-boat rather than stagecoach designs. These early carriages were more practical and usually more comfortable than their European counterparts. They were longer and were open plan rather than fitted with compartments, which reflected the American ethos of equality. (Equality, of course, only amongst white passengers. Black passengers were segregated until the second half of the 20th century.) Some carriages even had seats on the roof, open to the elements, but this idea was soon abandoned.

INSIDE CARRIAGE INTERIOR
English painter Thomas Musgrave Joy's 1861 painting is titled *Tickets Please* and depicts conductors about to enter a tightly packed third-class carriage.

American carriages were similar to long omnibuses: they could accommodate up to 50 people on two-by-two seats with reversible backs, which were reasonably comfortable. Right from the start, there was a little annexe with a hole that opened straight out onto the tracks to serve calls

COMBINED LENGTH OF TRACK IN THE US IN 1840

4,500 KM
(2,796 MILES)

of nature. Relief was only partial. The wheel sets were relatively close to each other, which meant that the ends of the coaches swung to and fro, inducing dizziness and even vomiting, especially among children. The problem was not helped by the fact that there were only four wheels on the early vehicles, but happily this soon changed. Four-wheel vehicles gave way to six and then eight, greatly improving stability.

Novelist Charles Dickens, an experienced rail traveller in Britain, visited the US in 1842 and was pretty dismissive of what he found. Travelling on the Boston and Lowell Railroad, he was dismayed by the lack of class differentiation: "There are no first and second class carriages as with us; but there is a gentlemen's car and a ladies' car: the main distinction between which is that in the first, everybody smokes; and in the second nobody does". He noted, too, that there was a "Negro" car, which was "a great blundering clumsy chest". Dickens particularly took against the American habit of spitting – a fellow author described the central corridor through the train as "an elongated spittoon". Poor Dickens also recoiled when his fellow passengers tried to strike up friendly conversations with him about subjects such as politics, blithely oblivious to the famed English reluctance to talk to strangers and fastidiousness about topics of conversation.

Heating in winter was provided by a pot-bellied stove, which was not only a terrible fire risk when there were mishaps but also according to Dickens filled the air with what he called "the ghost of smoke". The stoves were ineffective, making it too hot for those immediately next to them, but giving no warmth to those further away. Lighting, too, was inadequate. Initially, there were lanterns with candles kept alight by the conductors. The lanterns were placed just above each seat, but gave out little light. Much better kerosene lamps replaced them by the 1860s. They hung from the roof and gave adequate lighting for the whole carriage, but they too were a significant fire hazard.

Thanks to the open-plan arrangements, American trains attracted hawkers walking along the carriage, offering things to read as well as drinks and snacks. The first hawkers were self-employed young men who had spotted an opportunity to make money, but later they were officially sanctioned. Many belonged to the gigantic Union News Company. They would pass through the trains offering the day's newspapers, magazines, sweets, soda pop bottles, and cigarettes. They announced their arrival in a falsetto voice, compressing their wares into a single word such as "candycigarettescigars" or "newspapersmagazines". Another British writer, Robert Louis Stevenson, travelling a few years later than Dickens, was much impressed by these young men and was amazed that he could buy "soaps, towels, tin washing basins, tin coffee pitchers, coffee, tea, sugar and tinned eatables, mostly hash or beans and bacon". It was, he noted, much more entertaining than a ride on a British train. But the vendors were not universally welcomed as some ran scams. The favourite was to sell cheaply bound novels for twice the normal 25 cents, with the promise that one of them contained a $10 note.

The American open-plan model created another difference from Europe: conductors went through the train checking and selling tickets and generally policing the passengers. They were a fearsome bunch and some, who were often on the same train every day or week, became well known to their regulars and even beyond. The doyen of them was Henry Ayers, or "Poppy" as he was generally known, described as "a huge, genial teddy bear of a man, weighing nearly three hundred pounds... [who] hovered over his passengers with benevolent menace". Ayers achieved fame because he had a fierce dispute over the use of the emergency cord with his driver on the Erie Railroad. The driver refused to acknowledge that the conductor had ultimate control over the train. By winning the argument, Ayers established railway practice that remains universal to this day and went on to serve the Erie for 30 years. His favourite tale was that he convinced an old lady who had left her umbrella at her station that he had organized to have it sent

BADGE OF OFFICE
Railway conductors wore official badges on their uniforms. This one, dated 1880, is from the Baltimore and Ohio Railroad.

TRAVELLING IN STYLE
This luxurious interior of an American railway
carriage in 1870 resembles an elegant drawing
room on wheels.

on by telegraph. The truth was that lost items were dumped in the
baggage car, so Ayers simply retrieved the umbrella and presented it to
its grateful owner at the next station.

In the early days, train travel in the US was more comfortable than
in Europe because people had the freedom to move about their
carriages. There was also an outside area on the last coach, which
afforded some much-needed fresh air in the summer. At first, the
connections between the cars were too difficult for passengers to
negotiate safely, but they soon improved, so people could walk through
the whole train. European carriages only began offering the same
facility for their passengers in the last quarter of the 19th century, when
trains with corridors were introduced, but the layout was different.
Instead of an American open plan, the corridor was a passageway at one
side of the carriage — at first external and used only by rail staff or
intrepid passengers, but later internal. Introducing a corridor marked a
significant step forward in passenger comfort since facilities such as
toilets could now be provided and passengers could have access to a
refreshment car. This meant that trains no longer had to make
intermediate comfort stops. Although corridor trains became the
norm, compartment-type carriages lingered well into the last quarter
of the 20th century on some European local and commuter services.

Points and Passing Loops

Points, or railroad switches, are track arrangements that allow one set of rails to connect with another. The mechanism consists of a pair of moveable tapered sections of track, known as points, which can be pushed into one of two positions, enabling a train to remain on its course or to divert to another line. A common function of points is to control access to a passing loop, or turnout – a length of track that briefly diverges from a line, allowing a train to be temporarily housed while another train passes by. A loop is a type of siding, which is any low-speed section of track that branches away from a running line. Sidings can also be used for mashalling, storing, loading, and unloading vehicles, and for holding maintenance equipment.

SETTING THE POINTS
Traditionally, points were controlled remotely from signal boxes. However, some still had to be operated by hand well into the 20th century – particularly those that controlled access to sidings and goods yards.

Sharing the line

Passing loops allow multiple trains to run on the same routes. They are used primarily at stations to let trains vacate the main line so that express services can pass through, or on longer stretches of track to enable freight trains to be passed by faster passenger services. Safety signals ensure that only one train occupies a passing loop at any one time.

A FREIGHT TRAIN WAITS ON A PASSING LOOP,
LEAVING THE MAIN LINE UNOBSTRUCTED

Changing tracks

The key component of a modern railway is the points mechanism, which was invented by English engineer Charles Fox in 1832. The mechanism is activated by a lever connected to a pull rod, which moves the points from one track to the next. Most points are now electrically operated, but pneumatic versions are also used on some networks, particularly underground lines.

Main line open | Branch line closed
No signal for branch line
Point closed
Switch stand or lever
Pull rod extended
Point open

Main line closed | Branch line open
Branch line signal
Point open
Switch stand adjusted
Pull rod retracted
Point closed

STAYING ON TRACK
The points are set to keep the train on the main line. The lever is thrown, extending the pull rod to slide the moveable rails across the track, drawing the left-hand point away from the track and bringing the right-hand point parallel to it.

SWITCHING TO THE BRANCH LINE
The points are set to divert the train onto the branch line. The lever is adjusted, retracting the pull rod to bring the left-hand point flush with the main track and the right-hand point away from it. The signal indicates the right-hand branch is open.

GREENWOOD SIGNAL BOX, NEW BARNET
BRITISH RAILWAYS
ON EARLY SHIFT
BRITISH RAILWAYS

THE SIGNAL BOX
A signal box is an operational nerve centre from which signals are sent to incoming and outgoing trains and points are opened and closed to direct railway traffic. A single signalman can control an entire lever frame (left) to activate all the relevant signals and points.

Temples of Steam

T HE LATTER 70 YEARS of the 19th century are commonly known as the railway age. But it would perhaps be more apt to call the period the railway station age. Stations were a highly visible presence for travellers, and the first glimpse of a new place for visitors.

Railways were a revolutionary intrusion into people's lives. They introduced a whole new world of speed, noise, and bustle, all rather frightening to people more used to the gentle clip-clop of horse-drawn travel. But the vast majority of travellers were oblivious to the marvels of engineering that had gone into building the lines, the bridges, viaducts, cuttings, and other structures. The station was the passengers' point of contact with the iron road. Architects had to hit the right note – the stations needed to be solid and reassuring, laying a balm of soothing normality over an unprecedented and therefore alarming experience. Moreover, the buildings had to reflect the importance of the railway company responsible for the station, and its recognition of the town or society it served.

It took only a decade after the launch of the railways in 1830 for a quartet of stations to be built worthy of the term "Temples of Steam". The progenitors were the two men who pioneered the modern long-distance railway, Robert Stephenson and Isambard Kingdom Brunel. Stephenson ensured that both terminals of the railway he built between London and Birmingham would be worthy of his extraordinary engineering achievement. Stephenson's architect, the eminent Philip Hardwicke, built a noble Grecian-style building at Curzon Street in Birmingham. At Euston in London he constructed a Great Hall of elegant grandeur, with the world's first boardroom upstairs, but unfortunately the heavy Doric arch in front of the station overshadowed the graceful proportions of the Hall.

Brunel could not be outdone by Stephenson. In the early 1840s, his own design for a terminus at Bristol was unexceptional, but 10 years later he worked with a distinguished architect, Matthew Digby Wyatt, to produce Paddington Station in London. Brunel's innovative glass-roofed train shed was complemented by Wyatt's station buildings and 130-room Great Western Hotel, a handsome Renaissance building, and the largest hotel in the country at that time. The hotel and the separation of the station buildings and train shed served as a model for many others – most effectively at St Pancras in London where the contrasting neogothic hotel and glass-roofed train shed were larger and more dramatic than anywhere else in the world.

Stations were not just the temples of a new railway age; along with town halls, they showcased the character of a town or city. Railway companies and their architects continued to emphasize solidity but styles varied wildly as every country reflected its "inner self". Scots went in for Highland style, Germans chose a heavy, Teutonic look, while Spanish and Portuguese stations recalled their ancient Moorish past. Americans went furthest in providing a variety of styles. As railroad historian Lucius Beebe remarked, with only slight exaggeration: "Passengers were set down in storybook settings, Grecian temples, Moorish arches, French chateaux, the tombs of Egyptian dynasts, Turkish mosques, Palladian porticos, Gothic castles and Italian palazzi". The beautiful Antwerp Central station in Belgium is thought to reflect so many different architectural styles as to be unclassifiable; conversely, Flemish architectural style can be seen in the early-20th century Dunedin station in New Zealand. Whatever the style, reactionaries hated the new station buildings. The 19th-century British art critic John Ruskin was appalled at their pretensions to architectural beauty since they represented industry, which, for him, was inherently hideous.

The grandiose Temples of Steam formed only a minute proportion of the hundreds of thousands of stations built around the world during the 19th century. The smaller ones were often delightful examples of local architecture, sometimes standardized by the railway company itself, such as the handsome villas spread over much of western France. In Russia, on the Trans-Siberian Railway, there were five classes of station. The highest class were built of brick and had heated waiting rooms, while the lowest were little more than huts to shelter waiting passengers from the elements.

American stations were generally built in the middle of the city. Thousands of small towns owed their very existence to the railway, which often ran down the main street. Stations were at the heart of the

"Railway termini are our gates to the glorious and the unknown"

E.M. FORSTER, AUTHOR, 1910

community, full of "retired gentlemen, idlers of all kinds, champion talkers, crackerbarrel philosophers". Although there was powerful opposition to lines and stations near some city centres, in Europe, historic York allowed its ancient city walls to be breached to admit the iron horse, while in Cologne the station abuts the city's historic cathedral. However, if a station was not built in the centre it simply resulted in the creation of a new, important part of town. The railway companies also created their own towns, simply by locating the enormous workshops needed to build and maintain the trains there.

The shape and size of stations outside Europe and the United States often reflected the tastes of imperial masters or European immigrants, notably in Canada where there was a remarkable mix of French and Scottish heritage. In India, the station and its associated buildings such as the engine sheds formed part of an elaborate social and industrial complex, planned by the British colonists. The most impressive example of this is the massive Victoria Terminus (now renamed the Chhatrapati

VICTORIA TERMINUS, MUMBAI
Pictured in 1910, the splendid Victoria
Terminus is modelled on St Pancras
Station in London. It is still in use today.

Shivaji Terminus) in Mumbai, completed in 1888. In South America, however, architectural roots varied. Argentinian stations, usually built with British money, reflected their financiers' tastes, but in neighbouring Uruguay locals built stations in their own style. Stations could also fall prey to triumphalism: when the Prussians retook Alsace and Lorraine from the French in 1871, they imposed their own design on a new station at Metz in Lorraine, complete with statues of Teutonic warriors.

Railway stations provided the stage for poignant scenes of farewell and reunion, especially during wars. The departure to the Western Front of waves of soldiers from Waterloo Station in London and the Gare de l'Est in Paris left a lasting impression. Then, in 1939, millions of children were evacuated from cities across Europe, helped on to trains by their distraught parents. The emotional power of the station was not lost on film producers either, from the tear-jerking family reunion at a small country station in *The Railway Children*, to the highly charged meetings in a station café of *Brief Encounter*. The world's first film, *A Train Entering a Station*, made by Louis Lumière, depicted a train heading directly towards the camera, causing some of the audience to flee in terror. Artists were inspired by stations, too, such as Claude Monet, who painted a whole series of canvases at the Gare St Lazare, just below the Parisian café where he and his Impressionist colleagues used to meet.

Stations also created new markets. Two major companies, WH Smith in Britain and Hachette in France, were founded to cater for travellers' needs for reading matter – and so gave birth to the much despised but highly popular "railway novel". However, the glory of a major station could be marred by the inadequacy of the catering. In the half-century before the arrival of special dining or buffet cars on trains, passengers had to rely on refreshments or even whole meals snatched at stations. The owners of these establishments naturally exploited their monopoly. However, Europe led the way in station food, especially France. In Ian Fleming's novel *Goldfinger*, James Bond stayed at railway hotels because, "It was better than an even chance that the Buffet de la Gare would be excellent". Today, the sumptuously decorated Train Bleu restaurant at the Gare de Lyon in Paris is justly famous, as is the Oyster Bar at Grand Central Station in New York.

By the end of the 19th century, station architects – and the companies behind them – were confident enough not only to design afresh, but also to use architecture to express a political, social, or national vision. The modernist station with exciting clean lines designed by Eliel

Saarinen for Helsinki, Finland, in 1919 announced not only the arrival of the modernist movement but also proclaimed Finland's newly declared independence from Russia (1917). And after World War I, the French gloried in local Norman and Breton styles in a number of provincial stations, while at Perpignan in French Catalonia they erected a statue of Spanish surrealist artist Salvador Dalì. Even the new station at Milan, Italy, in 1930 was Mussolini's statement of fascist grandeur.

World War II destroyed many great stations, but postwar reconstruction programmes included the last true Temple of Steam, the Roma Termini in Rome, Italy. As the motorcar usurped the train, however, stations became neglected. The train services in many countries were scaled back, with some routes and stations permanently closed. A few stations were rebuilt but others were demolished – the most tragic victim was Penn Central in New York. The worst officially sanctioned railway vandalism occurred when the Belgian railways carved a cutting through the heart of Brussels to link the stations to the north and south, inflicting a permanent wound on the city. However, some disused stations were converted for other worthy purposes, such as the Gare d'Orsay in Paris, which now houses the Musée d'Orsay, a national art gallery, or Manchester Central Station in Britain, which was transformed into a convention and concert venue. In the US, some great union stations, such as St Louis, survived without any trains by becoming shopping, hotel, and entertainment complexes.

Today, many of the stations that survived destruction during the motorcar boom of the 1960s are now flourishing, with their architectural heritage preserved. St Pancras Station in London is a splendid example of the renaissance not just of trains but also of their stations. Until the end of the 20th century, it was best known as a decaying architectural masterpiece, which had been saved from demolition in the 1960s, but housed only a derelict hotel and a grimy set of platforms. Today, thanks to a substantial renovation completed in 2007, it is a world-beater. In Spain, the magnificent Atocha station in Madrid underwent a rather unique rebuild; originally designed in collaboration with French engineer Gustave Eiffel, during the 1990s its striking main hall was converted into a huge botanical garden, complete with turtles. Stations such as St Pancras, Grand Central Station in New York, Kyoto Station in Japan, the Berlin Hauptbahnhof in Germany, and Toronto Union Station in Canada are no longer used simply by travellers passing through, but have become destinations in their own right.

GRAND CENTRAL
Seen here in 1930, the majestic concourse at Grand Central Station in Manhattan, New York, looks remarkably similar today, thanks to a loving restoration.

Railway Signal Telegraphy

The telegraph transformed railway signalling, making it possible for train operators to send messages ahead of trains for the first time. American inventor Samuel Morse devised the earliest experimental telegraph, and the Cooke and Wheatstone needle telegraph, a later model, first entered commercial use in 1838 when it was adopted by the Great Western Railway in Britain. The system gained wider acceptance after its dramatic role in apprehending British murderer John Tawell in 1845: he had been seen boarding a train at Slough, and this information was telegraphed ahead to Paddington Station, where he was arrested. In 1844, Morse's telegraph transmitted the words "What hath God wrought" from Baltimore to Washington, DC, and brought about a revolution on the US railroads.

The needle telegraph

Inventor William Fothergill Cooke and scientist Charles Wheatstone patented their five-needle telegraph in 1837. It consisted of a receiver with needles that were moved by electromagnetic coils to point to letters on a board. Each letter was communicated via two currents flowing down two wires, causing the receiving telegraph's needles to swing to the left or right. Six letters were omitted – C, J, Q, U, X, and Z – a limitation that caused confusion when identifying the murderer Tawell (see above), who was described as wearing a "KWAKER" (Quaker) coat.

COOKE AND WHEATSTONE FIVE-NEEDLE TELEGRAPH (1837)

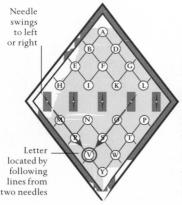

Needle swings to left or right

Letter located by following lines from two needles

READING THE MESSAGE

The five-needle telegraph was popular with users as it did not require any knowledge of codes: two of the five needles pointed to one of 20 letters laid out in a diamond pattern on the receiver to spell out words. Over time, the system was simplified to two needles and then to a single needle, mainly to reduce the cost of replacing wires as they deteriorated. However, systems with fewer needles required complex codes, so telegraphy became a specialized job.

Morse's telegraph

Invented in 1835, Morse's first telegraph used a pencil point attached to an electromagnetic pendulum. His partner Alfred Vail suggested using a lever and armature to print a code of dots and dashes – the precursor to Morse code – sending the message "a patient waiter is no loser" in 1838. This system, patented in 1840, was soon adopted in the US both for railway signalling and general use, with lines built alongside new railroads. It was cheaper and simpler to use than the needle telegraph, especially once adapted to an audio system.

MORSE KEY SOUNDER (1875)
The Morse telegraph had one wire and an earth connection, and used a single current switched on or off to send dots and dashes.

REPAIRING THE WIRES
A linesman repairs a telegraph line at Billericay, Essex in the UK in 1932. The telegraph remained integral to railway signalling, and was still in use as late as the 1970s.

Monopolies and Railway Barons

ACCUSTOMED AS WE ARE TO THE NOTION of national railways and large rail monopolies, it is hard to imagine today that the early railways were made up of hundreds of small companies, each serving its own limited local area. Local entrepreneurs created these railways, largely from a desire to improve transport for their own goods rather than as a result of any grand vision. However, as the railways expanded, they became more ambitious in scope, and economies of scale became evident. Not only was it convenient for people to travel long journeys on one train, it was also more profitable for the train companies to operate in this way. It was relatively cheaper to carry goods over a longer distance, as loading and unloading them was expensive.

Lines gradually grew longer. In Britain, the London and Birmingham Railway was the first railway more than 160km (100 miles) long, and a civil engineering project far larger than any that had gone before. Robert Stephenson, son of George Stephenson (see pp.22–29), was appointed chief engineer in 1833 and the railway, London's first main line, opened five years later in 1838. Other, longer, railways soon followed, such as the Great Western from London to Bristol, constructed by engineer Isambard Kingdom Brunel between 1835 and 1841 at a cost of £6.5 million (US$32.5 million), and the London and Southampton, completed in 1840. In the United States, both the pioneering railways – the 219-km (136-mile) Charleston and Hamburg, which opened in 1833, and the Baltimore and Ohio, whose first section ran from 1830 – were ambitious projects that extended far inland from the Atlantic Coast port cities they served.

The men who managed the railway companies were generally enterprising and progressive, and could see the benefits of far-reaching railway networks. As the railways became established, these men dreamed up ever-grander schemes, and railway promoters raised finance for their construction. These longer railways began to sprout branches, and the companies grew. Given the advantage of large networks, it was inevitable that railway companies should come together first to provide joint services. However, even as they extended their reach, the railway companies remained distinct until

THE BALTIMORE AND OHIO RAILROAD
Among the first American lines, the B&O was also
part of the heyday of the railway barons and the
battles between the first large companies. Pictured
here is the early B&O locomotive *Atlantic* in the 1830s.

competition between them made the creation of monopolies
attractive and they began to merge – a process that accelerated
when railways fell on hard times, and rivals took over their
struggling competitors.

Amalgamated railway companies soon became the biggest
enterprises in the world. In many respects, their development prefigured
the growth of capitalism. Before the railways, there were no large
companies in any industry, with the exception of quasi-government
organizations such as the Dutch East India Company. Factories were
still just small buildings where goods were made, owned by local
entrepreneurs and supplying their immediate area. These firms
employed local people and were part of the local community.

The railways were a totally new and different sort of enterprise. To
begin with, they stretched dozens and later hundreds of miles, taking
them across many different localities. Then, they demanded a new
style of management with complex organizational structures.
Furthermore, the companies needed bosses with vision and great
ability, able to see the bigger picture as well as being industrious. In
Britain, already off to a head start with the railways, the first larger-scale,

amalgamated, companies began to emerge. The new companies were powerful and self-important, as testified by the grand stations they erected in major cities (see pp.154–59). The first mega-company to spring from the dozens of smaller railways was the Midland Railway, created by entrepreneur George Hudson (see pp.54–55). In 1844, Hudson created the Midland by amalgamating three lines: the North Midland Railway, the Midland Counties Railway, and the Birmingham and Derby Junction Railway, all of which converged at Derby. The new, combined railway created the core of a line that ran all the way from London to York, offering a more convenient service to its passengers, with fewer changes of train. Hudson had also built the Newcastle and Darlington Junction Railway, which he now linked to the rest of his network via York, so that he had control of more than 1,600km (1,000 miles) of railway. He continued to consolidate the network throughout the 1840s by taking over other smaller Midlands lines. In 1842, Hudson cleverly created the Railway Clearing House, an organization that enabled all the railway companies – of which there were now more than a hundred in Britain – to collect revenues from each other when passengers used more than one company's trains on a journey. Until then, passengers had been obliged to change trains and buy a new ticket at each stage of the journey. Sadly, for all his entrepreneurial genius, Hudson turned out to be a fraudster. The ticket-sharing scheme, however, long outlasted his downfall and the collapse of his railway empire.

Despite the obvious advantages of amalgamation, British politicians were reluctant to let the railways merge, fearing that monopolies would exploit the public. However, the financial weakness of some railways forced the government to accept the idea, especially at times of economic downturn, so throughout the mid-19th century, companies continued to merge.

One of the merger beneficiaries, the London and North Western Railway (LNWR), was, for a while the world's biggest company, employing 15,000 people at its peak. Its brilliant manager, Captain Mark Huish, was a former Indian Army officer. He shrewdly negotiated takeovers, managed the company in an innovative manner, and introduced novel accounting methods essential for the company's size. The LNWR was created in July 1846 by the amalgamation of the Grand Junction Railway, the London and Birmingham Railway, and the Manchester and Birmingham Railway. This created a network of 560km (350 miles). The core route connected London with Birmingham,

Crewe, Chester, Liverpool, and Manchester. Although it covered less ground than rivals such as the Midland, the LNWR offered the best route between London and the main towns of northwest England.

Once it was in a position of strength, the LNWR bullied rivals into forced mergers or disadvantageous deals to run on their tracks. But the bully-boy tactics did not always work. Two small railways that combined to run on a shorter route between Birmingham and Chester than their big rival were warned off by Huish: "I need not say if you should be unwise enough to encourage such a proceeding, it must result in a general fight..." To his alarm, they resisted the threat, fought a three-year battle through the courts, and, surprisingly, won. However, this was an exception. For the most part, the big bullies effectively quashed their smaller rivals.

In continental Europe, too, major networks were soon created from the plethora of companies that had started running rail services. In France, six big regional companies were formed with government encouragement between 1858 and 1862. The most ambitious, the Paris–Lyon–Mediterranée (PLM), soon extended over the border to Switzerland and Italy, creating an international network. The Rothschild banking family owned the PLM, along with a second French company, the Nord, and it looked for a time as if the Rothschilds would establish themselves as the dominant force in European railways. At one point they also controlled the Austrian Südbahn, which included the Semmering Railway (see p.102–107), and had concessions on various Italian lines. After unification, however, Italy prevented the Rothschilds from expanding their railway empire and effectively blocked the creation of "the biggest international railway company that had ever been seen". Instead, four big Italian companies were formed, but the poverty of the

PARIS–LYON–MEDITERRANÉE
One of the big six railway companies in France, and one of the first international companies, the Paris–Lyon–Mediterranée promoted its services to tourists with posters designed by artists of the day.

country and its difficult terrain, with the Apennines running down its spine, made it hard to make a profit. The nation suffered a railway crisis every few years and, unwilling to allow foreign takeovers, Italy in 1905 became one of the first nations to nationalize its railway system. In the early days of Swiss rail, meanwhile, the plutocrat Alfred Escher (see p.55) more or less oversaw the explosion in rail construction from the 1850s, and became so powerful that he was nicknamed "King Alfred".

The American railways soon eclipsed all others in scale. The distances to be covered were huge, so big companies such as the Erie Railroad and the Pennsylvania Railroad emerged early in railway history. When the first transcontinental was completed in 1869 (see pp.120–27), the Union Pacific and Central Pacific railroads became the railway giants. After them, a series of American railways earned that accolade as railway barons consolidated the network.

By 1900, seven companies controlled most of the US railways. Many of their proprietors became infamous, among them Jay Gould and his son George, J.P. Morgan, Edward Harriman, and the Vanderbilts. William, the younger Vanderbilt, demonstrated the attitude of the new railway barons to their passengers when asked by a reporter why a popular fast train was no longer operating: "The public be damned! ... I don't take any stock in this silly nonsense about working for anybody but our own," he is alleged to have replied. Daniel Drew, one of the first of these "robber barons" – a term applied by *Atlantic Monthly* in 1870 to the new breed of capitalists — was also one of the biggest rogues.

OUR ROBBER BARONS.

OUR ROBBER BARONS,
***PUCK*, 1882**
In this cartoon from satirical magazine *Puck*, "R. Road Monopolist" Jay Gould, William Vanderbilt, and other barons divvy up their spoils by "Castle Monopoly".

"We hear now on all sides the term 'Robber Barons' applied to some of the great capitalists"

ATLANTIC MONTHLY, 1870

As company treasurer of the Erie, Drew agreed several times for the company to borrow money against newly issued shares, and then used his position as an insider to profit from the trade in these shares – insider trading was not regulated at the time.

J.P. Morgan was the most successful of these entrepreneurs, forging a railway empire that stretched across the US by taking over ailing companies and reorganizing them. Unlike Drew, Morgan actually improved the railways he acquired. So too did Harriman, who became known as the "greatest rail baron in America". His background, as with most of these moguls, was modest: he started out as a messenger boy, but made money on the stock exchange and invested in railways. He boosted his assets by purchasing rolling stock, improving tracks, and establishing good management. His first major acquisition was the Illinois Central Railroad. After the Panic of 1893 – the last of a series of major 19th-century recessions caused by boom and bust in the business cycle – he added the massive Union Pacific to his set. Harriman made it profitable by straightening out bends in the track – many added unnecessarily by the builders to take advantage of government subsidies – and reducing gradients, and it became a money-spinner. By the turn of the century, Harriman controlled more track than any individual in the history of American railways. He was the baron of barons.

All too soon, the advent of the motorcar brought about the decline of the railways, and empires were broken up or bailed out by the government. In the US, however, one last pair of barons emerged in the 1920s: the Van Sweringens. This strange pair of reclusive brothers were property developers who bought a railway for its development potential and ended up with an empire that included the Erie, the Chesapeake and Ohio Railroad, and the Pere Marquette Railroad, which operated a series of lines in the Great Lakes area. Following the 1929 crash, however, their empire was broken up even more quickly than they had built it up. With this, the era of the big railway barons finally came to an end.

Building Bridges

As the railways expanded, railway bridges were erected to enable lines to follow the most direct routes possible. Engineers devised a range of architectural and engineering strategies for overcoming the obstacles of local geography – from vaulting brick viaducts spanning valley floors to iron suspension bridges that dangled tracks above rivers and gorges. Concrete and steel are now the materials of choice, but the ingenuity of modern designs is no less impressive than the elegant blends of function and form deployed by the early railway builders.

The Tangiwai disaster

New Zealand's worst ever rail bridge disaster occurred on Christmas Eve, 1953, when 151 lives were lost in the catastrophic failure of the Whangaehu River bridge near Tangiwai, in the centre of the North Island. A mudflow from a collapsed dam destroyed a supporting pier of the beam bridge (see panel, opposite), which gave way under the weight of an express train.

ENGINEERING MARVEL

At the time of its completion in 1890, the Forth Bridge in Scotland was the longest steel bridge in the world. Its three 100m-(330ft-) high trapezoid cantilevers support the railway at a height of 46m (151ft) for the 2.5-km (1.6-mile) crossing of the Firth of Forth sea inlet.

Types of bridge

Different types of railway bridges have been developed to meet geographical and economic constraints. While there are multiple variations on – and combinations of – each design, the basic types of bridge can be grouped into four categories: beam, arch, cantilever, and suspension.

THROUGH-TRUSS BEAM

DECK-TRUSS BEAM

BEAM BRIDGE

The simplest of all bridges, a beam bridge, consists of a "beam" or girder laid across a gap, supported at each end by piers and often strengthened by a truss. A through-truss design uses iron or steel struts joined together in triangular sections to form the load-bearing superstructure, which carries the railway track beneath. A deck truss uses the same arrangement of struts, but supports the beam from below.

THROUGH-ARCH

CANTILEVER

ARCH BRIDGE

A classic arch bridge supports the railway from below, but in the more sophisticated through-arch design, the top of the arch rises above the deck, suspending the railway from vertical cables or struts.

CANTILEVER BRIDGE

Built from sections that are supported at one end only, cantilever bridges have the advantage of not needing "falsework" (temporary supports) in construction, so are ideal for wide crossings.

CLASSIC SUSPENSION

CABLE-STAYED SUSPENSION

SUSPENSION BRIDGE

Well suited to long crossings in exposed, windy locations, suspension bridges make use of cables to support the deck. The classic design stretches a cable laterally between one or more towers, with vertical suspension cables to support the deck. A cable-stayed bridge suspends the deck directly from one or more towers via a series of angled suspension cables.

The Pullman Phenomenon

THE NAME OF ENGINEER GEORGE PULLMAN is still used to refer to the sleeping carriage he developed for rail passengers. He was the American "genius of the bed on wheels", who destroyed all his competitors to establish a monopoly in the Unted States by the end of the 19th century. As with many such legends, the original idea was not his, but Pullman made it his own.

It was inevitable that the first sleeping carriages would be developed in the US rather than in Europe, as journey times were longer and trains were slower because of the sharper curves and higher gradients of the tracks. At first, trains simply stopped for the night and passengers stayed in local hotels and inns. This was clearly both unsatisfactory and inefficient, so the first sleeping carriage was introduced on the Cumberland Valley Railroad in Pennsylvania in 1839. Unfortunately, it did not provide a comfortable night's sleep. The sleeping accommodation consisted of a couple of carriages, each with four sets of three-tiered berths. They were no more than hard boards without bedding or mattresses, which were then folded away during the day.

A few years later, the New York and Erie Railroad devised an equally uncomfortable solution. Two carriages, known as "diamond cars" because of the shape of their windows, were equipped with iron rods that could be used to link facing seats to create a basic bed. The cushions were made of horsehair cloth that penetrated all but the thickest clothing and were invariably infested with all kinds of ravenous insect. As if that were not bad enough, the condition of the track, with its short, badly laid rails, made the experience akin to "sleeping on a runaway train", according to one early passenger.

By the 1850s, matters had begun to improve. Several railways advertised improved sleeping accommodation based on an idea by Webster

GEORGE MORTIMER PULLMAN
Born in New York State in 1831, Pullman achieved success at a relatively young age. He had developed his first railway sleeping car before the age of 30.

Wagner, a stationmaster on the New York Central. He went on to found the Wagner Palace Car Company, a rival of Pullman. Wagner developed the idea of a coach with a single tier of berths and bedding closets at each end, a definite improvement on all its predecessors. Several other

THE VALUE OF PULLMAN'S PATENTS IN 1875

US$100,000
(TODAY, US$2 MILLION, OR £1.2 MILLION)

competitors emerged, building sleeping carriages to a variety of designs. But it was Pullman who transformed night-time travel on trains, making it not only comfortable but even respectable.

Like many railway entrepreneurs, Pullman had already been successful in a different enterprise — that of moving houses (not their contents, the buildings themselves). Several low-lying houses in New York State were in the way of a planned extension to the Erie Canal, so Pullman, along with his father, contrived to move them to higher ground by putting them on wheels. Pullman then moved to Chicago, where he started a fledgling railcar business in 1858, building two carriages for the Chicago and Alton Railroad that provided upper and lower sleeping berths.

The radical aspect of Pullman's design was that the upper berth was suspended from the ceiling by ropes and pulleys. When not in use, it could be hauled up to the roof, leaving plenty of seating space during the day — unlike older designs, in which the bunk was fixed and made life uncomfortable for passengers when they were not in bed. Curtains around the berths created privacy, but these carriages were still crude affairs. Candles provided lighting and a wood stove generated heat, but both were a great fire risk given the large number of flapping curtains. Each carriage accommodated 20 people, and blankets and pillows were provided, although not sheets. The experiment was successful. Soon the carriages, which ran between Bloomington, Illinois, and Chicago, filled up every night. The only problem was dirty footwear. The conductors had to convince the male passengers — who were the majority of travellers at this time — to take off their boots at night so that they didn't soil or damage the bedding. There was a great reluctance to do so, presumably because of fear of theft, so for many years every Pullman carriage carried notices politely requesting, "Please take off your boots before retiring".

PULLMAN PALACE CAR
Nicknamed "palace cars", these sleeping cars were modelled on the packet boats that a young George Pullman had seen travelling on the Erie Canal.

In 1861, in association with local authorities, Pullman supervised the raising of many of Chicago's buildings in an attempt to improve the city's street sewerage system. His most spectacular feat was the four-storey Tremont House Hotel, the tallest building in Chicago at the time. The hotel was in line for demolition, but Pullman devised a clever scheme to save it. He put the whole building on 5,000 jacks, then a team of 1,200 workers turned the screws 180° each time Pullman gave the signal. They successfully raised the hotel by 1.8m (6ft), while the house band continued playing and the hotel guests happily ate their lunch.

Perhaps raising the Tremont House Hotel helped to inspire Pullman to create a moving hotel for rail passengers. In 1863, he set about building what he claimed, with some justification, would be the finest and most luxurious sleeping carriage ever. Pullman had realized that he needed to attract the rich and famous, and his efforts were rewarded with good fortune. His new carriage, called the *Pioneer*, cost $20,000 to build, perhaps four times the cost of any other railway vehicle at the time. Mary Todd Lincoln, the First Lady, saw it on a visit in early 1865 and was enchanted by the style and elegance of the luxurious train, with its hand-carved seats and panels, and thick pile carpet. When she was called upon to organize the funeral of her assassinated husband a few months later, she remembered the vehicle, and it was used as the hearse for the funeral procession along the Chicago and Alton Railroad.

The *Pioneer* attracted national attention, and soon Pullman began building vehicles for other railway companies. Before long, many other railway companies, such as the Michigan Central, the Burlington, and the Great Western, were attaching luxurious

Pullman carriages to their trains. Pullman's company also sold the tickets for the berths, which cost 50 cents more than the railway's own sleeping accommodation, but were far superior. Passengers were carried in comfort in Pullman sleepers to almost every part of the US. The carriages were all built to the same design, equipped for both day and night travel, and served by Pullman's employees. It was a great business model, and highly profitable as Pullman did not have to pay any of the costs of hauling the trains or using the tracks.

Oddly, despite the luxurious surroundings, the Pullman carriages were inferior to those in Europe in one key respect: they did not provide the same level of privacy. Pullman's design was open plan, with makeshift folding seats, pull-down berths, only curtains for privacy, and nothing to stop a loud snorer from keeping the whole carriage awake. In Europe, compartments were retained, containing up to six beds on three levels, although a few open-plan carriages were introduced for third-class passengers, notably on the Trans-Siberian Railway (see pp.180–89). The open-plan design survived in the US up until the second half of the 20th century, and can be seen in several famous scenes in the Billy Wilder classic comedy *Some Like It Hot*, starring Marilyn Monroe. Although the carriages were popular, some commentators disapproved of such close-quarters living arrangements.

In 1867, Pullman developed a combination sleeping-and-eating car, with a kitchen at one end and removable tables set between the seats at mealtimes. Although this was not the first time that meals had been provided on board trains, the quality, Pullman's selling point, was undoubtedly superior to anything that had gone before. Sugar-cured ham was 40 cents, a Welsh rarebit 50 cents, and steak with potatoes just 60 cents – cheap even at the time. Pullman was a great publicist and introduced his first hotel carriage on a journey

"It is considered tolerable that [women] should lie with the legs of a strange, disrobing man dangling within a foot of their noses"

KARL BAEDECKER, GUIDEBOOK AUTHOR, DESCRIBING PULLMAN'S COACHES

LINCOLN'S FUNERAL RAILCAR
Hundreds of thousands of people lined the railway as Lincoln's funeral train passed by, providing Pullman with excellent publicity and many new customers.

around the eastern US from New York to Chicago that took seven days. Next, he put self-contained dining cars on trains. The first was called *Delmonico*, after an eminent restauranteur of that name. Pullman tried it out on the Chicago and Alton, his home railway, on which he always tested his ideas. It was another great success, and Pullman subsequently both built dining carriages for other railways and operated them himself on some lines. The selection of meals for sale on the best trains was sumptuous. The hotel carriages on the Chicago-Omaha service in the 1870s offered a choice of 15 seafood and fish dishes, together with 37 meat courses, including a huge variety of game. One only wonders how often the waiters had to say: "Sorry, that's not available today".

While Pullman's customers greatly enjoyed the quality of service, it was a terrible idea to die on one of his trains. Pullman ruled that if a passenger passed away, the corpse had to be put off at the next station, regardless of whether the town had an undertaker, leaving the travelling companions of the deceased to deal with the situation. Fortunately, most of the attendants were more compassionate than Pullman, and would ensure the body was dispatched at one of the larger towns, where funeral facilities were more likely to be available.

Later, Pullman devised simpler carriages, which were cheaper but still clean and comfortable with good service. Whatever the level of luxury, the attendants were always black and male, and all known as "George". At first, they were not paid and relied on tips to earn a living. Although this changed later, tips remained a key part of their wages. It was a tough job, according to one historian: "a cross between a concierge, bellhop, valet, housekeeper, mechanic, babysitter, and security guard". To make it tougher, Pullman sent inspectors incognito, to ensure that the attendants carried out their tasks properly. These inspectors would "mislay" jewellery, and the female ones would even make romantic overtures to tempt the attendants into breaking the rules. Attendants who failed to respond appropriately were sacked instantly. Despite the many indignities, being an attendant was stable and reasonably well-paid job, so was much sought-after.

By the early 1870s, Pullman had become, according to one railway historian, "the foremost industrial name in the United States". He was to remain so for more than 20 years. Pullmans were introduced in Europe and Asia, too, but it was the dining-carriage concept that really caught on. Pullman's influence spread outside the

TRAVELLING IN STYLE
This 1910 poster promotes the
comforts of Pullman Palace dining
cars on the Chicago and Alton
Railroad, the first railway Pullman
ever worked on.

US, though railway companies
tended to provide their own
sleeping carriages or use those
of Pullman's rival. Pullman's
carriages also spawned the trend
for luxury that was continued by
the Palace on Wheels in India,
the Blue Train in Africa, and
most famously on the Orient
Express (see pp.190–97).

The name of Pullman also
lives on in a town he built east
of Chicago to house the workers
at his factory. The factory is
long abandoned but the pleasant, well-laid-out houses survive. The
housing, however, was a source of friction between Pullman and his
employees. When the economic panic of 1893 reduced demand for
new carriages, Pullman announced redundancies in the factory, but
refused to reduce the rents on the houses he provided for them. A
bitter strike ensued and spread across the country after 250,000
railworkers joined the action in sympathy. Violence broke out in
several cities across the US and the strike eventually collapsed, but it
left a bitter legacy. Pullman's reputation was so tarnished among
workers that when he died, his family arranged for his remains to be
placed in a lead-lined mahogany coffin, which was then sealed inside
a block of concrete for fear that it would be dug up by angry trade
unionists. It was not a comfortable end for a man who brought a good
night's sleep and a decent hot meal to millions of rail passengers.

Railways
Come of Age

TEE SAPHIR
CLASS VT 11.5
DIESEL (DMU), 1957

By the last quarter of the 19th century, the iron road had become so profitable that many railway companies were using their profits to create new lines. It was an adventurous period that saw the construction of many extraordinary railways, including the Trans-Siberian — a 9,250-km (5,750-mile) line between Moscow and Vladivostok, which remains the longest railway in the world.

Railway technology was now tried and tested, and promoters were driving it to its limits. In South America, several lines were built through the Andes to help exploit the region's mineral wealth — becoming not only the highest railway lines in the world, but also the most spectacular, cutting through mountains and running along perilous cliffs and precipices. In India, the British desire for a cooler climate in summer led to the construction of a series of narrow-gauge hill railways that climbed slowly but surely up the steep inclines far quicker than the road traffic ever had. One of the most ambitious ideas was to run a railway line across the whole of Africa, from Cape Town to Cairo. Cecil Rhodes, the prime minister of Cape Colony (in what is today South Africa), had hoped to link the whole continent by a railway that travelled through only British colonies, but was stymied by difficulties with construction, lack of finance, and the unwillingness of the British government to support the scheme.

It was also a time in which services were greatly improved to encourage passengers (particularly the rich) to use the trains. The most notable luxury service was the Orient Express, which crossed the whole of Europe from Paris to Constantinople (Istanbul). In the United States, competition between railways led to the launch of rival services between New York and Chicago, offering the red carpet treatment to their passengers. And further south, in Florida, the "overseas express" to Key West — one of the most astonishing railways ever built — was completed by Henry Flagler. It was an exciting time for planners and passengers alike.

The Trans-Siberian Railway

WHEN PRINCESS MARIA VOLKONSKY sped across Russia from Moscow to join her husband in exile in 1827, it took 23 days before she saw the churches of Irkutsk, the capital of eastern Siberia, looming out of the snowy atmosphere. That was extremely fast by contemporary standards, and she had travelled night and day on the trans-Siberian Trakt – a crude road that was easier to travel in winter. At other times of the year, when the road was muddy, travellers could take up to nine months to reach Irkutsk, which was barely two thirds of the way to Vladivostok, the port on the Pacific that would become the terminus of the Trans-Siberian Railway.

Siberia had long been equated with exile and little else. It was a distant part of Russia, a huge region encompassing all Russia east of the Ural mountains. A spartan land, its small population was concentrated on a few river and road arteries, and was mostly employed to maintain the Trakt or guard the territory. They were supplemented by two types of exiles: criminals sent to Siberia as an alternative to prison or execution; and political exiles like Prince Sergei Volkonsky, Maria's husband, who had been involved in a failed coup attempt in December 1825.

The terrible transport situation between Siberia and European Russia provided the impetus to build the Trans-Siberian Railway, which was by far the most ambitious railway project ever attempted. Russia had first established a base on the Pacific as early as the 17th century, but its control of the land between the Urals and the ocean was maintained only tenuously. Indeed, Russia's ability to retain its vast Eastern territory began to look tenuous in the mid-19th century, as the development of efficient steamships in the 1840s and the completion of the Suez Canal in 1869 made it easier for its European rivals – France, Britain, and Prussia – to access the Pacific. The completion of the first American transcontinental, also in that year, followed in 1885 by its Canadian equivalent, raised fears among the Russian elite that an invasion from the East was imminent.

There had been discussions about a possible trans-Siberian line as early as in the 1850s, and a succession of plans and projects were presented to the Russian government over the following decades.

THE TRANS-SIBERIAN TRAKT
Before the Trans-Siberian Railway, the main route
through Siberia was a primitive road known as the
Trakt, seen here as it reached the outskirts of Irkutsk.

Several were madcap ideas dreamt up by foreigners intent on
making a fast buck by exploiting what they perceived to be Russian
naivety, but others were sane and realistic suggestions. Some of the
tales of these schemes may have lost accuracy in the telling. A
favourite is the idea that a British gentleman going by the name of
Mr Dull was the first to suggest a trans-Siberian railway.
Unfortunately, the truth is more prosaic, or, rather, duller. The
individual was in fact Thomas Duff, an adventurer who went to
China and returned to St Petersburg in 1857, where he knocked on
the door of the transport minister, Constantine Chevkin, and
suggested the construction of a "tramway" from Nizhny Novgorod,
426km (265 miles) east of Moscow, to the Urals. The line would be
horse-drawn, and some of the four million wild horses that roamed
western Siberia could be enlisted to provide the traction.

Duff was quietly shown the door, as was a succession of both
Russian and foreign entrepreneurs. Even Nikolay Muravyov-
Amursky, the governor-general of eastern Siberia, who had managed
to establish Russia's control over previously disputed territory and
who wanted to build a line connecting the Pacific Ocean with the
Siberian interior, had no better luck than Duff. Neither did three
Englishmen (about whom little is known except that they were called

Sleigh, Horn, and Morrison), nor Peter Collins, an adventurer from New York, who was reportedly the first American to cross the entire breadth of Siberia. Collins also suggested a line in eastern Siberia, from Chita, 400km (250 miles) east of Lake Baikal, to the navigable section of the Amur River, which flows into the Pacific.

Despite rejecting all these suggestions, controversy raged within the Russian government throughout this period about the need for a trans-Siberian line. While there were many reasons not to build the line — such as the expense and the technical difficulties of creating a railway 9,256km (5,750 miles) long between Moscow and Vladivostok — the supporters of the project eventually won the argument on both military and nationalistic grounds. The military motives for the line were both defensive and offensive. It would not only allow a much quicker response to any attack on Vladivostok but, and this was not discussed openly, it would also make it easier for Russia to establish control over its vast but at the time very weak southern neighbour, China.

Consequently, in 1886, after some three decades of prevarication, the tsarist government, despite being ruled by the very conservative Alexander III, took the radical step of deciding to build the line. The immediate catalyst for the decision seems to have been a fear that large numbers of Chinese were infiltrating Transbaikalia, the region around Lake Baikal. In fact, this had little basis in reality, but somehow it was the crucial development that finally made the government decide to give the go-ahead to the scheme.

Inevitably, finding the money and getting the unwieldy Russian government behind the scheme delayed the start of construction for a further five years. Finally, however, the tsar despatched his son, the future Nicholas II, to Vladivostok, where on 31 May, 1891, he wielded a shovel to fill a wheelbarrow with clay soil, which he emptied onto an embankment of what would become the Ussuri line. Having done so, however, there was still no agreement on how to complete the work, or how it could be funded. What the project needed was a man of vision and drive to see it through to its completion — and that is just what it received. His name was Sergei Witte, and he was briefly transport minister in the Russian government, but was finance minister by August 1892. Normally such posts were held by people of limited vision, with an interest only in keeping the purse strings tight — not so with Sergei Witte.

Using his skills as a maths graduate, he both managed the country's finances with acumen and ensured that there were plenty of funds for work on the Trans-Siberian Railway.

Born in the Georgian capital, Tblisi, Witte came from a minor aristocratic family that had fallen on hard times, and he had to work as a railway clerk – a very lowly task for a man of his birth and ambition. His ability was soon recognized, however, and he was swiftly promoted to manage a railway company, and then obtained a senior government post in St Petersburg. When he became finance minister, work on the railway had come to a halt due to a famine in the Volga region and lack of funds. Witte's masterstroke was to create a Committee for the Siberian Railway, headed by the young tsarevitch (heir to the Russian throne) Nicholas, which effectively guaranteed that the project would enjoy the continuing support of the monarch. Witte thus became the father of the railway. He took a constant interest in its progress, ensured that money was available, fought off any resistance to the project within government, and appeased the Chinese, who were highly suspicious that the line would be used against them.

The difficulties facing the railway's builders can hardly be exaggerated. Although the terrain the line had to cross was not as difficult as the Alps (see pp.102–107) or the Andes (see pp.198–203), nor as barren as the American deserts (see pp.32–39), the sheer length, the extreme temperatures, and the absence of a local labour force made the railway's construction an unprecedented challenge. To illustrate the scale of the task, the 9,250-km (5,750-mile) route was 3,200km (2,000 miles) longer than the Canadian transcontinental – and the US equivalent was not only shorter overall, it only required 2,800km (1,750 miles) of new track, since a great deal of railway had

SERGEI WITTE
Russian finance minister Sergei Witte oversaw the industrialization of much of the Russian Empire. He was the driving force behind the building of the Trans-Siberian Railway.

HARD LABOUR
Workers lay tracks for the central portion of the
Trans-Siberian Railway, in the Krasnoyarsk region
of Russia. This section of the line runs between the
Ob and Yenisey rivers.

already been laid in the east. By contrast, Russia's railways only
reached as far as the Urals, and so the Trans-Siberian Railway needed
an entire 7,240km (4,500 miles) of new track.

Although there were no enormous mountain ranges in the way –
the Urals and the Siberian ranges were relatively easy to get through –
there was no shortage of other difficulties. In the vast steppe, neither
stone for ballast nor wood for sleepers could be sourced locally, so
materials had to be brought from afar, mostly by river. The rails, too, had
to be transported from factories in the Urals and eastern Russia, as did
the steel for the bridges, which had to cross the massive Siberian rivers.
Then, two-thirds of the way from Moscow, was the biggest obstacle of all
– Lake Baikal, Russia's biggest lake by volume and the deepest in the
world. The northern shore was too much of a detour and the southern
one was lined with steep cliffs right to the water's edge, which meant
that a shelf for the railway had to be blown out of the stone.

Time was at a premium, with the Tsar intent on seeing the project completed within a decade. As a result, the surveys of the route were cursory, carried out only on a narrow belt that had been drawn thousands of miles away by St Petersburg bureaucrats who had never been to Siberia and had only inaccurate maps. The ethos behind the construction was to "muddle through", since it was reckoned that building the perfect railway would simply take too long. That strategy worked well in terms of ensuring that the job was done on time, but the result was a very basic railway that could only carry a handful of trains per day and was dogged with technical problems in its early years.

For construction purposes, the railway was divided into three main sections, each of around 2,400km (1,500 miles) – the western, the mid-Siberian, and the far eastern – and it was the latter that had the most difficulties. Work started first on the western section in 1891, from Chelyabinsk, the easternmost point of the existing railway, and the main difficulty was a lack of local workers. It was estimated that some 80,000 men would be needed to build the first two sections, so workers were recruited not only from western Russia but as far afield as Persia, Turkey, and even Italy. The work was onerous, but well paid – agricultural workers could get far more than they did on the fields, but even then they would often return to their villages at harvest time to help their relatives. Oddly enough, the main shortage of material on this section was wood – the local timber was deemed unsuitable – and supplies had to be brought in from western Russia.

Construction on the mid-Siberian track began in 1893, and the labour shortage was so acute that it proved necessary to call on an obvious local source of workers – convicts who had been exiled to Siberia. This proved to be an excellent decision, for they were keen

"We must give the country such industrial perfection as has been reached by the United States of America"

SERGEI WITTE

workers, not least because a year of their sentence was remitted for every eight months they worked on the railway, and they had access to tobacco and even occasionally alcohol in the work camps.

Conditions were harsh for the workers, but they were generally better than those of other 19th-century railway projects – largely because workers were in short supply and their employers had to keep them happy. In the summer months, between May and August, the hours were long, with men being expected to work from 5am to 7:30pm, broken only by a lengthy lunch period of an hour and a half. In the winter, work was confined to the daylight hours, but since the line was quite far south – roughly on the same latitude as London, Berlin, and Prague – this still meant a seven- or eight-hour day in mid-winter.

The work was dangerous, too. The death rate was calculated at around two per cent, which was less than on other projects such as the Panama railway (see pp.110–19) and the never-completed Cape to Cairo railway (see pp.214–221), but it is still shocking by today's standards. The most perilous work was constructing the major bridges, which was particularly perilous in winter, when men had to perch high above the rivers with no safety equipment and were dangerously exposed to the elements. Often men became so cold that they fell unconscious and plunged to their deaths in the icy waters.

The two western sections were completed by 1899, enabling trains to reach Irkutsk, but the eastern section proved more difficult. Witte agreed to a fateful change in plan – to run the eastern section through Manchuria, part of China, rather than building the planned Amur Railway, which would have kept it on Russian soil (the Amur line was eventually built between 1907 and 1916). The Manchurian route was shorter, but it was dangerous politically. Although the Chinese government acquiesced to the arrangement, it would prove politically troublesome and eventually lead to the Russo-Japanese war, which broke out in 1904, soon after the completion of the line.

After the opening of the Chinese Eastern Railway in November 1901, there was still one section left to be built. This was the 180-km (110-mile)-long Circum-Baikal Railway, along the southern shore of Lake Baikal, which presented the most severe difficulties. Work did not start until 1895 and, because of the need to create a shelf in the cliffs, it did not finish until 1905. Until then, passengers travelling east of Irkutsk had to take a train ferry across the lake in summer, or a sledge over it in winter. In fact, it was not until 1916 – when the Amur

Railway, which required the erection of the longest bridge on the line at Khabarovsk, was completed – that the whole journey from Moscow to Vladivostok could be undertaken entirely on Russian soil.

Even the most optimistic promoters of the railway could not have anticipated the impact that it would have on Siberian – and indeed Russian – history, and it has not all been good. Not only was the line the catalyst for the Russo-Japanese war, it played a key role in several other conflicts, most notably two world wars. Also, the tsarist regime that created it paid a heavy price. By concentrating so many of its limited resources on the project, it neglected other areas of spending, and this imbalance helped trigger the revolution that led to the overthrow of the monarchy in 1917. This also led to the execution of Nicholas II and his family at Ekaterinburg, which, ironically, is one of the main stations on western section of the line. Nevertheless, the project must be counted as a success, despite its cost, and the sometimes unusual conditions endured by its early passengers (see p.146). The Trans-Siberian remains the main artery between Siberia and the rest of Russia. It is a double-track, electrified line and is heavily used by both freight and passenger trains. It is the longest railway in the world, and arguably the most important.

RUSSIAN STEAM LOCOMOTIVE
The USSR stopped producing steam engines in the 1950s, but a few are preserved at stations on the Trans-Siberian Railway. This model remained in service until the 1970s.

RUSSIAN TIME ZONES

Such is the length of the Trans-Siberian Railway that the journey from Moscow to Vladivostok crosses seven time zones. Timetables and station clocks are set to Moscow time (MT), which results in discrepancies between local and railway time. These discrepancies increase from two to seven hours the further one travels east.

MOSCOW

VLADIVOSTOK

KEY

- ■ MT
- ■ +2
- ■ +3
- ■ +4
- ■ +5
- ■ +6
- ■ +7

ST PETERSBURG

Lake Ladoga

KARA SEA

VOLOGDA

NIZHNII-NOVGOROD

MOSCOW

Kirov

URAL MOUNTAINS

RAZAN'

PERM

SYZRAN

UFA

EKATERINBURG

SAMARA

Tiumen

Zlatoust

Mass

Cheliabinsk

Kurgan

OMSK

Ob'

Tomsk

Petropavlovsk

Novosibirsk

KAZAKHSTAN

SIBERIAN RAIL BRIDGES

Hundreds of bridges were built along the route of the Trans-Siberian Railway. Many of these are of unsual design, such as this lenticular bridge, otherwise known as a "fish-bellied truss". The longest bridge of all, which crosses the Amur River at Khabarovsk, is 2,612m (8,570ft) in length.

The Trans-Siberian Railway

Russia's railway network is exceeded in size only by those of the US and China, so it is perhaps fitting that it features the world's longest continuous railway line. At around 9,250km (5,750 miles) in length, the Trans-Siberian Railway straddles the Russian interior, linking the country's heartland in the European west to its hinterland in the Asian east. A broad-gauge, double-track line that was fully electrified in 2002, it is a vital artery that has spread industry and commerce across this vast territory.

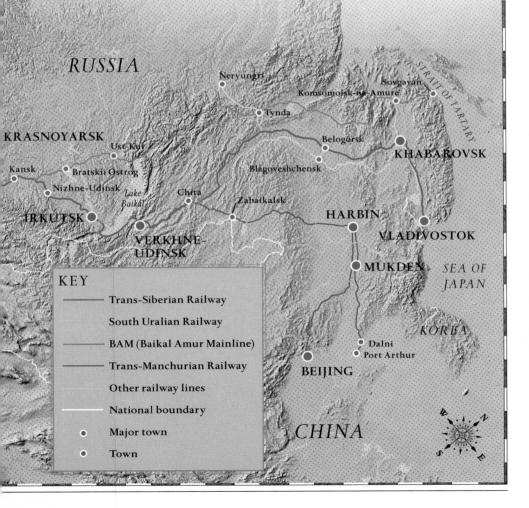

RUSSIA

Neryungri

Sovgavan

STRAIT OF TARTARY

Komsomolsk-na-Amure

Tynda

KRASNOYARSK

Ust-Kut

Belogorsk

KHABAROVSK

Kansk

Bratskii Ostrog

Blagoveshchensk

Nizhne-Udinsk

Lake Baikal

Chita

Zabaikalsk

IRKUTSK

VERKHNE-
UDINSK

HARBIN

VLADIVOSTOK

MUKDEN

SEA OF JAPAN

KOREA

Dalni
Port Arthur

BEIJING

CHINA

KEY

—— Trans-Siberian Railway

South Uralian Railway

—— BAM (Baikal Amur Mainline)

—— Trans-Manchurian Railway

Other railway lines

—— National boundary

○ Major town

○ Town

The Orient Express

DISAPPOINTINGLY FOR SOME, there never was a murder on the Orient Express, but there is no doubt that Agatha Christie chose a fitting setting for her "whodunnit" mystery novel. The Orient Express was the most exciting and exotic train service in the world, crossing the whole of Europe and entering territories – particularly in the east – that were little known to western Europeans. Indeed, the service was one of the wonders of the age, and like so many railway innovations it owed its existence to the tireless efforts of one individual, in this case Belgian engineer Georges Nagelmackers.

Nagelmackers was the founder of the Compagnie Internationale des Wagons-Lits, a popular service that offered compartments instead of the open-plan carriages of Pullman's sleeping cars (see pp.170–77). However, Nagelmackers' real genius lay not in the trains he built but in the routes he established. He wanted a Europe *sans frontières*, one that travellers could cross quickly and in style in his well-appointed trains. To that end, in 1872, he created a service that ran from Ostend on the North Sea coast of his native Belgium more than a 1,600km (1,000 miles) south to Brindisi on the tip of the Italian heel. The venture proved successful, and with the East and the Balkans opening up as the Ottoman Empire declined, he saw that a service linking Europe and Asia would also be profitable. And so he began work on his Orient Express – a 2,989-km (1,857-mile) passage from Paris to Constantinople (now Istanbul), bridging east and west and crossing six countries en route.

Dealing with the railways of six diverse nations was no easy task, and Nagelmackers had to use all his skills as a negotiator to solve a whole range of problems. Most importantly, he had to ensure that each

GEORGES NAGELMACKERS
Belgian industrialist Georges Nagelmackers was the founder of the Compagnie Internationale des Wagons-Lits, the company best known for its Orient Express service.

THE ORIENT EXPRESS

country had locomotives that could haul his trains, and that the tracks were of standard gauge (see pp.90–91). Other issues included the width of the route's tunnels, and arcane matters such as the security of wine lockers. He was also a great publicist and generated huge interest in his venture, not least because the route passed through the Balkans, an area that was still recovering from numerous wars, having struggled for independence from both the Ottoman and Austro-Hungarian empires.

The inaugural train, for press and VIPs, left the Gare de L'Est in Paris on the evening of October 4, 1883, and was scheduled to take three and a half days to reach Constantinople. Nagelmackers had created what *The Times* correspondent Henri Opper de Blowitz described as a level "of comfort and facility hitherto unknown". There was a smoking room, a ladies' boudoir, and a library, and each compartment (or coupé) had a miniature drawing room in the style of Louis XIV, complete with a Turkish carpet, inlaid tables, and plush red armchairs. In the evenings, the compartment walls could be folded down to reveal beautifully upholstered beds. The *cabinet de toilette* had a mosaic

ALPINE ADVENTURE
The Orient Express passes through the Austrian Alps shortly
before World War I. Here it is hauled by an Austrian locomotive –
one of six different engines that would take it to Constantinople.

floor, and a special coach at the rear of the train had cubicles for showers that were supplied with hot and cold water – certainly a railway first. According to one account (and numerous tales were published) the *piéce de résistance* was the dining room:

> [It] had a ceiling with embossed leather from Cordoue [Cordoba], walls lined with tapestries from the Atelier des Gobelins, founded by the Sun King, and drapes of finest Gènes [Genoa] velvet.

The tables were covered with white damask cloths and intricately folded napkins, and ice buckets filled with champagne bottles were at hand – and if the five-course meal were not enough, iceboxes full of exotic foods and cold drinks were available at the end of each carriage.

Nagelmackers was a stickler for detail, and set out a series of rules to maintain high standards. Attendants had to be smart at all times and on special occasions had to dress like footmen from the time of Louis XIV, complete with blue silk breeches and buckled shoes. Even the engine crew had to dress up on occasion, often in white coats that were highly impractical in the boiler room.

That first journey was one long party. At Strasbourg, Vienna, and Budapest the train was met by brass bands and local dignitaries, while at Tsigany, in Hungary, a gypsy orchestra came aboard and serenaded the passengers all the way to the border with Romania. The only drawback was that the track was incomplete. The bridge over the river Danube was unfinished, so the crossing from Romania to Bulgaria had to be made by ferry, and even then the line only reached as far as the port of Varna, where passengers had to take a ship to Constantinople. This last section of the journey was, according to Blowitz, through a land full of "brigands" who had recently attacked one station and "garrotted the stationmaster and his subordinates in order to get hold of the money they expected in his till", and only fled when they were disturbed by workmen. Consequently, Blowitz and his companions armed themselves with revolvers, although they never had occasion to use them. They arrived at Constantinople precisely 82 hours after their departure from Paris and were met by the Sultan, with whom Blowitz conducted a newspaper interview, the ruler's first.

It was another six years before it was possible to take the train all the way to Constantinople. The trip took just under three days, leaving Paris on a Wednesday at 7:30pm and arriving at 5:35pm on the Saturday in Constantinople. The service became popular, attracting a wide range of travellers as it was quicker and more convenient than travelling by ship. Subsequently, a variety of other routes were opened, running trains that bore some variant of the name "Orient Express". Various connecting trains were also introduced, including one from London via a train ferry. Inevitably, when war broke out in 1914, the Orient Express was suspended, but as soon as the war was over in 1918 a second line was opened – the Simplon Orient Express, on which Agatha Christie's tale is set. Using the Simplon Tunnel between Switzerland and Italy, this second line was a more southerly route via Milan, Venice, and Trieste, and soon became the more popular route from Paris to Constantinople. A third line was

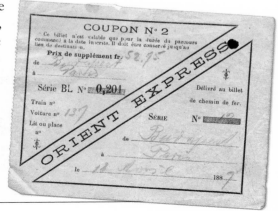

BOUND FOR PARIS
On 18 April 1887, a traveller bought this ticket for Fr52.95. It afforded passage from Budapest to Paris aboard the Orient Express.

LUXURY DINING
The dining carriage of the Orient Express, set for dinner. The very first menu included oysters, turbot with green sauce, chaud-froid of game animals, chicken à la chasseur, and a buffet of desserts.

added in the 1930s (the heyday of the Orient services) – the Arlberg Orient Express, which ran via Zurich and Innsbruck to Budapest, with sleeper cars continuing on to Bucharest and Athens. The outbreak of the World War II in 1939 again interrupted the service, although the German Mitropa company ran trains through the Balkans until Yugoslav partisans destroyed the line.

While there were no recorded murders on the Orient Express, there was at least one mysterious death – when a US agent fell from a train at the height of the Cold War in the 1950s – and there was no shortage of mischief. Sleeping car attendants were regularly called on to hire prostitutes, not just for gentlemen, but for princes and even bishops who found that a train offered more privacy than a brothel. Indeed, many men took the train simply for these services alone. There was plenty of spying, too, given that the trains linked east and west. Between the wars, "King's Messengers" – effectively couriers for the British Foreign Office – travelled in compartments where they guarded their diplomatic bags with their lives – and later claimed that they were immune to the wiles of the beautiful young spies who were sent to entrap them, although we only have their word for that.

For all its luxuries, however, the service did not remain exclusive for long. On the contrary, although there was only one class of carriage in the original service, which cost 300 Francs (the equivalent of two weeks' average wages at the time), second and third class carriages were opened for poorer

EASTERN PROMISE
A French poster displays the timetable of the Orient Express over the winter of 1888. Its seven main stops are advertised, plus a connecting service to London.

"Peasants in half a dozen countries would pause in their work in the fields and gape at the glittering cars and the supercilious faces behind the windows"

E.H. COOKRIDGE, *THE ORIENT EXPRESS*

people who used it for shorter, mostly domestic journeys. In these packed carriages, as one writer put it, "the pulse of Old Europe beat, with its almost medieval characters: the tramp, the peddler, the gypsy-musician…" Indeed, although the service continued to operate even after the Iron Curtain divided Europe, the communist countries increasingly replaced the luxurious Wagon-Lits cars with more spartan carriages run by their own railway networks.

By 1962, the Orient Express and the Arlberg Orient Express had stopped running, leaving only the Simplon Orient Express, which was replaced by a slower service, the Direct Orient Express, which ran daily trains from Paris to Belgrade and twice-weekly services from Paris to Istanbul and Athens. The service through to Istanbul finally came to an end in 1977, killed off by the ubiquitous spread of the motorcar. A service called the Orient Express stuttered on between Paris and Vienna, and between Budapest and Bucharest, but that closed with the opening of the high-speed line between Paris and Strasbourg in 2009 (a service called the Venice-Simplon Orient Express still operates between London and Venice, but it is a separate entity). By the time of its swansong in 2009, the original Orient Express was an anachronism – a relic that had perhaps done well to last as long as it did.

The Most Spectacular
Railways in the World

HENRY MEIGGS WAS A SCOUNDREL who made good building railways. When he arrived in Chile in 1855, he was a 44-year-old outcast who had fled San Francisco amid accusations of fraud, but by the time he died 22 years later, this handsome, larger-than-life character had been honoured with the unofficial title of "Don Enrique". By then, he had conquered some of the world's most difficult railway terrain – the seemingly impossible slopes of the Andes – for which he also earned the nickname "Yankee Pizarro", after the Spanish conqueror of the Incas.

In his youth, Meiggs demonstrated a remarkable capacity for hatching imaginative schemes, but he was never entirely honest – if a venture failed, he was not above lying and manipulating others to avoid being exposed. He had an early success in the timber business, setting up his own company in New York City and relocating to San Francisco during the Gold Rush. After that he went into property and developed land near the Golden Gate, but he soon fell into debt and only avoided bankruptcy by raising cash with illicitly obtained warrants. When his fraud was discovered, he fled to Chile, where his devious reputation preceded him. The only work he could find was overseeing a gang of labourers building the railways, but he proved to be so efficient that he was soon given charge of entire railway projects. Two of his predecessors, a New Englander called William Wheelwright and the great Richard Trevithick (see pp.20–21), had dreamt of building lines inland from the west coast of South America, but it was Meiggs who finally built them. This achievement had enormous consequences for the region, for it opened up vast deposits of copper, silver, and minerals for exploitation, and made fortunes for Chile and Peru.

HENRY MEIGGS
Charismatic American entrepreneur Henry Meiggs pioneered the railway lines of Chile and Peru. Doing so required scaling the heights of the Andes.

To help him with construction, Meiggs engaged engineers who shared his own daring outlook on the fearsome terrain. His first big success came with the laying of a 145-km (90-mile) line from the Pacific coast to San Fernando, which involved bridging the Maipo River, previously a major obstacle separating north and south Chile. On completing the line faster than his contract required, Meiggs successfully bid for the most important route in the country – from Valparaiso, on the west coast, to Santiago (the capital), a mere 89km (55 miles) inland as the crow flies, but in practice 185km (115 miles) due to the mountainous terrain. Wheelwright had begun the route, but after spending a million pesos (or tens of thousands of dollars) only 6.5km (4 miles) had been completed by the time Meiggs took over. To finish the route, the government borrowed money from Barings Bank of London, and Meiggs did a speedy deal with the Minister of the Interior, promising to complete the route in three years for six million pesos – so long as he received an additional half million pesos if he finished early, plus an extra 10,000 pesos for every month gained. Backed by a workforce of 10,000 men, Meiggs completed the line in just two years and three days, a triumph that proved his astonishing capabilities both as a contractor and a negotiator.

Having thus "conquered" Chile, Meiggs moved on to even bigger schemes in Peru, a country that was just striking rich thanks to its enormous deposits of guano, or bird droppings, which made an excellent fertilizer. Understandably, Peruvians wished to use their new-found wealth to build a railway system that would unify the country, just as the Belgians had done forty years earlier (see pp.43–44), and as the Canadians (see pp.125–27) and the Italians (see pp.46–47) were doing at the time. For that reason Meiggs was welcomed with open arms – or open palms, in the case of the ruling class, who demanded huge amounts of money in bribes.

Meiggs's big opportunity came as the result of an episode that was typical of Peru's dramatic political history. In 1868, Colonel José Balta, the type of buccaneering officer often found in South America at the time, was elected president. Immediately after his election, Peru suffered a devastating earthquake, and Meiggs cannily donated US$50,000 (£7,300) to the government, or rather to Balta personally, ostensibly for crisis relief. Balta had already upset the local oligarchy by giving a French company a monopoly on the sale of guano, and now he used money raised by the deal to pay another foreigner –

HEIGHT ABOVE SEA
LEVEL OF GALERA
STATION IN PERU

4,777 M
(15,681 FT)

THE WORLD'S
HIGHEST STATION

Meiggs – to build Peru's railways. And so, in the three years following Balta's election, Meiggs signed six contracts to build over 1,600km (1,000 miles) of railways, on terms that were highly favourable to him. The result was that, having had a mere 98km (61 miles) of track in 1861, Peru had 1,524km (947 miles) by 1874, and nearly 13,200km (2,000 miles) by 1879, two years after Meiggs' death.

Meiggs built two lines in Peru, and both are wonders of the railway world. The first runs from the southern port of Mollendo to Arequipa, Peru's second-biggest city, and then up to Lake Titicaca and the mining area of Juliaca. Meiggs estimated that it would cost him 10 million soles to build it (around US$300 million or £185 million today), then told the government that it would cost 15 million, and proceded to build it for 12 million, even completing it early. The second line, the Central Peruvian, rises from Callao, the port of Lima, up through the steepest and highest sections of the Andes, following precipitous llama paths to the copper mines of Huancayo and the fabled silver mines of Cerro de Pasco.

Unfortunately, the lines were built at a time of great financial turmoil. As the country's guano ran out, so the supply of money from the government dried up, and Meiggs was forced to use his own bills of exchange – the so-called "Billetes de Meiggs". Sadly, too, Meiggs died during construction, but by then he had shown how it was done, and had conquered the steepest slopes. He followed the British idea of zig-zagging railways uphill (see pp.204–205), but did so on an unprecedented scale. In India, the British lines reached 760m (2,500ft) – Meiggs's trains scaled mountains over 4,250m (14,000ft) high, and zig-zagged 25 times in a matter of 160km (100 miles).

Being a foreigner, Meiggs was an easy scapegoat for Peru's economic woes, one journalist even writing that the "the ruin of Peru is the monument [to] Henry Meiggs". However, he was mostly considered a hero, and one of the country's highest peaks was soon named after him. His success was due not only to his ability to find the best route

BRIDGING THE ABYSS
To access the remoter parts of Peru, Henry Meiggs constructed numerous bridges, such as this seemingly precarious viaduct in the mining region of Juliaca.

BILLETES DE MEIGGS
In the 1870s, Henry Meiggs effectively created his
own currency to finance his railway projects in
Peru. Around a million soles' worth of banknotes
known as Billetes de Meiggs were put in circulation.

for a railway, but also to his formidable organisational skills and his ability to bring out the best in his workers. One Peruvian journalist described his "railway army" battling the elements:

> The 'army' (distributed along the line in eleven camps), consisting of Don Enrique's engineers and labourers, was attacking the Andes. The scouts went ahead to determine the best and least costly route; the advance guard followed in their tracks, staking out the exact route to be followed; next came the main body, levelling the barriers, making fills and cuts and piercing tunnels; lastly, there was the rear guard, putting down ties and laying rails.

Meiggs was famously generous to his workforce, particularly the *rotos* – the much-feared, much-despised, Chilean working class. According to James Fawcett, in *Railways of the Andes*, a typical *roto* was notorious: "for his hardihood, his skill in the handling of the sharp, curved, disembowelling knife that all his tribe carried, his hatred of any sort of discipline, his love of cane sugar as a beverage and his addiction to gambling". Meiggs succeeded by treating his workers as men rather than slaves, and he was even more successful with the 5,000 Chinese workers he hired and who were normally treated worse than the *rotos* (see pp.88–89). According to one observer, quoted by Fawcett: "some of them were fat, the only fat Chinese in the country! Meiggs fed them well with rice and beef in plenty and a good breakfast of bread and tea before starting the day's work".

Towards the end of his life, Meiggs wanted to return to the US, claiming that he had repaid his San Francisco debts, but the governor of San Francisco vetoed a bill that was passed to exonerate him from his offences. In 1977, a century after Meiggs's death, the California Supreme Court quashed the indictment against him, declaring that he "had gone to a higher court", but his death was not the end of his family's influence. His nephew, Minor C. Keith, went on to complete a railway his uncle had started in Costa Rica. Its major source of income was carrying bananas, and Keith went on to found United Fruit, the colossus that dominated the sale of bananas for a century.

Going Uphill

The first railway lines were laid along the flattest routes possible, but the requirements of industry – particularly mining – soon demanded that trains could travel uphill. The earliest solution was the "incline" – a pair of parallel tracks that enabled a descending train to haul an ascending train uphill by means of a chain that connected the two via a pulley. This worked particularly well on the short sections of track that were used to draw raw materials up from pits and quarries, and variants were powered by horses or stationary steam engines. The basic premise lies behind modern-day funicular railways, and other engineering solutions, such as spiral loops and switchbacks, have also been developed.

Spiral loop

Building a railway track on a spiral allows a train to gain elevation in a much shorter length of track than would be possible with a conventional curve. Spiral loops also avoid the inconveniences of reverse travel and interrupted movement that are necessary when climbing switchbacks, the other railway engineering method by which traction trains climb hills (see right). Popular in challenging terrain, such as mountainous regions in which level ground is limited, spirals are set at a constant grade and degree of curvature, and allow the track to pass over itself as the line ascends.

THE BRUSIO SPIRAL VIADUCT IN SWITZERLAND WAS BUILT IN 1908. IT DESCENDS 20M (60FT) AT A GRADE OF 7 PER CENT.

SWITCHBACKS

The railway linking Ecuador's coast with its capital, Quito – at 2,850m (9,350 ft) – crosses the Nariz del Diablo escarpment via a series of switchbacks. By this method, trains gain height in a short length of track by entering a dead-end siding, and then reversing to climb the next switchback.

Funicular railways

The first funicular railway – a form of cable car operating on similar principles to a railway incline – opened in 1862 in Lyon, France, and featured a four-rail track layout on which two cars travelled on separate parallel tracks. The development of passing loops allowed later designs to economize on the space and materials used. First came a three-rail layout, in which cars shared a central rail – then came a two-rail layout in which the cars shared both rails on either side of the passing loop.

HOW IT WORKS

Two- and three-rail funiculars contain a passing loop at the halfway point. Each car has "blind" (flangeless) inner wheels and double-flanged outer wheels to prevent them from switching rails.

Descending car

Two-rail funicular

Weight of upper car hauls lower car up the slope

Passing loop

Pulley cable

Flangeless wheel rides on top of the inside rail

Outer wheel with flanges on either side of outside rail

THE KIEV FUNICULAR, UKRAINE, OPENED IN 1905. IT CLIMBS 238M (781FT) OF TRACK AT A GRADE OF 36 PER CENT.

Henry Flagler and the Overseas Railroad

HE WAS UNIQUE in the history of the United States. He could have been as rich and as famous as John D. Rockefeller. Instead, Henry Flagler chose to spend the last 30 years of his life building a railway line in Florida and establishing Florida's tourist industry. His final triumph, completed only a year before he died in 1913, was the construction of the world's most ambitious "overseas railroad" – a line stretching all the way from the mainland across the Florida Keys to the southernmost tip of the US, Key West.

For decades before his great Florida adventure, Flagler had been a key partner in the creation of Rockefeller's gigantic Standard Oil monopoly. According to Flagler's biographer, David Chandler, Rockefeller readily admitted that Flagler was an inspiration. Indeed, Flagler had contributed more than Rockefeller to the organization of the Standard, and was wholly responsible for the clever legal structure that protected it against antitrust lawsuits. However, Flagler craved an outlet for his colossal creative energies, and that was just what he found in Florida, which he explored in 1883 while on honeyoon with his second wife, Ida.

At the time, Florida was still a young state and was keen to sell its land rights, and Flagler saw that even underdeveloped St Augustine, the oldest European settlement in the US, was attracting plenty of wealthy tourists. Sensing a golden opportunity, he gave up his daily involvement in the Standard, and set about building a chain of hotels along the east coast – the first of which, the 540-room Ponce de León, opened in St Augustine in 1888.

Designed by the architects of the Metropolitan Opera and New York Public Library, the Ponce de León was the height of luxury and immediately attracted visitors. However, the local railways were a deterrent, for they ran on a variety of gauges (see pp.90–91) and so demanded frequent changes of train. What was needed was a reliable railway that would link the town directly to New York, so Flagler bought up the existing lines and converted them to standard gauge. As he noted: "the average passenger will take a through car ninety five times in a hundred in preference to making a change".

FLORIDA'S EAST COAST RAILWAY

Another problem was that the lines only ran to Daytona, a beach about a third of the way down the coast — beyond that, Flagler would have to lay his own tracks.

Flager's next port of call was Palm Beach, a natural harbour that he explored in 1893. As always, he inspected the site incognito, to avoid attracting attention, and then returned openly to buy the land he wanted. Within months he opened the 1,100-room Royal Poinciana hotel, which Chandler called "the largest resort hotel in the world... equipped and staffed in the most luxurious manner imaginable", and extended the railway south to reach it. The guests did full justice to the luxury of the accommodation, with a hundred private railway cars arriving each winter for the George Washington Birthday Ball – an event at which the most powerful men in America, including Flagler himself, dressed in the most elaborate drag costumes, complete with fishnet stockings, powdered wigs, and strings of diamonds. Another great draw was an annex called the Breakers, which proved so popular that Flagler turned it into a casino.

To foster local industry, Flagler also established a "Model Land Company", which, in Chandler's words, "did more perhaps to actually building up the Florida East Coast than any of his other undertakings". He encouraged people to plant vegetables, citrus fruit, and pineapples, and when an unprecedented snowstorm wiped out the fledgling industry in the winter of 1884 he secretly spent a fortune helping the affected farmers. He even arranged a link-up with weather forecasters, and if a serious drop in temperature was predicted, his engine drivers sounded six long blasts on their whistles as they thundered through the orange groves, calling on farmers to hurry out with their "smudge pots" – oil-burning heaters that prevented frost from forming on the fruit trees.

Another consequence of these freezes was Flagler's decision to extend his railway south, for only 100km (60 miles) away the climate was warmer and better suited to farming. Extending the railway also entitled him to land grants, and on the basis of these he accumulated over two million acres of territory, including Biscayne Bay, a beautiful spot protected from the Atlantic by a barrier island and watered by the little

Miami River. At the time, the area was "mostly swamp, and was filled with mosquitoes, snakes, mangrove thickets and Spanish Bayonet" (a nasty type of cactus), but Flagler tamed it and brought water and electricity to the town he established there. The locals wanted to call the town "Flagler", but Flagler declined the honour, preferring to name it after the river. Thus Miami was born. The following year he set about building another luxury hotel, the Royal Palm, which was as popular as the Royal Poinciana. The railway arrived at Miami in 1896, completing a 800-km (500-mile) line that ran south from the neighbouring state of Georgia through Jacksonville and the resorts Flagler had built. Anyone glancing at a map could see that Miami was the end of the line, but Flagler kept on going, out to sea, away from the mainland and over the Florida Keys — an archipelago that sweeps southwest from Miami to Key West, far out in the Gulf of Mexico. "There is an impelling force within me", he told a friend, "and I must carry out my plans" — and the result was his 206-km (128-mile) "overseas railway".

In one respect Flagler was lucky. By the time his plans were ready, President Theodore Roosevelt had authorized the construction of the Panama Canal, making Key West a potentially vital transport hub. As for getting the work done, Flagler simply found the right man for the job and left him to it, ignoring the question of cost, even though there were no more grants to be had. His chosen engineer was Joseph Carroll Meredith, who had already built the massive docks at Tampico on the Gulf of Mexico. However, before he got started on the offshore part of the route, Meredith had to lay 146km (91 miles) of railway through the Everglades, an ordeal in which every kind of danger and annoyance was encountered, from apparently bottomless swamps and uncharted lakes to snakes, alligators, mosquitoes, and obstacles that only the

"But that any man could have the genius to see of what this wilderness was capable and then have the nerve to build a railroad here…"

GEORGE W. PERKINS OF J.P. MORGAN, ON FLAGLER'S ACHIEVEMENTS biggest dredgers in the country could move. Then he faced the 60km (37 miles) of the "overseas" railway itself, a route demanding 27km (17 miles) of bridges and 32km (20 miles) of embankments — a feat of engineering that has never been equalled. The Long Key viaduct alone measured 4km (2½ miles), and was second only to the 11-km (7-mile) Knights Key viaduct, which rested on 366 concrete columns and had a swing bridge to allow ships to pass through it. Without dry land for accommodation, the 4,000 workers were housed on enormous barges, which contained all the facilities needed for survival, including vast quantities of fresh water. However, there was still a high casualty rate, both from accidents and disease, and a hospital was built in Miami to treat the afflicted. The elements also caused havoc, not least in 1906, when a hurricane sank an accommodation barge, causing at least 70 deaths, and delaying construction for a year.

The whole Florida East Coast Railway project was completed at a cost of US$20 million (US$500 million in today's money) and in less than seven years. This was largely thanks to the loyalty of Flagler's men, one of whom told a reporter "there isn't one of us who wouldn't give a year of his life to have Mr Flagler see the work completed". And see it he did, opening the line to the public on 22 January 1912, tearfully exclaiming: "my dream is fulfilled, now I can die happy". He had never expected to see the project completed, predicting 20 years earlier that it would take 30 years to finish, and accurately forecasting: "I have only 20 more years to live". The line's completion was celebrated by the introduction of the Havana Express, a regular through service that arrived at Key West only 52 hours after leaving New York, giving passengers the luxury of strolling across the quay to take a ship to Cuba, a mere 45km (90 miles) away. Flagler, his life's work accomplished, died a happy man the following year.

Sadly, however, the line never prospered. It failed to attract many passengers, and proved to be unreliable since it was affected by bad weather. Consequently, the railroad went bankrupt in 1932, and the offshore track was destroyed on Labour Day 1935, during the worst storm of the century. Nevertheless, Meredith had built his railway well. Highway 1, which replaced it, was constructed on the roadbed that Flagler had financed. Indeed, Florida, the Sunshine State, has much to thank him for. When he started work it was one of the poorest states in the Union — today it has one of the strongest economies in the world.

OVERSEAS EXPRESS
An express train thunders over the Long Key Viaduct — a 4-km (2½-mile) stretch of arches that links two islands of the Florida Keys. Today, the structure supports the Overseas Highway, or Highway 1, which follows Flagler's railway route.

Hauling Freight

The workhorses of the railways, freight locomotives require high power output rather than speed. The use of containers to convey goods has increased demand for freight trains, and rail is still the preferred method for moving bulk cargo, such as coal, grains, and liquids.

UNION PACIFIC NO.25408 CABOOSE (1959)
Common on US and Canadian railways, cabooses were the last carriage on a freight train, and housed the crew. Thought to be named after the Dutch *kabuis* ("ship's galley"), their use has declined as automatic signalling has reduced the need for crews. The pictured model has a cupola for watching the train's cargo.

B&O NO.3684 (1966)
No.3684 is a General Motors GP40-class diesel-electric, a versatile locomotive that could be used for "manifest" freight – hauling a range of different units in a single train – as well as heavy loads. It was the first engine capable of a power output of 2,240kw (3,000bhp) to be used by the Baltimore & Ohio Railroad.

Front-facing cab

Mounted on a 16.8-m (55-ft) frame

B&O NO.7402 (1964)
One of 24 Baltimore and Ohio SD35-class diesel-electric locomotives, No.7402 was powered by a 16-cylinder engine that yielded a power output of 1,900kw (2,500bhp). Its two three-axle bogies are typical of low-speed, high-weight freight trains.

NORFOLK AND WESTERN NO.522 (1962)

No.522 was the first of a series of the GP30 class from General Motors to be put into service by the Norfolk and Western Railway. It achieved a power output of 1,680kw (2,250bhp) through its diesel-electric engine.

SANTA FE SOUTHERN NO.92 (1953)

A diesel-electric "switcher" used to shunt trains at rail yards, Santa Fe Southern's No.92 is a GP7-class built by General Motors. It was one of the first locomotives to use the "hood unit" design, in which a narrow body is surrounded by external walkways.

NORFOLK AND WESTERN NO.1776 (1970)

With a power output of 2,680kw (3,600bhp), No.1776 was one of 115 SD45 diesel-electrics produced by General Motors for the Norfolk and Western Railway. It was painted in a stars-and-stripes livery to mark the 1976 bicentenary of the US Declaration of Independence.

Three 121-cm (48-in) radiator fans

Locomotive weighs 141 tonnes (139 tons)

Geared to travel at 104kph (65mph)

External walkways

SBB CARGO TRAXX F140 AC (2003)

Built by Bombardier, the TRAXX class is a modular family of trains that can be adapted for a range of functions, and is the most economically successful train ever produced. The pictured model is of an electric freight train operated by SBB Cargo of Switzerland.

Cape to Cairo:
the Railway that Never Was

IT WAS THE MOST ABSURD, the most ambitious, and the most improbable of all railway dreams, and it failed – but only just. No continuous line from Cairo to the Cape of Good Hope – which would have linked Britain's African colonies (coloured pink on global political maps of the era) – was ever built. Nevertheless, construction started on a through-rail route in the 1880s, and one did eventually emerge 40 years later, although hundreds of miles of transfers via lakes and rivers were necessary to complete the journey. However, even the project's most optimistic protagonists had accepted that maritime interruptions would be necessary. Indeed Cecil Rhodes, the godfather of the idea, stated that the project was never for a railway that depended on traffic all the way through, but one that would "pick up trade all the way along the route", and, crucially, would run entirely through British Imperial territory.

The idea represented a microcosm of the various impulses behind the British Empire in the late-Victorian era. It combined private megalomania, commercial and financial greed, and military necessity, although it had relatively little support – especially not of the financial kind – from London. Whether the project is viewed as a failure or as a partial success, the motley band of imperialists, contractors, and engineers who worked on it built thousands of miles of railway that are still vital for the African continent today. The route incorporated separate lines to both the Atlantic and Indian oceans and, as a by-product, created a number of new towns and cities. Lusaka, now the capital of Zambia, was described in railway

CECIL RHODES
British imperialist Cecil Rhodes was the man behind the dream of a railway from the Cape all the way across the "red line" of British colonies in Africa to Cairo.

historian George Tabor's *The Cape to Cairo Railway* as no more than a "lion-infested siding", and Gaberone, the future capital of Botswana, was a "remote watering hole on the edge of the Kalahari desert".

GEORGE PAULING
Larger-than-life engineer George Pauling worked with astonishing stamina and speed to build Rhodes' railways across southern Africa.

The idea of an all-British railway through Africa was first suggested in 1876 by the explorer H.M. Stanley (of "Dr Livingstone, I presume" fame), in a letter to the *Daily Telegraph* newspaper. As Stanley later put it, "the railroad is the answer to Africa's pressing problems. It is the only answer to the wagon trails, decimated by rinderpest and the tsetse fly; and the one way to defeat slavery by opening up the continent to commerce and communication". Stanley's idea became a reality through the unbridled ambition of Cecil Rhodes, an imperial and political megalomaniac who made his fortune from the lucrative diamond trade of southern Africa. Rhodes was supported throughout the project by Charles (later Sir Charles) Metcalfe, an unusual blend of aristocrat and consulting engineer, who had been a friend since the pair were students at Oxford University.

To carry out his ambitions, Rhodes required someone with the engineering skills to build a railway over thousands of miles of virtually impassable country. He was lucky to find the right man in British railway engineer George Pauling, head of family-owned engineering contractor Pauling & Co, which already had a decade of experience building railways overseas when it was established under that name in 1894. The firm also included George's brother Harry, four cousins – Harold, Henry, Willie, and Percy – and his brother-in-law Alfred Lawley.

In every respect, George was a larger-than-life character. He was a very big man who professed that he was "never able to reduce my weight below 16 stone [100kg]". This was perhaps not surprising given his enormous appetite – on one occasion he consumed 300 bottles of German beer with two friends while stuck for 48 hours on a railway line; on another he ate a thousand oysters ("small but of delicate flavour") in one sitting. As his banker Emile d'Erlanger put it (Pauling relied on the d'Erlangers' financial backing, as Rhodes depended on the Rothschilds'), he was "endowed with a physique that made light of any feat of strength and enabled him to defy fatigue or illness".

His stamina was combined with a readiness to build rough-and-ready lines, leaving bridges to wait until later. He knew that his work would prove to be durable, and it was this confidence that ensured his promises of apparently impossible speeds of construction would be kept. His financial success came from his capacity to identify almost at a glance the shortest and cheapest route for a line. Although he based his estimate on an initial outside survey and charged a fixed fee per mile, he profited greatly from his ability to find shortcuts.

The first railways had opened in the Cape Colony, at Africa's southern tip, in 1863. To save money, they were built to a narrow gauge of 1,076mm (3ft 6in), which became known as "Cape Gauge". Development of the lines was limited by financial constraints, and the narrow gauge resulted in speeds that never averaged more than 56kph (35mph). It was the 1872 diamond rush at Kimberley, 965km (600 miles) to the north, that sparked more ambitious railway-

CONSTRUCTION OF THE CAPE TO CAIRO
Work started on southern Africa's first railway at Cape Town in 1859. By the time the tracks reached the Congo River in 1918, the dream of a trans-African railway had been abandoned.

building schemes, adding a solid financial rationale to the young Rhodes' imperial ambitions.

The rails reached Kimberley by 1885 while Rhodes, still only in his thirties, was busy building up a diamond monopoly through his company, De Beers. This first stage of the line was no easy feat, with a climb of more than 1,000m

DISTANCE FROM CAPE TO CAIRO AS THE CROW FLIES

6,750KM

(4,200 MILES)

(3,500ft) to the dry, dusty uplands of the Karoo. Pauling ensured that the pace of construction was far faster than the eight years it had taken to lay the first 650km (400 miles) from Cape Town to Worcester. Progress was easier on the plateau of the Karoo, and Pauling's men could advance as much as a kilometre (half a mile) a day. Pauling pushed ahead despite opposition from the region's Afrikaner population, who hated the railway as a symbol of British imperialism and as "an invention of the devil". But Pauling had an unexpected trump card to play. His family had welcomed in a couple of stranded Afrikaners who had been turned away by English hoteliers, thus ensuring the permanent gratitude and support of President Kruger of the neighbouring South African Republic.

By 1890, Rhodes, a politician as well as an entrepreneur, had become Prime Minister of Cape Colony. A year earlier he had founded the British South Africa Company, which was to control the two countries later named after him – Northern and Southern Rhodesia. He planned to lay rails north to the Zambezi River and, eventually, to the Nile Valley. The first step was Mafeking, 160km (100 miles) to the north of the existing end of the rails at Vryburg; the line was opened to traffic in October 1894. The next step was the 850km (530 miles) to Bulawayo. Pauling made good his promise to build the railway at an amazing speed – more than a mile a day – and the line arrived at Bulawayo in 1897 to a banner reading "Our two roads to progress: Railroads and Cecil Rhodes".

The next step was to connect the Cape line from Bulawayo to Salisbury (now Harare in Zimbabwe), the capital of Southern Rhodesia. Two links were required: one connecting Salisbury to Beira on the coast of Portuguese-controlled Mozambique, and another running directly from Salisbury to Bulawayo. Construction was delayed by tension between the British and Portuguese authorities, which culminated in a diplomatic incident involving British forces and a Portuguese gunboat. The discord was resolved by a treaty between the two sides, and construction was permitted to proceed in 1892. Even by 19th-century standards it was a very risky project, crossing both swamp and forest terrain. In the first two years of construction more than half the white men died of fever, as did virtually all of the 500 Indian immigrant workers, who had less immunity to the local diseases. However, this did not deter Pauling & Co's project manager, Alfred Lawley, himself an excellent engineer, from achieving what Tabor describes as an "amazingly successful 2-feet [60cm] gauge miniature line, almost 'thrown together'... on the rough and ready earthworks", even though "at times it ran like a fairground switchback". The line would be improved a year later in 1899, when it was widened to the "Cape Gauge". The first train reached the Rhodesian frontier in February 1898 carrying the slogan "Now we shan't be long to Cairo". By 1902, the Bulawayo stretch of line was connected to Beira on the Indian Ocean, creating a continuous link of more than 3,200km (2,000 miles) to Cape Town on the Atlantic.

Meanwhile, there was considerable progress on the northern section of the railway, which stretched south from the Mediterranean coast of Egypt. There had been railway lines in Egypt since the mid-1850s, but financial and political problems ensured that they did not stretch into Sudan, the country's southern neighbour. In 1898, a major and entirely unexpected breakthrough took place when Major General Sir Herbert Kitchener, commander-in-chief of the British-controlled Egyptian army, arrived with an army to retake Khartoum, the capital of Sudan. The city had been captured 15 years earlier by the Mahdists, a rebellious local militia who had murdered General Charles Gordon and all the British inhabitants. To reach Khartoum from Egypt, Kitchener needed a railway to convey the troops south from Wadi Halfa on the Nile, in order to bypass hundreds of miles of unnavigable sections of the river. Experts dismissed the idea as impossible, but Kitchener found his equivalent of Pauling in a much more orthodox character – a brilliant and experienced young French-Canadian railway engineer called Percy Girouard.

Girouard identified a route that included a 400-km (250-mile) shortcut across the desert to Abu Hamed instead of following the winding river Nile, which took nearly 1,000km (600 miles) to reach the same point. It was not easy terrain, as the young Winston Churchill – who combined the roles of journalist and officer in Kitchener's army – explained: "it is scarcely within the power of words to describe the savage desolation of the regions into which the lines and its constructors plunged". Kitchener took the long view and decided that the line should be built using the "Cape Gauge", in view of the possible link up with Rhodes' line. Girouard established a veritable "railway town" at Wadi Halfa on the Nile, as well as a railhead – a mobile town complete with a station, stores, and a canteen – and reached half-way to Khartoum in a mere six months, coincidentally on the same day that Pauling reached Bulawayo.

The line reached Atbara near Khartoum nine months later, in time to enable Kitchener to avenge Gordon at the Battle of Omdurman in September 1898. The battle was a virtual massacre that cost only 50 British lives, while several thousand Mahdi followers perished. As Churchill pointed out, such a war "was primarily a matter of transport. The Khalifa [the Mahdi's official title] was conquered on the railway". The conquest had a major political repercussion for the British Empire. Joseph Chamberlain, the imperialist Colonial Secretary, later told a reporter: "you will live to see the time when a railroad will be built

BATTLE OF OMDURMAN, 1898
General Kitchener took bloody revenge for the killing of General Gordon by the Mahdist militia at Omdurman. His army reached the battlefield by train, on a purpose-built line.

"Build the bridge across the Zambezi where the trains, as they pass, will catch the spray of the Falls"

CECIL RHODES

through that country to the Great Lakes, the Transvaal, and the Cape". Back in the south of the African continent, just before the Boer War broke out in 1899, Pauling had promised to fulfil Rhodes' dream to build a yet-more-ambitious line. He committed to extending the tracks from Salisbury to the Zambezi River at Victoria Falls, and then on to the Congo border at Likasi – more than 1,600km (1,000 miles) of track. It was projected that this track would take 14 years to lay. However, plans were delayed for three years by the war.

The railways, commanded by the ubiquitous Girouard, proved to be vital for British communications during the conflict, but required a high proportion of British troops in order to guard the lines against attack. The first stretch of the new line was relatively simple, and the 480km (300 miles) of track across open savannah countryside arrived at the Zambezi in 1904. Soon the Zambezi Express from Cape Town was providing a regular service to the north. The seemingly impossible task of crossing the 200-m (650-ft) span of the Victoria Falls was achieved when the Cleveland Bridge & Engineering Company of Darlington in northeast England built a bridge to specifications set out by the British engineer George Hobson. It took five months to build, and was then shipped to the heart of Africa, where it was constructed in situ.

The next extension of the line had a sound economic object: the enormous reserves of coal at Wankie, and the equally staggering riches of copper in the so-called Copper Belt at Broken Hill. Both areas were in Northern Rhodesia (now Zambia), and the route to reach them required a bridge even longer than that at Victoria Falls. Designed by Hobson, the structure that crossed the Kafue river had 13 steel spans and was completed in 1906 in a mere five months. Pauling and his colleagues had become even more adept at managing these huge construction projects, and completed the 450km (281 miles) from Kalomo, the existing railhead 80km (50 miles) north of the Zambezi, to Broken Hill (now Kabwe) in just 277 working days. The impetus behind the project, however, had been greatly reduced

ZAMBEZI BRIDGE
The suspension bridge over the Zambezi River at the
Victoria Falls was an astonishing feat of engineering,
originally constructed in England and reassembled in
situ. Rhodes did not live to see it erected in 1905.

following the death of Rhodes in 1902 at the age of just 48. His
successor was Robert Williams, a Scottish mining engineer who
lacked Rhodes' British imperial vision. However, after three years
of negotiations, Williams obtained concessions from the Belgian
authorities to continue the railway into the recently annexed
Belgian Congo. The line finally left British-controlled territory in
1909 on its way north to the Katanga region – which had even bigger
deposits of copper and other minerals than Northern Rhodesia –
rather than east to Tanganyika, which was a colony of German East
Africa at the time. It eventually reached Bukama, 725km (450 miles)
further along the Congo River, in 1918, the year before a defeated
Germany was divested of all of its East African territories.

By the end of World War I, the idea of a grand imperial railway all the
way down the spine of Africa was abandoned. Instead, efforts were
concentrated on building the shortest route to export the Congo's
minerals to Europe; to this end, the Benguela railway in Angola was
extended to Lobito Bay on the Atlantic. However, this appallingly
difficult route of more than 1,200km (800 miles) would not be complete
until 1929. Until then, a tenuous – and somewhat roundabout – rail link
did indeed run from the Cape to Cairo, also using ferries to cross lakes
and the River Nile. A few hardy travellers succeeded in travelling along
the entire route – that, surely, could count as a success for Rhodes'
vision, given the monumental scale of the task of crossing the continent.

Cape to Cairo

A Victorian imperial ideal with the goal of opening the African continent up to commerce, Cecil Rhodes' ambitious plan for a north–south railway across British colonial Africa was never fully realized. The challenges of the terrain, local opposition, and a lack of finance to meet the huge material demands of laying iron rails across mountain, jungle, and desert meant that, by the close of World War I, pragmatism had overcome idealism. Africa's abundant natural resources of diamonds, gold, and copper became the main destination of its railways. This map shows the sections of the Cape to Cairo line that were completed between the 1880s and the 1920s, and its connecting railways.

ALGERIA

FREN WES AFRI

NIGERI

KEY

- City
- Town
- —— Main line
- Regional line
- ------- River route
- —— Colonial boundary

N
W · E
S

ATLANTIC OCEAN

LINE OPENING
A branch of the Cape to Cairo line from Beira on the Mozambique coast to Salisbury (now Harare) in Northern Rhodesia (now Zimbabwe) opened on 19 June 1899. The arrival of the first train in Salisbury was celebrated by the line's engineers, George Pauling and Alfred Lawley, with British imperial pomp.

MEDITERRANEAN

Alexandria
CAIRO Port Said
Suez

LIBYA

EGYPT

Aswan

RED SEA

SAUDI ARABIA

PERSIAN GULF

River Nile

Wadi Halfa

Abu Hamed Port Sudan

Atbara

Massaua

Omdurman Asmara

KHARTOUM

GULF OF ADEN

Kosti

DJIBOUTI

ANGLO-EGYPTIAN SUDAN

ADDIS ABABA

BRITISH SOMALILAND

Diredawa

Akaki

ABYSSINIA

FRENCH EQUATORIAL AFRICA

CAMERUN

ITALIAN SOMALILAND

UGANDA *BRITISH EAST AFRICA*

Jinja
Tororo
Eldoret
Nakuru
Thika

BELGIAN CONGO

Kisangani *KAMPALA*

INDIAN OCEAN

RUANDA Kisumu
Mwanza *NAIROBI*

URUNDI

Moshi

Loudima

Brazzaville

Kigoma Arusha
Shinyanga *MOMBASA*

Kinshasa

Matadi Kananga Kalemi Mpwapwa *DAR ES SALAAM*

Luanda

Bukama

GERMAN EAST AFRICA

Dondo
Lobito Kolwezi Likasi

ANGOLA

Lubumbashi

Vila Cabral

Benguela Silva Porto Kitwe Broken Hill Moçambique

Vila Luso

NORTHERN RHODESIA

Moçâmedes Lusaka Nampula

Kalomo Mazabuka

Victoria Falls

SALISBURY Entre Rios

Kafue River

MOZAMBIQUE

GERMAN SOUTH WEST AFRICA

Zambezi River Que Que

Livingstone

MADAGASCAR

Tsumeb Wankie
Bulawayo Gwelo Beira

Windhoek

Vila Pery

Swakopmund *SOUTHERN RHODESIA*

Walvis Bay *BECHUANNALAND*

Mafeking *PRETORIA*

Maputo

JOHANNESBURG

SWAZILAND

Vryburg Benoni

Kimberley Pietermaritzburg

UNION OF SOUTH AFRICA Bloemfontein *DURBAN*

Worcester *BASUTU LAND*

CAPE TOWN Oudtshoorn Queenstown

East London

Port Elizabeth

Mossel Bay

CAPE OF GOOD HOPE

Electricity
Lightens the Load

STEAM LOCOMOTIVES WERE ALMOST UNIVERSAL on the railways by the end of the 1830s, once horses had been seen off the tracks. It was not until the end of the 19th century that electric power began to challenge steam's supremacy on the rails. Although electricity has numerous advantages over steam – it is cleaner, more efficient, and ultimately cheaper – it requires greater capital investment, as power has to be provided either by an external delivery system, most commonly an overhead wire or third rail, or by an internal system such as an onboard power generator – technologies that demand a high initial outlay. However, once its benefits had been seen, it superseded steam.

Britain was again a pioneer with electric trains, as it had been with the steam engine (see pp.22–29), although it lost out in the technological race once electricity was more widely adopted. As early as 1837, a chemist from Aberdeen, Robert Davidson, made the first electric locomotive. It was battery-powered, as was a second version named *Galvani* (after its galvanic cells, or batteries) that was exhibited at the Royal Scottish Society of Arts Exhibition in 1841. This massive, 7.7-tonne (7-ton) vehicle managed to haul a load of 6.7 tonnes (6 tons) at 6.5kph (4mph) for a distance of 2.5km (1½ miles), and was tested on the Edinburgh and Glasgow Railway the following year. However, the perennial problem of batteries of running out of power — which still limits their use in transport today — meant *Galvani* was not much practical use. Railway workers also opposed it, fearing electric trains would ruin their livelihoods, and destroyed the engine in a fit of Luddite pique.

German industrialist Werner von Siemens developed the first electric passenger train in 1879, and exhibited it on a 300-m (985-ft) circular track in Berlin, Germany. The train operated for several months, using a third-rail system to reach a speed of 13kph (8mph). Britain's first electric passenger railway, the narrow-gauge Volk's electric railway (named after its inventor, Magnus Volk), was completed in 1883 and, remarkably, still survives today, running 2km (1¼ miles) along Brighton's seafront. A low-voltage electric generator originally supplied a 50-V current to the small engine via the two running rails. Later the voltage was increased and the gauge widened from a narrow 60cm (2ft) to 80cm (2ft 8½in).

Some fascinating early experiments with electricity took place elsewhere. In Ireland, William Traill used hydro-electricity from a local waterfall to power a railway for visitors to the Giant's Causeway

SIEMENS' FIRST ELECTRIC PASSENGER TRAIN
Werner von Siemens' train was exhibited at the Berlin Trade Fair in 1879, to the excitement of visitors. Over a four-month period, 86,000 passengers took a trip on it.

BRITAIN'S FIRST ELECTRIC PASSENGER RAILWAY
High seas crash around the Volk's electric railway along
Brighton's seafront. Opened in 1883, it carried 30,000
passengers in its first six months, and still runs today.

tourist attraction. Traill built the 15-km (9¼-mile) Giant's Causeway,
Portrush, and Bush Valley Railway on a 3-ft (90-cm) gauge, and
installed turbines and dynamos to provide the power. However,
electricity generation was unreliable when the railway opened in 1887,
and steam engines were used to supplement the electric power.
Reliability improved once the supply was converted to overhead wires
rather than the third rail, which was also hazardous to people crossing
the line – in 1895, a cyclist died from electric shock after touching the
live rail. Despite its mixed success, Traill's railway was ahead of its day
in ecological terms, and many lines since, especially in the mountains,
have been powered by more sophisticated forms of hydro-energy.

The exception to the near universal adoption of steam for railways
at their inception had been the tramways – omnibuses that used tracks
through towns, so that they would not get stuck on muddy roads.
Steam engines trundling through towns would have been not only
dangerous but also impractical, as they operated poorly at slow speeds
when they had to stop and start a lot, so horses remained the sole form
of traction. Consequently, horse-drawn trams were the norm until the
electric tramways began to emerge – skipping a technological step. The
first commercial electric tram line opened in Lichterfelde, a suburb of
Berlin, in 1881. It was built by Werner von Siemens, who had exhibited

the first electric train two years earlier. In 1883, the Mödling and Hinterbrühl Tram – the first regular service in the world powered from an overhead line – opened near Vienna, in Austria.

In the US, electric trolleys (the American name for tramways) were pioneered in 1888, on the Richmond Union Passenger Railway in Virginia. The new technology encouraged rapid expansion and in just over 10 years, trolleycars had become almost universal across the country: there had been just 4,800km (3,000 miles) of horse tramways prior to electrification; by 1905, there were more than 33,000km (20,000 miles) of electric tramways and the trolleycar became the most common form of urban travel. Although there was a potential hazard associated with trams powered from overhead lines, which occasionally resulted in electric shocks, in practice this seems to have been rare.

Elsewhere, the increasing use of tunnels, especially in urban areas and through mountainous regions, stimulated the need for electric locomotives. Despite the success of London's Metropolitan Railway (see pp.130–37), which opened in 1863, it soon became apparent that steam engines in tunnels caused dangerous levels of smoke, leading local authorities to prohibit their use within city limits. Once again Britain, which had developed the first underground railway, blazed the trail, with a line using electricity. The 5.1-km (3¼-mile) City and South London Railway, the world's first deep tube line, which opened in 1890, was bored through the London clay, so the whole railway was below ground. Steam could not be used in the poorly ventilated tunnels. At first, cables were suggested as an alternative form of traction, but in the end electricity was used. Small engines provided the power, and at times they could not cope with the heavily loaded trains on the line, which had proved to be an instant success. As a result, it was not unknown for trains to fail to make it up the incline at King William Street, the terminus for the line in the City, and to have to roll back for a second attempt. Nevertheless, electricity rapidly became the power supply of choice for underground railways and soon the power units were fitted under the passenger cars, eliminating the need for a separate locomotive. The early lines of the London Underground, which had been steam-powered (see pp.130–37), were all converted to electricity in the first decade of the 20th century.

The mountains and tunnels of Switzerland made it an obvious site for electric-powered trains. In 1896, the first commercial electric trains ran on the Lugano Tramway and, by 1899, a 40-km (25-mile) stretch of

AMERICAN TROLLEYCAR
An electric trolleycar, or streetcar, in Washington DC, in 1895. Within 10 years of their introduction, electric trolleycars had become the most popular form of urban transport in the US.

main line between Burgdorf and Thun had been electrified. It was on its mountain routes, however, that Switzerland pioneered electrification. The Simplon Tunnel line was powered by electricity when it opened in 1906 and the St Gotthard line demonstrated the advantage of electric traction when it was introduced in 1920. Whereas two steam engines struggled to climb up the steep gradients pulling a 224-tonne (200-ton) load at 32kph (20mph), one electric locomotive could haul a load of 336 tonnes (300 tons) up at 48kph (30mph). After that, electrification became the norm in Switzerland and began to spread rapidly across Europe. The Swiss success with electricity, combined with a coal shortage after World War I and an abundance of cheap hydro-electricity, drove its progress. Italy, which had already electrified a couple of its mountain lines, and France both drew up ambitious plans to electrify many of their main lines. Technical problems combined with the resistance of railway managers who still favoured steam held up France's programme. Italy, however, rapidly expanded its electrified services, driven by Mussolini, the nation's dictator after 1925, who saw electric trains as epitomizing modernity.

The United States had just beaten Switzerland to become the first country to electrify a main line when, in 1895, it opened a 6.5-km (4-mile) stretch of the Baltimore Belt Line of the Baltimore and Ohio Railroad – a connection from the main line to New York through a series of tunnels around the edges of Baltimore's downtown. A 1903 decision by the New York State legislature to outlaw the use of smoke-generating locomotives on Manhattan and in rail tunnels under the Hudson River boosted electrification in the US. As a result, electric locomotives began operation on the New York Central Railroad in

1906. In the 1930s, the Pennsylvania Railroad, which had introduced electric locomotives because of the regulation, electrified all its lines east of Harrisburg, Pennsylvania.

Despite the obvious advantages of electrification, the conversion of railways to electric power remained patchy. This was partly because railway managers were resistant to change, but also because it was hard for them to know which of the plethora of incompatible systems to choose. Many different kinds of electric technology were used: as well as various delivery systems, there was a wide variety of voltages, different phases (one-, two-, or three-phase), and types of current — DC (Direct) and AC (Alternating). Even today, there are numerous systems in operation, which hampers the integration of services, especially across national borders.

The most difficult choice that promoters of electrification had to make was whether to use a third-rail or an overhead system. For the most part, overhead was used for main-line railways, while commuter lines and suburban systems were generally equipped with a third rail. Sir Herbert Walker, the general manager of Britain's Southern Railway from 1923 to 1937, was a great pioneer of electrification in the country. He decided on the use of a third-rail rather than an overhead system — indeed, on the Brighton line, he replaced the existing overhead with a third-rail system. Nowadays, this is seen as outmoded and inefficient, as it relies on low voltages. However, with a network of more than 1,600km (1,000 miles) of suburban and regional railway equipped with a third rail, it would now be prohibitively expensive to convert to overhead operation. The London Underground is unusual in that it operates on a four-rail system — one of the only ones in the world (the fourth rail helps to increase the total voltage available).

It was not until after World War II that new railways were almost invariably powered by electricity and the majority of existing main lines in Europe were electrified. Oddly, however, despite its early adoption of electric-powered trains, very little of the US rail network is electrified today — a few passenger lines in the northeast, and some commuter services — while most mainline trains are powered by diesel engines. In India, too, many trains are still diesel-powered, but in most modernizing Asian countries, electrification of busy lines is now standard, and all high-speed trains around the world are electrically powered.

Going Electric

In the 19th century, electric trains were seen as a cleaner alternative to smoke- and soot-belching steam locomotives. The first electric trams appeared in the 1880s, with electric trains following in the 20th century. Cheaper diesel-electric engines arrived in the 1930s.

NER NO.1 (1904)
One of two Class ES1 electric locomotives run by North Eastern Railway (Britain), No.1 featured a "steeplecab" – a centrally mounted cab – and could be powered by overhead lines or an electrified third rail.

ENGLISH ELECTRIC NO.788 (1930)
A small locomotive used for shunting at the English Electric engineering works, No.788 drew its power from rechargeable batteries. This class was used for a range of light industrial applications in Britain.

PENNSYLVANIA RAILROAD NO.4465 (1963)
No.4465 was an E44-class electric freight locomotive built by General Electric. A versatile and reliable engine, the E44's six traction motors could produce a top speed of 112kph (70mph).

PENNSYLVANIA RAILROAD NO.4935 (1943)
Nicknamed "Blackjack", No.4935 was a GG1-class electric passenger locomotive that was later pressed into freight service. Industrial designer Raymond Lowey's distinctive streamlining hides a powerful locomotive with concrete ballast for greater traction.

Body shell welded rather than bolted for streamlined look

Steeplecab design for bi-directional travel

"Cat's whiskers" paint scheme

Three-axle bogie

SNCF BB9004 (1954)
The BB9004 was a high-speed electric
locomotive built for French national railway
SNCF. In 1955 it set a world speed record of
331kph (205mph) on the same day that another
SNCF engine, the CC 7107, achieved the same
feat. The record was not beaten until 2006.

DB CLASS 160 "BUGELEISEN" (1927–34)
German national railway Deutsche Bahn
operated a fleet of 14 Class 160 electric
shunting locomotives between 1927 and
1983. Its distinctive appearance led to the
nickname *bugeleisen* ("iron"), due to the
placement of the cab behind the engine.

CONRAIL NO. 2233 (1963)
Consolidated Railways arose in the 1970s out of
the wreckage of six failed railroad companies.
This general-purpose GP-30 diesel-electric
locomotive was one of the "second generation"
of diesel engines, and was first unveiled by the
Electro Motive Division of General Motors.

JRF FREIGHT EH200 DC (2001)
The EH200 class was an electric freight train
built by Toshiba for JR Freight, Japan's main
cargo carrier. With a top speed of 110kph
(70mph) and a power output of 4,520kw
(6,061hp), its primary uses are for hauling
oil tanks and working steep grades of track.

Pantograph collects
AC from overhead
power lines

The GG1-class was
24m (79ft 6in) long
and 4.5m (15ft) high

Articulated frame for negotiating curves

The People Who Ran
the Railways

RAILWAYS NEEDED MASSIVE NUMBERS of people to keep them running. Once the tracks were laid and the labour force of navvies had dispersed, a whole range of new personnel was required: drivers, firemen, porters, conductors, engineers, track workers, signallers (known initially as policemen), and level-crossing keepers. From their inception, many railways were responsible for the largest workforce in their country. During the early days, and in many countries well into the 20th century, this workforce was almost exclusively male, and it was only during and after the World Wars that women began to be employed on the railways in any number.

When the Liverpool and Manchester Railway opened in England in 1830 (see pp.25–29), it was not only the first commercial passenger railway line in the world, but it also introduced many standards and practices that other railway companies all around the globe would follow. Strict discipline and attention to detail were vital in order for the trains to run on time and to ensure the safety of the new railways, so employees were expected to follow military-style rules and wear smart uniforms. Since the armed services were the only contemporary organizations comparable in size and scale to the railways, inevitably their ex-personnel became a major source of trained, well-disciplined labour. Indeed, many of the first workers who took up posts as porters, drivers, firemen, and track workers were former soldiers or sailors.

As the railway business boomed in the mid-19th century, running the increasingly large companies required new skills and new types of professional workers, such as specialist engineers, accountants, lawyers, and managers. Many of these workers were also recruited from the armed services, but this time from the officer ranks. This did nothing to lessen the military character of the early railways, and issuing "orders of the day" – setting out the daily tasks to be undertaken – became a popular practice at this time. However, the railways were not solely the domain of military men; white-collar jobs such as ticket-office clerks were snapped up by anyone with a modicum of education, and the rapidly expanding industry was so different from any other that training mostly consisted of learning on the job.

STATION MASTER, 1904
The role of station master was a much-sought-after white collar job. This station master at Finmere Station, Oxfordshire in England would have been an important, well-respected figure in his local community.

In many countries, the structure of the railways simply reflected the dominant social or political hierarchy. When India was under British colonial rule (pre-1947), the labourers and unskilled staff were native people, but managers were predominantly white Europeans, or Eurasians with an Indian mother and a European father. Recruiting people to work on the railways was more difficult in parts of the world where the tracks traversed inhospitable and sparsely populated territory. On the Trans-Siberian Railway, completed in 1916 (see pp.180–89), some of the local workforce consisted of convicts who had been sent east to Siberia as punishment, but the railway company could not afford to be too selective in its recruitment. Thus, many of the watchmen hired to guard property at night had been banished to Siberia for robbery, passengers were often served by conductors and ticket clerks who had committed violent crimes, and large stretches of track were maintained by murderers and rapists.

The rules of the railways were strict and workers would be sacked instantly for serious offences, such as falling asleep on the job, or have their wages docked for more minor transgressions, such as "deserting" their post to fetch a cup of tea. It was hardly surprising, however, that some people fell asleep at work: workers toiled for up to 16 hours a day, six days a week. Furthermore, some of the restrictions placed on railway workers were notoriously harsh. Drivers on delayed trains received no extra pay, or time off in lieu, even if they worked several extra hours. Employees could be sacked without any warning, but they were required to give employers three month's notice if they wanted to leave.

PENN STATION LUGGAGE, 1910
Porters were a vital part of the early railways. They carried out of a variety of duties, including carrying the passengers' luggage.

A London and South Western Railway Company employee who failed to give the required notice was prosecuted and sentenced to three weeks hard labour in a case that served as a warning to others.

Discipline was largely the domain of special police forces, employed by individual railway companies. A railway policeman's duties included keeping order at stations, on the railway, and in the local area around the railway; removing trespassers; and ensuring staff adhered to company rules at all times. Most policemen carried a truncheon as a weapon, but equipment such as watches, flags, lamps, shovels, and wheelbarrows was also issued and frequently called into action.

In most countries, working for the railways was highly regarded, especially at the beginning of the railway age. Even unskilled men could earn relatively high wages – railway labourers earned twice as much as farm labourers. The relatively good pay, strict rules, and the smart uniform gave the new industry prestige and afforded its workers a certain level of respect. Corporate loyalty was also strong as working for the railways offered long-term stability, a permanent job in a world where that was a rarity, particularly in rural areas. Many men spent their whole working lives in the railway industry and jobs were often kept within families for several generations. Railway companies were usually keen to employ multiple members of the same family because they saw it as another way of fostering loyalty. The companies also devised other ways of keeping their employees happy: many jobs required working in remote areas so tied accommodation, at a very reasonable rent, was also a common perk for railway workers. In towns, too, where workers had to start very early, housing was often provided near depots and stations. Providing cheap, convenient housing meant that workers would be reluctant to leave their jobs since it would make them,

POLICING THE RAILS
Railway police certainly looked the part; they wore smart uniforms and had military-style ranks. Even lowly constables carried ornate truncheons, featuring the crest of the railway company, such as the Midland Counties (England) left. Senior police, such as inspectors, carried a brass or ivory staff with a crown at the tip.

and their families, homeless. Moreover, the most efficient and most loyal workers were rewarded with the best homes. As Frank McKenna puts it in his history of railway workers, "from the earliest days, the companies used housing policy as a means of staff control and for the preservation of company loyalty". Free or concessionary fares for employees and their families were also a widespread benefit in kind that still exists today.

The railway companies, therefore, took a paternalistic approach, controlling their employees with a firm but seemingly generous hand. However, railway work was often very dangerous (only mining and fishing had a higher casualty rate), although most employers did not feel inclined to address the problem. The most hazardous jobs were shunting and coupling or decoupling wagons, as this involved working on the track right next to moving trains, but all track workers faced a high risk of being hit by a train. Moreover, in the early days of the railways, individual carriages didn't have brakes, so when the driver stopped the locomotive, the carriages simply bumped into each other to stop. On average, more than five times as many workers were killed in railway accidents as passengers. In Britain in the first half of the 1870s, for example, there was an average of 782 worker deaths per year. In the US, the number of fatalities was even greater, with more than 2,000 dying in 1888 alone, a toll which belatedly led to the sponsoring of the Railroad Safety Appliance Act in 1893, which gradually began to reduce the number of accidents.

"The great object… is, to place the two rival powers of capital and labour on an equality so that the fight between them, so far as fight is necessary, should be at least a fair one"

BRITISH PRIME MINISTER HENRY CAMPBELL-BANNERMAN

ON THE 1906 TRADES DISPUTES ACT

USE BOTH
HANDS

When entering
or leaving a
locomotive always
keep both hands
free. If you are
carrying anything,
put it on the cab
floor–don't climb
up or down with it.

PUT YOUR
FOOT RIGHT
ON THE STEP

play it
safe
today

London Midland Region

CLIMBING THE LADDER
During the latter part of the 20th
century, health and safety at work
became a serious issue. As trade
unions grew, the welfare of workers
became a major concern at last.

Eventually, the loyalty of the railways'
employees was simply pushed too far.
Concerns over safety, wages that
hadn't kept pace with other industries,
and autocratic management led
railworkers to join together to form
trade unions, which could co-ordinate
campaigns for improvements to pay
and conditions. The traditional loyalty
that workers felt towards the railway
companies began to erode. In Britain,
trade unions started to be organized in the 1860s. In 1867, workers on
the North Eastern Railway went on strike over working hours – they
wanted the company to agree to a maximum ten-hour-day or sixty-
hour-week, which does not seem unreasonable by modern standards.
However, the company reacted aggressively by employing
strikebreakers and sacking the strikers, so the strike collapsed.

However, trade unionism could not be held back for long and
gradually organized labour movements gained a foothold over the
ensuing couple of decades. Membership of unions grew quickly, and
employers had to take notice. The unions were able to wrest a few
concessions from the railway companies, principally over the long
hours and lack of overtime pay, but the companies were far from happy
about it. In Britain, matters came to a head on the small Taff Valley
Railway, a line serving several coal mines in South Wales. The
Amalgamated Society of Railway Servants union had successfully
negotiated a 60-hour-week in 1890, following a brief strike, but the Taff
Vale Railway Company still failed to recognize the union officially.
This provoked a second strike by the workers in 1900, but the company
decided to sue the union. In 1901, the strike was judged to have been
illegal and the union was ordered to pay £42,000 (US$205,000) in
compensation to the company, a judgment that made any further
industrial action in Britain impossible. This incident provoked a bitter

public reaction and as a result the Conservative government was heavily defeated in the 1906 general election. The new government, led by the Liberals, introduced the Trades Disputes Act, which effectively gave trade unions immunity from being sued in such circumstances. This resulted in a rapid growth of union strength.

Other countries followed a similar pattern. In the US, railway workers began to organize into trade unions in the 1860s, but this was strongly opposed by the railway companies. Railway workers were involved in three major strikes in the last quarter of the 19th century and although all of them ended in defeats for the unions, union membership nevertheless increased and the rail companies were forced to recognize them. The US public largely supported the workers' desire for basic rights and in the early years of the 20th century trade unions grew across the rail industry, and they remain relatively strong in the 21st century. Similarly, in the Netherlands, railway companies were initially resistant to any legislation that would restrict the number of hours that employees worked. So, in the late 1890s, brotherhoods began to form and in 1901 they coalesced into a single trade union, the Federatie van Spoorwegorganisaties. The union's first strike, in January 1903, was in support of dockworkers and immediately won concessions, but a second strike in April over working conditions resulted in mass sackings. Eventually, though, hours were reduced and workers' wages increased.

Today, railways require far less labour. Signal boxes have been replaced by control centres covering vast regions; electric and diesel trains only require a single driver as firemen are no longer necessary (although in some countries, such as the US, two people are still required to be in the drivers' cab at all times); stations no longer employ porters; ticket sales and collection are often automated; and machines have replaced people for some track safety and maintenance tasks. Some modern metro systems are even "driverless", with trains controlled by computers. The days when the railways were the largest and most prestigious employers are largely over, although Indian Railways is still the ninth largest employer in the world. However, with more than 1,000,000km (620,000 miles) of railways around the world, a significant, skilled workforce remains vital to build, maintain, and operate the railways.

The Wrong Side of the Tracks

FROM THE 1830s ONWARDS, railways became potential sources of huge profit. People and goods could be transported further, faster, and for less money than ever before. Those local merchants who had invested in the earliest railways, such as the Liverpool to Manchester line (see pp.25–29), reaped the financial rewards. Further railway expansion was needed, and many people saw it as the perfect opportunity to make lots of money. By the 1840s, the rapidly expanding railway system was attracting many new businessmen, entrepreneurs, and investors, all hoping to see fat returns for their money, if not always by honest means.

In 1859, a pioneering investigative journalist, D. Morier Evans, described the situation in his book *Facts, Failures and Frauds*: "It is with the railway mania of 1845 that the modern form of speculation may be said to begin and the world has not yet recovered from the excitement caused by the spectacle of sudden fortunes made without trouble". It was finance capitalism at its most primitive, with George Hudson (see pp.54–55) typical of those who, in Evans' words, were "pioneering new lines through every difficulty" and establishing the many and various ways in which he and his successors could defraud the public. Hudson embezzled a fortune and ruined many investors along the way, including the famous English literary family, the Brontës.

By modern standards of corporate governance, the promoters responsible for many of the world's railways were dishonest. Yet many of them, such as Henry Meiggs in South and Central America

"A man who has never gone to school may steal from a freight car; but if he has a university education, he may steal the whole railroad"

THEODORE ROOSEVELT

(see pp.198–203), made innovative contributions to the development of the railways. Even George Hudson belonged to the class of railway promoters who actually cared passionately about railways, as well as feathering their own nests. So perhaps the worst scoundrels were those who contributed nothing to the actual development of the railways. John Sadleir, a successful Irish financier and Lord of the (British) Treasury, who issued £150,000 (around US$750,000) worth of forged shares in the Royal Swedish Railway Company, certainly belonged to the latter category.

While John Sadleir eventually ruined himself, his railway fraud ensured that the Swedish government assumed responsibility for its country's rail system for the next 150 years. In this the Swedes were typical of many European governments whose control over their railways was far more complete – and more honest – than the British. The French, for instance, operated a system of controlled regional monopolies. Nevertheless there remained opportunities for those involved to enrich themselves, and some politicians often made handsome, if completely unethical, profits from the railways. In Prussia (later part of Germany), Chancellor Otto von Bismarck had no qualms about instructing his banker to buy shares in the railways he was proposing to nationalize – a process that made him a tidy profit, but that would now be deemed illegal insider trading.

Perhaps inevitably, it was the US, with the biggest rail network in the world (at that time), that provided crooks with the greatest opportunities. The battle for control of the Erie Railroad in the late 1860s really laid bare the world of railroad speculation – the varied characters, the complex legal dealings, and the level of political involvement. The battle was immortalized by Charles Francis Adams, a grandson and great-grandson of presidents and himself a railwayman, in his book *Chapters of Erie* (1871). The Erie Railroad had never been profitable, he explained, but industrialist Cornelius "Commodore" Vanderbilt saw an

JOHN SADLEIR
John Sadleir was immortalized by several writers, including Charles Dickens and Anthony Trollope, who are believed to have based on him the characters of Mr Merdle in *Little Dorrit* and Melmotte in *The Way We Live Now* respectively.

opportunity to create a monopoly of the tracks to Lake Erie and make some money. However, he came up against a formidable trio of directors and speculators – Jay Gould, who had acquired a reputation as the most sinister and corrupt of railroad barons, and his two associates, Daniel Drew and Jim Fisk. The Gould gang issued masses of stock – and bonds convertible into stock – in order to dilute Vanderbilt's holdings. The ensuing battle spread to the courts and the politics of New York State. When the battle reached the State legislature at Albany, Vanderbilt looked like winning the hearts, minds, and pockets of the legislators, but Gould got there first – at an estimated cost of US$1 million (around £150,000). In the end, Vanderbilt gave up.

ERIE SATIRE
Puck, a popular American magazine, published this cartoon satirizing the struggle for control of the Erie Railroad. Vanderbilt gleefully watches Jay Gould drowning in a flood of his own watered-down stock.

Russia, too, was ripe for corruption. During the railway boom in the latter part of the 19th century, many lines were built by private enterprise with the government guaranteeing a generous rate of return on their investment. This proved highly lucrative. One of the big railway barons of the Russian railways, Samuel Polyakov, manipulated the companies he ran to ensure that he owned all the shares, thereby reaping all the dividends. Polyakov also amassed shares in other railways, which he used as collateral against loans from foreign bankers, betting on the expected rise in share value. While these activities might just have been on the right side of the law, he also artificially inflated costs of railroad construction in return for bribes to state officials, usually paid with railroad shares. And he was not the only one. In *A History of Russian Railways* J.N. Westwood writes: "Many other important civil servants and even members of the royal family (including apparently Tsar Alexander III's brother, the Grand Duke Nikolai Nikolaevich) received bribes in the form of shares from railway promoters". This corruption was endemic at all levels—even conductors, who were poorly paid, would often allow a passenger to travel for a "consideration", usually around half the proper fare.

German philanthropist Baron Maurice von Hirsch died both respected and respectable, yet he was also a railway profiteer. Today, his fortune, most of which he made on the Constantinople-to-Vienna railway, would be counted in billions. Hirsch was awarded a concession by the Sultan of the Ottoman Empire to build lines in the open country, which did not touch any towns. This left gaps that had to be filled, which Hirsch did – expensively – and he was reckoned to have made several million pounds from the construction contracts alone. To make matters worse, the lines were built so shoddily that they required extensive improvement. Hirsch increased his profits by issuing "loans" to himself at cheap rates, then selling them on to banks at a profit. (The banks then sold them to the public even more expensively.)

Every aspect of railway promotion, construction, management, and operation attracted its own type of crimes and criminals. Unsurprisingly, given the crowds, stations were favourite haunts of pickpockets and other opportunistic rogues. The managers of the London and North Western, Britain's largest railway company, were, according to the historian of the line, "at their wits' end to find out the blackguards. Not a night passes without wine hampers, silk parcels, drapers' boxes or provisions being robbed; and if the articles are not

RAILWAYS COME OF AGE

valuable enough they leave them about the station". In the US, card sharps proliferated on the railways, including the infamous "Poker Alice" Ivers, a petite, blue-eyed beauty whose winning combination of card skills and feminine wiles made her a very successful gamester.

Access to the files of a railway company also provided rich pickings for forgers and fraudsters. None was more successful than Leopold Redpath, a British clerk at the Great Northern Railway, the company that owned the tracks between London and York. Redpath was assisted in his deception by the fact that the company had numerous kinds of stock, bearing various rates of dividend, and therefore intricate calculations were required to determine the level of payments to which the owners of the certificates were entitled. Redpath forged share certificates in which he was both buyer and seller, or, more cunningly, added the figure "1" to genuine documents bought by him, transforming, say, £250 to £1,250. In total, Redpath is believed to have embezzled an astonishing £220,000 (about £18 million/US$29 million in today's money) through forgery and speculation on the company's stocks and shares (which was also forbidden). Interestingly, although he used his ill-gotten gains to live a comfortable and luxurious life, Redpath also became a philanthropist; as Evans summarizes:

> never was money obtained with more wicked subtlety; never was it spent more charitably. A greater rogue, so far as robbery is concerned, it were difficult to find; nor a more amiable and polished benefactor to the poor and the friendless.

Ultimately, it took the revelation of anomalies in the affairs of another business, the Crystal Palace Company, to prompt a similar investigation at the Great Northern Railway. This lead to the discovery of Redpath's deception and resulted in his conviction and sentence to transportation in 1857. Redpath was not alone, however; his defence counsel revealed that when Redpath joined the Northern "he found in the office of the company a widespread system of speculation and of trading in

WILLIAM ROBSON STOLE

£27,000

(US$132,000) FROM THE CRYSTAL PALACE COMPANY IN 1855

stocks and shares under other people's names — names not infrequently entirely utterly fictitious". It is impossible to know how many similar frauds occurred during this time, but have remained undetected.

One railway crime from this era stands out for its cunning execution — the theft of £12,000/US$58,600 of gold bullion (around £1 million or US$1.6 million in today's money) in 1855 from a South-Eastern Railway train travelling from London to Folkestone, Kent. It was largely an inside job involving Messrs. Burgess, a guard, Tester, a clerk, and Pierce, a ticket-printer and fraudster, together with Edward Agar, a long-time professional thief. The plan was devised by Pierce and Agar: the gold was bound for France, and would be transferred from the train to the ship at Folkestone. On the way to Folkestone, it was carried in a guard's van in safes with two separate locks and was then weighed at the docks to ensure that nothing had been stolen. The gang managed to acquire impressions of both sets of locks and enough lead to counter the weight of the gold. They were able to board the train, open the safes, extract the gold, and replace it with the lead, all before the train reached Folkestone. It was so wonderfully simple and the scheme only unravelled when Agar was arrested for an unrelated crime. He asked Pierce to provide for Fanny Kay, the mother of one of his children, but Pierce failed to do so. Kay then revealed the plan to the railway company and Agar confessed, implicating the other three to reduce his own sentence.

Thus the early commercial railways attracted a wide range of crooks and cheats, forgers and fraudsters, speculators and schemers from every echelon of society, all looking to line their pockets while emptying others'. As Samuel Smiles put it in his 1857 biography of "father of the railways", George Stephenson: "Folly and knavery were for a time in the ascendant. The sharpers [card sharps] of society were let loose and jobbers and schemers became more and more plentiful. They threw out railway schemes as lures to catch the unwary".

WHAT A CARVE UP!
Entrepreneurs Cornelius Vanderbilt, Jay
Gould, Russell Sage, and Cyrus W. Field
are shown dividing up the United States'
railways in 1882, as European royalty
watch from across the Atlantic Ocean.

Indian Hill Railways: Climbing Out of the Heat

THERE WERE MANY REASONS to build railways: to carry passengers and freight; to unite towns, villages, and nations; to make money; or simply to stop other companies from building them. The famous Indian hill railways, however, owe their existence to a very particular phenomenon – the British colonists' dislike of the hot Indian summer.

Since their inception in 1853, the railways in India had quickly become a vital part of the way of life in the subcontinent, used by both the Indians and the British, though mostly in separate carriages or trains. As the railway network grew, the British realized that it could also be the answer to the nagging question of how to avoid the oppressive heat during the summer months. Leaving the towns in the summer for cooler areas in the hills had long been a habit of the colonists, but it was a long and arduous journey. Building the Indian hill railways, which would climb perilously steep inclines to link the hill towns with the plains below, seemed the obvious, if ambitious, solution. Such a venture seemed impossible at first, however, as the hills in question – which included the foothills of the mighty Himalayas – had gradients that appeared too steep to tackle. Yet as the 19th century wore on and railway engineering became more and more sophisticated, it was soon felt that no mountain, ravine, or river could present any serious obstacle to the iron road's inexorable progress.

The first, and still the most famous, hill railway to be built in India was the Darjeeling Himalayan Railway (DHR). It linked Siliguri in the plains of the Himalayas (122m/400ft above sea level) with Darjeeling in the Lesser Himalaya mountain range (2,045m/6710ft above sea level), climbing nearly 2km (1¼ miles) in its 88-km (55-mile) journey. Construction began in May 1879, just months after the mainline railway had reached Siliguri, and it aroused great interest in India. In March 1880, Lord Lytton, the British Viceroy of India, travelled on the first completed stretch of track, cheered on by huge crowds. The line was completed in two years, which is truly remarkable considering the challenges the engineers faced. For most

CHUNBATTI RAILWAY LOOP, 1914
Originally the third loop of the Darjeeling Himalayan,
the Chunbatti loop is now the first and lowest after
the others were removed in 1942 and 1991.

of its length, the DHR ran alongside a newly built path, but while the
first 11km (7 miles) was a gentle incline, after that the gradient became
much steeper, up to 1 in 23 (or 4 per cent). This level of incline can be
problematic for a railway without extra support, such as a rack or a
cable, but the DHR engineers avoided this by building a lighter,
narrow-gauge railway. Later they also added loops, in which the track
passed over itself, and zigzags, in which it reversed back on itself, to
reduce the sharpness of the gradient further. One of the four loops on
the DHR was named Agony Point because of the perilous tightness of
the bend and its proximity to the precipice of the hill.

Perhaps surprisingly, the DHR was extremely profitable right from
the start. Not only did it carry British residents keen to escape the
summer heat and tourists who immediately flocked to see the
wonderful scenery, it also carried vast amounts of tea. In fact, the
arrival of the railways helped the local tea industry to thrive. Although
the railway was very slow, rarely reaching speeds of more than 24kph
(15mph), it was still much faster than the bullock carts that used the
road. As with the mainline Indian railways, the hill railways also had

AGONY POINT, 1910
The fourth loop on the Darjeeling Himalayan
Railway, Agony Point also has the tightest
curve. It is located just north of Tindharia
station, on the steepest part of the line.

a military function: building railways deep into the Himalayas enabled the British to establish control and create garrison towns that would protect the most remote parts of the subcontinent.

In the early days, the mail train left Siliguri at 8:25am and passengers were treated to an unparalleled experience as the train climbed up through the cloud and early morning mist, steadily navigating the steep gradient to find the warmth and blue skies of Darjeeling. An early description in *Railway Magazine* in 1897 recounts an amazing climb up the Himalayan foothills:

> And now we approach the culminating wonder of the line. At one place, we have been able to count three lines of rail below us which we have just traversed, and to see three more above us, up which we are going to climb, making in all seven lines of track (counting the one we are on) visible at one time, nearly parallel with each other at gradually rising heights on the mountain side. But now the wheels groan with the lateral pressure caused by a tremendous series of curves, and for a few breathless seconds, the train seems transformed into a veritable snake, as we pass 'Agony Point' and in so doing traverse two complete circles of such incredibly small diameter that the train, if at rest, would stretch round more than half of the circumference of one of them.

Today, the DHR is a designated UNESCO World Heritage Site, honoured for its innovation and socio-economic impact. It is also still a functioning railway, carrying both local passengers − there is even a special school train, which transports children to schools in local towns − and countless tourists. The trains can be heard anywhere on the mountain up to Darjeeling, thanks to the loud horns that sound constantly, even managing to drown out the trucks and buses. If they are lucky, passengers can see Mount Everest in the distance, although the frequent mists and clouds make this relatively rare (this author spent a week there without so much as a glimpse of Everest). Incredibly, some of the original steam locomotives supplied by the British company Sharp, Stewart & Co. are still running, although they spend much of their time in the workshop at Tindharia, a third of the way up the line. The line has suffered from subsidence and landslides over the years and the lower section was closed in 2010 following a major landslide, which also washed away the adjoining road. Today, only the upper section from Kurseong to Darjeeling remains in operation.

The next hill railway project in India was the 1-m (3ft-3⅜-in) gauge Nilgiri Mountain Railway (NMR) from Mettupalayam to Udhagamandalam (more commonly known as Ooty) in Tamil Nadu, South India. It had initially been proposed as a garrison line way back in 1854 at the start of the Indian railway age, but construction did not begin until 1894. The NMR was even steeper than the DHR, as the railway had to climb more than 1.6km (1 mile) from the plain to the summit, over a distance of 42km (26 miles). Consequently, it took much longer to build than the Darjeeling line and entailed far more major structures, including 108 curves, 16 tunnels, and a staggering 250 bridges. It did not open fully until 1908. The steepness, which at some points reached 1 in 12 (or 8 per cent), was too great for a locomotive to manage on its own and consequently for the first 27km (17 miles), between the towns of Mettupalayam and Coonoor, the line used a rack and pinion system to navigate the steep gradient. This involved installing a third rail in the middle of the track, with teeth similar to those on a gear mechanism. A special toothed wheel on the locomotive then locked in to the rail, enabling it to grip and help to pull the train up the hill (see pp.108–109). Given the steepness of the line and its sharp curves, it was a very slow journey, taking five hours to reach Ooty at the top. As with the DHR, some very old steam locomotives still

DHR TRAIN
Due to the railway's narrow gauge and the distinctive blue trains that resembled beloved fictional steam locomotive Thomas the Tank Engine, the Darjeeling Himalayan Railway also became known as the "Toy Train".

travel on the line today. In honour of that fact, the NMR joined the DHR as a UNESCO World Heritage Site in 2005, and they became known collectively as the Mountain Railways of India.

The third famous Indian hill railway to be completed was the Kalka to Shimla line, opened in 1906. Shimla (or Simla as it was then known) was a much more important centre for the British than Darjeeling or Ooty. By the 1830s, it had become a well-established summer residence for the British and was noted for its balls and other social highlights, attended by colonial officers and senior administrators. Although the roads up to the station were widened and improved with the construction of the Hindustan–Tibet highway in 1850, it was still a four-day journey

RACK AND PINION
The Nilgiri Mountain Railway adopted a Swiss-designed rack and pinion system, involving a third rail in the centre (see below) to cope with the steepness of the gradient.

from the plains up to Shimla. When, in 1863, Shimla became the official summer capital of India it meant that the whole paraphernalia of government, even the military, was moved between Calcutta and Shimla twice a year.

Due to Shimla's importance to the colonists, it was vital that a railway should be built up to the town, but it was a far more complicated proposition than the other two hill railways. As with the DHR and the NMR, the Kalka to Shimla Railway was built to a very narrow gauge (in this case 762mm/2ft 6in) to make it lighter and to save construction time. Nevertheless, the railway route from Kalka to Shimla involved the construction of more than 806 bridges and, although many were little more than culverts over streams, several were arched, multi-tiered structures rising from the bottom of deep valleys.

In fact, there is a sad legend about the longest tunnel on the line (number 33), which is nearly 1.2km (¾ mile) long. Colonel Barog, the engineer of this tunnel, ordered digging to begin at both ends, but the two sections were not properly aligned so they didn't join up. Barog was fined a nominal amount (1 rupee) by his employers, but he could not cope with the stigma of his failure and committed suicide. Another engineer completed the tunnel, but it was named the Barog Tunnel in memory of the original engineer. Despite this minor mishap, the 97-km (60-mile) line was a feat of engineering and came to be known as the "British Jewel of the Orient". The prolific railway writer O.S. Nock travelled on the line in the 1970s and was amazed at the difficult terrain that the line traversed. He wrote:

> The geology of the area is highly erratic. The formation consists of a heterogeneous mass of boulders, clay containing small quantities of sand and other debris, while in other locations it is a solid rocky mass. There is frequent trouble during the monsoon season from slips and subsidence, and these sometimes occur without any preliminary warning because of the peculiar geology and the unpredictable hydrology of the area.

WHEN IT IS EVENTUALLY COMPLETED THE KASHMIR RAILWAY WILL EXTEND

345KM
(214 MILES)

He goes on to explain that he found the use of the word "erratic" by local geologists rather strange until he travelled up the line and saw for himself that the area posed particularly unique difficulties for the construction of a railway. It was worth it though. The line is one of the most impressive in the world with spectacular views of the Himalayan foothills and in 2008 the line was added to the UNESCO World Heritage Site, the Mountain Railways of India.

Several other hill railways were built during this era and are still thriving today. These include the Kangra Valley Railway (opened to passengers in 1929) in the sub-Himalayan region; the Matheran Hill Railway (built in 1907), which ascends the western Ghats mountain range in south; and the Lumding to Silchar line, built at the turn of the 20th century, lying deep inside the state of Assam, in the Barak river valley of the Cachar Hills. All of them are spectacular railways, providing a vital connection between remote hill towns and the lowlands. However, Indian hill railway-building is not just a thing of the past: the Kashmir Railway, which aims to connect the region in the outer Himalayas with the rest of the country, is an ongoing challenge. First mooted in 1898, the proposed route includes major earthquake zones, extreme climates, inhospitable terrain, and is subject to continued conflict between India and Pakistan over territorial rights to Kashmir. These geographical and political difficulties combined to delay the start of building work until the late 20th century and completion is not estimated to happen until 2017, well over a century after the line was first proposed.

KALKA TO SHIMLA RAILWAY
As well as more than 800 bridges of varying sizes and complexity, the Kalka to Shimla line also featured 107 tunnels, a figure which has since been reduced to 102.

War and
Uncertainty

MALLARD, NO.4468
LNER Class A4 PACIFIC
STEAM, 1938

The railways reached their apogee just before the outbreak of World War I. Trains were now safer, cheaper, and faster than they had ever been, and reached virtually every sizeable town and village in the developed world. The United States was the world's leader, with more than 400,000km (250,000 miles) of line. Inevitably, it was the railways that bore the brunt of coping with the huge transport demands of the war. Not only did they take virtually all the war materiél to ports for despatch overseas and to the front, they carried millions of men off to war, and brought the casualties home. Indeed, the armies built whole networks of narrow-gauge lines to carry men and supplies right up to the front line. Railways inevitably became targets during the conflict, notably in the Middle East, where Lawrence of Arabia led a series of assaults on the Hejaz Railway controlled by the Ottoman Empire.

After the war, the railway companies began to realise that they had to look for alternatives to steam locomotion. There had been some electrification before the war, but now diesel was being considered, and both the Germans and the Americans created fast new diesel services in an effort to improve journey times. Attempts were still made to modernize steam locomotives, however, and the fastest ever speed by a steam engine was reached in 1938 by the British locomotive *Mallard*.

The railways remained prominent in World War II, in which they saw their darkest hour – millions of Jews and other minority groups were transported by train to the German concentration camps, and thousands of prisoners died while constructing the Burma–Siam railway. Elsewhere, they played a vital part in the eventual Allied victory over the Germans and the Japanese. However, the railways were poorly treated after the war – as soon as hostilities ended, services closed in many countries as competition from road transport and aviation intensified.

The Golden Age of
the Railways

IN MANY WAYS, THE IDENTIFICATION OF a "golden age" of rail is difficult. At various times there were many incredible railways in operation, and several companies undoubtedly enjoyed relatively long periods of prosperity, but trouble always seemed to be around the next bend. The problems came in varied forms – safety issues, worker dissatisfaction and unrest, the need for further investment to improve services and cope with new technology, the whims of hostile governments, and, perhaps most crucially, the arrival of new methods of transport, such as the car and the lorry, and later the aeroplane.

Initially, however, the railways had a crucial advantage: for nearly the whole of the first 100 years following the opening of the Liverpool to Manchester line in 1830 (see pp.25–29) they were the only feasible form of transport for many types of journeys. Thanks to the railways, passengers could travel across whole continents, journey between a nation's major cities, commute between town centres and suburbs, and even reach remote villages – and freight, too, could be moved swiftly over great distances. By the beginning of the twentieth century, the railways had become a sophisticated industry – larger and more influential than any other in existence at the time – and in the years leading up to World War I in 1914 they reached the apogee of their power. It was a time when the car was still the province of the rich and the lorry was an unreliable contraption, and both had to cope with roads that, for the most part, were rutted muddy tracks. It was a brief heyday for the railways, but it was one that had deep and lasting effects.

By 1914, virtually every country in the world had entered the railway age. There were no absolute boundaries to the spread of the railways, and even the toughest natural obstacles – jungles, mountains, rivers, and deserts – could be overcome by clever engineers. Latecomers, ranging from Costa Rica (1890) to Hong Kong (1910) and Morocco (1911), joined the established railway nations in Europe and the Americas, extending the iron road across most of the globe. The United States, Europe, and Asia could boast transcontinental lines. Even some small islands had substantial systems. Sicily, the biggest island in the Mediterranean Sea, had more than 2,400km (1,500 miles) of line at the peak of its railway age, and even the Isle of Wight, measuring just 380sq km (150sq miles), boasted 89km (55 miles) of line by the turn of the 20th century. In the Caribbean, the island of Cuba had 103.5km (64 miles) of railway by 1849, mostly for carrying sugar.

Most countries embraced the railways, particularly as their spread seemed so inevitable, but there were some exceptions. China was the last major nation in the world to give in to the incursion of the iron road. Even when the first line was finally built between Shanghai and Woosung in 1876, opposition to it was so strong, partly because it had been financed by foreign interests, that it was dismantled a year later. Gradually the powerful Chinese mandarins, or administrators, were persuaded of the necessity of joining the railway age, although by 1895 a mere 30km (18 miles) had been completed. In contrast, today China has more high-speed rail lines than any other country (see pp.372–81).

For the most part, railways played a key role in connecting the world in the 19th and early 20th century. Thanks to their facility for carrying both passengers and freight in large numbers, railways began the process of globalization that was carried forward in the late

CROSSING THE WILDERNESS
Finished in 1890, the Costa Rican railway traversed dense jungles, mountainous terrain, thick jungle, and raging rivers. The line was built to make the export of the country's main export – coffee – more efficient.

RULING THE RAILWAYS
During the Mexican Revolution (1910–20),
the railways had great strategic importance,
and whoever controlled the tracks,
controlled the country.

20th and early 21st centuries by aeroplanes and information technology. In the latter years of the 19th century and the start of the 20th, railways across the world grew on average by 16,000km (10,000 miles) per year, making many towns and villages accessible to the outside world for the first time.

The precise impact of the railway varied across the world, but it was invariably profound. Unlike roads, which need little day-to-day attention, railways require constant maintenance, such as patrols that ensure the good condition of the track, and investment, such as replacement of rails and signalling equipment. Therefore, once the railways arrived, they transformed the economy and, inevitably, the character of a region. In fact, the railways were a revolutionary force in both predictable and unpredictable ways. The most obvious advantage was a reduction in the cost of transport. Consequently local produce, whether it was crops, minerals, or manufactured goods, could be transported more cheaply to national or global markets. The mail-order industry grew hugely at this time, as the railways transported all sorts of mail-order goods to the newly connected citizens. The railways also stimulated international population movement: immigrants arrived in the US by ship but then transferred to trains to fan out across the country. Indeed, many of the tracks were built especially to transport the influx of workers to industrial or agricultural centres, and then to transport away the results of their labours. Within countries too, the railways were a catalyst for the vast migration of people — the towns became honeypots for people from the countryside who could now relocate far more easily.

British economist Alfred Marshall, writing in 1890, summed up the influence of the railways and the industrial boom they had stimulated: "the dominant economic fact of our age is the development not of the manufacturing but of the transport industries". Another important outcome of the railway boom concerned the workers and industries that supported the railways themselves. The railways required a whole set of new skills to enable them to run very large enterprises so, according to the railway historian Terry Gourvish, "it is not an exaggeration to say that the [rail] industry played a key role in encouraging the growth of occupational professionalism based on specialized work. Engineering, law, accountancy, and surveying all received an important stimulus". Banks developed new loan systems in order to provide investment capital, universities stepped up to

BY 1914 THE IRON ROAD SPANNED

1,200,000 KM
(750,000 MILES)

supply competent engineers and surveyors, and factories of all kinds were built to manufacture the vast array of equipment needed, ranging from huge steel components such as boilers and wheels for locomotives to soft furnishings for seats and panels for train roofs.

Furthermore, the railways affected other industries. By making transport cheaper, they enabled similar factories to be concentrated in particular areas, which enabled the easy transfer of skills and experienced workers. The railways also stimulated small-time capitalism, empowering many people previously restricted by their geographical isolation. In Mexico, Teresa Miriam van Hoy, the author of a social history of the railways, found that the railways introduced local competition in more remote regions since they:

> prompted the arrival of multiple suppliers, thereby breaking any monopolies or market strangleholds, and provided smallholders affordable access to markets beyond their local community.

In Russia, the village usurer (money-lender) became redundant because the local peasants were now able to travel to the town market by train to sell their produce and turn it into cash. The new stations, according to one contemporary writer:

> swarmed with a mass of small traders, exporters, and commission merchants, all buying grain, hemp, hides, lard, sheepskin, down, and bristles – in a word everything bound for either the domestic or the foreign market.

Many of the lines built, especially in the latter stages of the railway boom, were unprofitable but nevertheless had a lasting effect on the region they served. A railway built in Senegal in 1885 as a way of establishing French colonial rule became a vital lifeline for the economy as, according to one historian of the African railways, it allowed "the rubber, the cereals, and the peanuts from a rich hinterland to reach the Senegal river and transported [back to] the interior manufactures produced on the coast, such as textiles, foodstuffs and machinery". This story of economic opportunity was replicated across the world.

The railways not only revolutionized existing industries, they also helped to create new ones: in the US, Birmingham in Alabama was a sleepy backwater until it was transformed into an industrial centre by the Louisville and Nashville Railroad, which provided favourable freight rates, thus enabling the iron ore deposits at nearby Red Mountain to be exploited. The wine industry also developed, and not solely because of the cheaper transport. In Argentina, wine production centred on the inland town of Mendoza and, as European immigrants arrived by train, they modernized the small existing vineyards and then exported their vastly increased yield via the railways. Italian favourite Chianti became a regular feature of French and British restaurant tables thanks to quicker, easier access to wider markets. In

TRANSPORTING WHEAT IN DAKAR
The railways revolutionized modern commerce.
Dakar station in Senegal became a thriving centre
of trade, transporting wheat and other commodities.

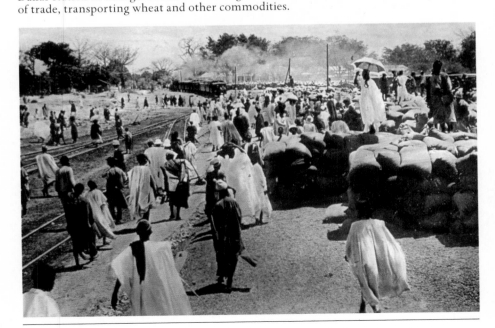

other regions the taste of wine improved notably thanks to the railways. As the rail historian and wine writer Nicholas Faith recounts, "in pre-railway days, many wines tasted decidedly resinous because they had been carried on mule-back in hog skins painted with pitch".

It was not only industries and economies that were affected by the railways. Even the lives of those who could not afford train fares were improved by the railway's existence. In many countries, particularly in South America, Asia, and Africa, the railway provided the only safe thoroughfare for walkers – provided they did not get in the way of the trains, of course. The railway lines forded rivers and canyons and cut through mountains far more efficiently than the old mule paths that were circuitous and badly maintained. Pipelines also followed many railway routes, bringing water to many towns and villages for the first time. Even the station buildings became prominent local landmarks.

ICE TRAIN
One strange industry facilitated by the railways was the transport of ice in the US. Until the advent of refrigeration, natural ice was harvested in cool northern regions and transported via railway to the warmer south.

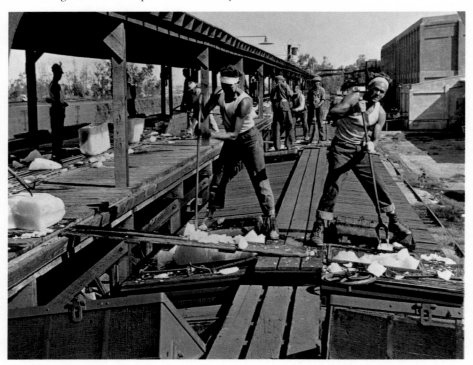

They were often the most imposing building in the area, or even the only permanent ones, and they were frequently used as community meeting places. Every railway also had a telegraph system, which allowed faster communication than ever before. Finally, thanks to the iron road, people were free to travel around spreading ideas, and information and newspapers could be distributed easily. Thus, the wider dissemination of democracy, and other political and social ideas, can be attributed – at least in part – to the railways.

By 1914, in many countries, the railway network was virtually complete. Consequently, the railway companies were able to focus investment on improvements, such as faster locomotives or straighter track. Moreover, they could also devote substantial resources to making life more comfortable for passengers, especially those at the luxury end (see pp.170–77) of the market. These included elegant restaurant cars, comfortable sleeping facilities, and luxurious waiting rooms. At the other end of the scale, however, there were still lots of lousy trains. A branch line shuttle might run only a couple of times a day, and was not only slow but also subject to regular delays – the passenger cars might be pulled next to freight wagons, which could be shunted off at various stops along the way, slowing progress. The "stoppers" that meandered between mainline towns often used the oldest stock (trains) and made their way in a desultory fashion, waiting patiently for express trains to pass at every siding. Timetables were also subject to all kinds of vagaries, and were often designed for the convenience of the railway company rather than its passengers. The railways were unchallenged and the companies took full advantage, with many making healthy profits by charging high fares and bullying their smaller rivals to improve their own position. Worst of all was the grime – steam locomotives were messy beasts, spewing smoke and grit wherever they went.

So, while for a short period the railways were king, their dominance could not last. By 1914, the railways had done their job as the catalyst for the creation of the modern world. The world would never be the same again, but nor would the railways. By the end of the World War I in 1918, lorries had become more sophisticated and would soon offer viable alternatives to rail freight transportation. Moreover, in the coming years the car would become ubiquitous, further reducing the dominance of the passenger railway.

WORKING IN THE DEPOT
Workers at the Longsight locomotive sheds in
Manchester, England, polish a set of locomotives
in preparation for the Whitsun holiday rush of
1936. At the time, the railways were still the most
popular means of long-distance travel.

The Field Railways of World War I

A S STRATEGIC ASSETS, railways came of age during World War I. At the start of the war, they were used chiefly to transport troops as close to the front as possible, after which soldiers still had a long march to their posts, usually burdened with supplies and equipment. However, as the two sides fought themselves to a stalemate on the Western Front, smaller, narrow-gauge lines began to proliferate locally, serving as connections between the main lines and the trenches. The Germans, possibly having anticipated the stalemate, were better prepared than the Allies. They had stockpiled huge quantities of 60cm- (2ft-) gauge railway, having devised the concept during a successful but bloody campaign to colonize South West Africa (now Namibia) in a three-year war that began in 1904. The *Feldbahn* – literally "field railways" – were very flexible, and could be laid very quickly to transport troops across the vast Namibian plains.

The *Feldbahn* trains carried both troops and supplies, and were powered by little steam – or even petrol-driven – locomotives which, by virtue of having eight wheels, the leading and trailing pairs of which could swivel and move sideways, could cope with short-radius curves of track. They could also be hauled by horses, of which there were plenty in each infantry unit. When they invaded Belgium and France, the Germans took enough 60cm- (2ft-) gauge railway equipment to lay several hundred kilometres of track. The French, too, were well prepared. They regarded themselves as the inventors of the mini-railway, having used it extensively in their invasion of Morocco in 1911. And so, as soon as trenches began to be dug in 1914, the French brought some 645km (400 miles) of narrow-gauge track (manufactured by Decauville) out of storage. The standard French narrow-gauge locomotive was the Pechot double-bogie, double-boiler, eight-wheeler, but this was soon supplemented by vast numbers of small, saddle-tank locomotives from the great US engine manufacturer, Baldwin.

The Russians – despite the many inadequacies of their army and their preparation for war – had also anticipated the need for railways, having used them in their war with Japan in 1904–05. In that conflict, they had built a 48-km (30-mile), horse-drawn, narrow-gauge line

HEADING FOR THE EASTERN FRONT
German troops travel by train to the Eastern Front in 1914.
Large troop-carriers such as this took the soldiers to the
railhead, from which light railways took them to the front.

near Mukden, which had greatly facilitated troop deployment. In
1914, the Russian army had nine railway battalions, of which three
used narrow-gauge tracks. Once the Eastern Front, which was longer
and more fluid than the Western Front, was established, a staggering
number of lines were built. In addition to some 900km (560 miles) of
pre-existing track, a further 4,000km (2,500 miles) were laid, about
half of which was used by horse-hauled trains, and most of the rest
by steam engines. The Russians had the most need for this flexible
railway system, since they were fighting both the Germans and the
Austrians across a wide swathe of Eastern Europe. The Austrians
also had a well-developed field-railway system, especially for their
campaign in the south against Italy. In the mountains of the
Dolomites, they added to the existing narrow-gauge lines – which
were, in fact, slightly bigger than the standard 60cm (2ft), as they
used a 75cm- (2½ft-) gauge – to keep their mountain troops supplied.
As historian John Westwood writes in *Railways at War*:

> Anticipating war in the Dolomites, the Austrians had realized that it
> would be hard to build standard-gauge lines on the Italian–Austrian
> front, so a proportionately heavier task had been allocated to the narrow-
> gauge lines, which were expected to be quite long. Indeed, in the long

and usually fairly static campaign against Italy from 1915 to 1917, three substantial narrow-gauge lines were built by the Austrian army: the line from Auer to Predazzo, for instance, was thirty miles long, and included six tunnels and fourteen big bridges.

All of this was a far cry from the attitude of the British. British military strategists had expected a fluid war of movement, with troops attacking and counter-attacking each other across large areas, and so they were ill prepared when the Western Front became entrenched. According to a report into the British Army's use of transport during the war, the authorities could not believe that the stalemate would continue:

> For the first two years of the war, the British transport arrangements were dominated by the idea that the war would soon revert to one of movement, that it was useless to embark on any large scheme which might be left far in the rear and become valueless before it had materialized, and become of use.

VITAL SUPPLY LINE
Allied troops lay a light railway on the Western Front in 1918. The line brought supplies to the front and enabled troops to move swiftly between the trenches.

As a result, the British Army devoted more energy on trying to harness road transport for the war effort than either their allies or their enemies. It was a hopeless task – what roads there were in rural France soon became impassable, and very often there were none to the front line. A British official report described the situation surprisingly eloquently:

> ... beyond the roads lay a nightmare quagmire of pulverized fields, ruined ditches, and flooded shell holes, threaded by temporary duckboard tracks and communications trenches. Through this muddy wasteland, every single item needed by the troops – food, water, clothing, medical supplies, tools, timber, barbed wire, mortars, machine guns, rifles, ammunition, and yet more ammunition – had to be carried.

It was an unedifying and perilous task. Many men died as they wandered off the duckboards in the dark and into flooded shell craters, where they were weighed down by their huge backpacks and drowned.

Narrow-gauge railway lines were the perfect answer to this logistical problem. Their main advantage was that in the precarious conditions of the front line, they were more flexible and efficient than any other form of transport. They could be laid easily, with a minimum of ballast and only basic sleepers, and were also very easy to repair if they were shelled or damaged by the constant traffic they had to carry. As the name "field railway" implies, they could easily be lifted up and used elsewhere if the front line moved. The British, seeing the French success in using light railways, belatedly began to develop their own from the summer of 1915.

The initial British light railways were crude affairs that were mostly man-hauled, although mules were occasionally used. However, the beasts were at times reluctant to do their job, especially at night, when most of the operations were carried out. Far more sophisticated networks were later developed, and gradually two different types of narrow-gauge railway emerged. The first type mainly ran from railheads to depots near the front line, and was normally worked by petrol or petrol-electric locomotives, or even steam engines in some cases. The second type of line – sometimes even narrower than 60-cm (2-ft) gauge, which made it seem almost like a toy train track – was a cruder design that reached right up to the trenches. Often called "tramways", these lines mostly used men or mules for traction, partly because they were so close to the enemy that the noise of the engines might attract attention and possible shellfire. The two systems were supposed to be kept independent of each other, since the lines nearer the front were not sufficiently robust to carry the larger loads used by the lines from the railhead. All the lines were necessarily short, usually between 8 and 24km (5 and 15 miles) long, and required almost constant maintenance. Derailments were common, particularly when tanks and artillery were being transported, and were usually dealt with by manpower alone – a few men would be called upon to heave the engines or carriages back onto the tracks.

Trains were forced to operate under the cover of darkness, and the only light – if one were used at all, which was impossible near the front – was the size of a small torch. Yet nearly all the lines were single-track, and there was no signalling system, so operations were carried out on a tramway-type system of "line of sight". This meant that the drivers had to stay constantly alert, checking whether there was a train ahead that had unexpectedly halted or broken down. A telegraph system could be used to contact the controller, but only if there were problems. The unsophisticated nature of the system is best revealed by the fact that the drivers often had to resort to finding water for their steam locomotives from the nearest shell hole, as there was often no other water source. One mad-cap scheme inspired by the lack of rolling stock was to adapt Model T Ford automobiles. They were fixed to a rail chassis, but proved too light for the task – they slipped on the rails due to insufficient adhesion, so the idea was abandoned.

Given the poor state of the lines and the frequent use of men or mules, speeds were very slow. Nevertheless, these little toy-town railways were infinitely better than any other form of transport at the front. There were, though, limitations. The maximum load of a narrow-gauge train was 33.5 tonnes (30 tons) and consequently, when

"The Russians had perhaps the greatest need of such lines... given their exceptionally long front line"

JOHN WESTWOOD, *RAILWAYS AT WAR*

MULE TRAIN
French soldiers of the 11th Artillery
Regiment complete a 60-cm (2-ft)
narrow-gauge railway near
Soissons, France, in 1917. Mules
stand ready to haul the wagons.

supplies were transferred at the
railhead, at least ten such trains
were required to take the load
from one mainline service.
Nevertheless, the lines carried huge loads. An officer of the railway
corps reckoned that one line could carry up to 1,340 tonnes (1,200
tons) of materials each night, representing up to 150 trains each run by
a couple of men. Even large guns were carried, often straddling more
than one wagon. Towards the end of the war, a new use was found for
the lines: field guns were set up on wagons, enabling the gun to be
moved after a few shots were fired, thus preventing the enemy from
locating them. And it was not only ammunition and supplies that
were carried – whenever possible, the trains carried troops to and
from the front, saving the men hours of trudging through heavy mud
where, in darkness, they risked falling into shell holes.

John Westwood concludes that "all the belligerents, even the
Germans, made greater use of the narrow-gauge railways than they
had expected". This was partly as a result of the stalemate that lasted
for three and a half years on the Western Front, but also because of
the state of transport technology at the time. Field trains were an
ideal solution for the logistical problems of the war's muddy
battlefields, and they became ubiquitous. It was only when the
Germans, at last, broke through the lines in the spring of 1918 and the
Allies then counter-attacked that the lines lost their purpose. Because
of their temporary nature, very few survive today, with just a handful
of sections of line in northern France preserved to show what *Les Petits
Trains*, as the French call them, achieved in that terrible conflict.

American Luxury

Passenger services began in the US in the 1830s, and by 1869 the first journeys across the whole continent were made. Long-distance travel led to innovations such as Pullman sleeper cars (see pp.170–77) and observatory carriages.

WM NO.203 (1914)
A luxury Pullman sleeping carriage used by the president of the Western Maryland Railway, No.203 had a steel frame with wood-effect exterior styling. It had an observation lounge, a dining area, and four sleeping berths.

RDG NO.800 (1931)
No.800 was the first electric multiple unit (EMU) to be put into service by the Reading Company on its Pennsylvania commuter routes. An EMU train consists of self-propelled carriages – No.800 was powered by 11,000 volts of AC current, collected via a pantograph from overhead lines.

NW NO.512:
***POWHATAN ARROW*(1949)**
No.512 was a 51-class lightweight steel carriage built by Pullman. It was one of the units that made up the *Powhatan Arrow*, Norfolk and Western's streamliner passenger service that served a 1,088km (676-mile) route from Norfolk, Virginia, to Cincinnati, Ohio.

66-seat coach

Smooth-sided design for improved aerodynamics

Twin-axle bogie

Imitation gold trim applied in early 1950s

NW NO.1489 *SCIOTO COUNTY* (1949)
Named after a county in Ohio, *Scioto County* was built by Budd Company for the Norfolk and Western Railway as a sleeper equipped with 10 roomettes and six double-bedrooms. After several refits and spells as a commuter car and snack-bar coach, it was retired in 2001 before returning to service on a heritage line.

BOMX NO.130: *HERSHEY WARE* (1949)
Named *Hershey Ware* by the Baltimore and Ohio Railroad Museum after a restoration, No.130 was a passenger carriage built by Budd Company in Philadelphia. Originally used as a 21-berth sleeper by the Pennsylvania Railroad, it was refitted as a commuter car in 1963 for the New York World's Fair.

RDG OBSERVATION NO.1 (1937)
This Budd Company observation car was the tail carriage in Reading Company's flagship *Crusader* train, a streamliner service that linked Jersey City and Philadelphia. It boasted ultra-modern features including air conditioning, sound proofing, and movable arm-chair seating.

Original Tuscan red and black livery

Hauled by NW J-class locomotive (see p.293)

Powhatan Arrow comprised seating, dining, and lounge-observation carriages

BALTIMORE AND OHIO NO.1961 (1956)
A Budd Company self-propelled dining car, No.1961 was powered by two underfloor diesel engines. The rear of the car could seat 24 regular passengers, while the eight-table dining area was served by a full kitchen. It was converted for conventional passenger duties in 1963 before being retired in 1984.

Wartime Railway Disasters

IT IS NO COINCIDENCE THAT A HIGH PROPORTION of the world's most serious rail disasters occurred during wartime. Britain, France, and Italy all experienced their worst accidents in terms of fatalities during the two world wars – although interestingly, none involved enemy attack – and the highest death toll of any rail accident in Europe occurred in Romania during World War I. Each of these disasters was wholly or partly caused by the overuse of the railways due to the imperatives of war, combined with a general decrease in safety. Wartime censorship meant that information on these incidents was withheld at the time, and even today the details are sketchy. Consequently, many wartime disasters have been largely forgotten.

The first of this series of tragedies occurred during World War I at Quintinshill, near the English–Scottish border. In terms of loss of life, it remains by far the worst train accident in British history, and while the direct cause was a series of mistakes by signalmen, a contributory factor was the enormous pressure placed on the railways due to the war. The Caledonian main line approaching Carlisle from the north – one of two main rail connections between England and Scotland – was one of the busiest stretches of railway in the country during the conflict. A huge number of "Jellicoe specials" – freight trains carrying coal for Admiral Jellicoe's Royal Navy – used the line when returning empty from Scotland to England, as well as local and express passenger services.

On the morning of 22 May 1915, the two overnight sleeper expresses from London were late, as often happened in the war due to the intensity of traffic. The small signal box at Quintinshill, 16km (10 miles) north of Carlisle, controlled a section of the main line as well as the sidings on either side of the track, which were used to temporarily accommodate slower freight trains or local services so that faster trains could overtake. That morning, the sidings were full of empty Jellicoe specials waiting to return to the mines to collect more coal. Consequently, the signallers

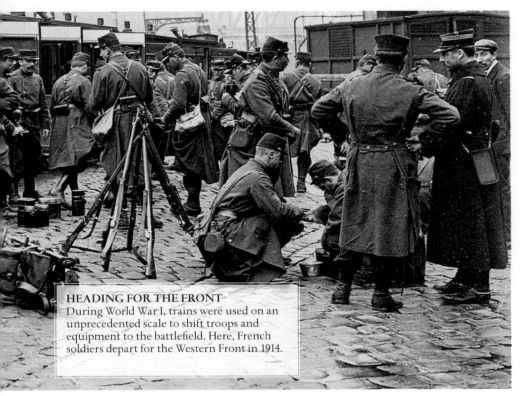

HEADING FOR THE FRONT
During World War I, trains were used on an unprecedented scale to shift troops and equipment to the battlefield. Here, French soldiers depart for the Western Front in 1914.

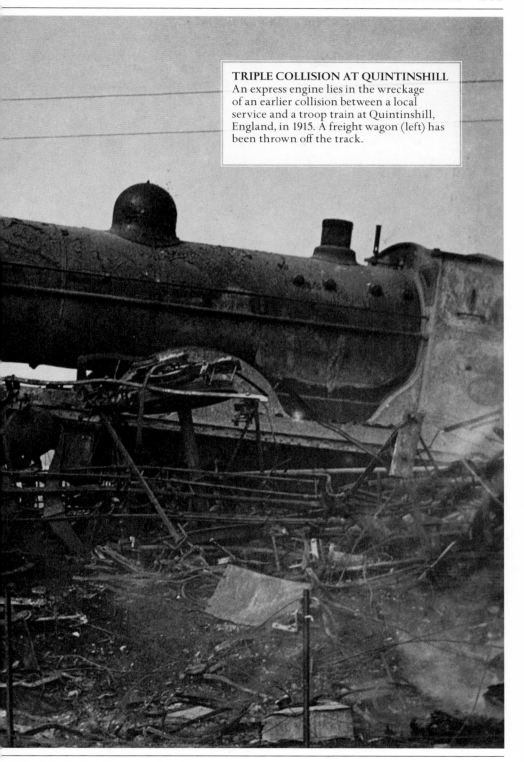

TRIPLE COLLISION AT QUINTINSHILL
An express engine lies in the wreckage of an earlier collision between a local service and a troop train at Quintinshill, England, in 1915. A freight wagon (left) has been thrown off the track.

decided to direct a slow local train off the northbound main line and onto the southbound track, in order to allow the sleeper express trains to pass through.

Disastrously, the signalmen then forgot that the southbound track was occupied, even though the parked train was within sight of the signal box. It was just after 6am, and the signalmen were about to change shifts – George Meakin giving way to James Tinsley. However, against the rules, the two men had agreed to swap shifts a little later than scheduled to give Tinsley time to take the local train to the signal box. Tinsley, therefore, was busy filling in the register – to cover the fact that he had not started work until after 6am – and chatting about the war when he gave the signal "line clear" to a southbound troop train. He had forgotten that the local train – on which he had just travelled – was sitting on the southbound main line.

The troop train was carrying 485 soldiers of the Royal Scots, who had just finished their training and were bound for the fighting at Gallipoli in Turkey. The driver had no chance of stopping when the troop train came down a slight gradient at more than 110kph (70mph). The train smashed into the local service head on, with such force that the troop train's carriages were concertinaed into a length of just 64m (210ft) – a third of their original size. To compound the disaster, the old rolling stock that had been commandeered for the troop train was made of wood and acted like a tinderbox – a fire quickly broke out and was fuelled by gas-lighting cylinders and coal from the engines. But worse was yet to come. The northbound express for which the local service had been waiting was unable to stop, and ploughed into the wreckage from the two earlier trains, which had been strewn across the northbound main line. The death toll from the incident was 227 – by far the worst British rail disaster, and nearly twice the total of the second-worst, at Harrow in 1952 – but fatalities on the two passenger trains were light, although the figures may have been massaged by the wartime official sources. The two signalmen were jailed for manslaughter, with relatively light sentences given the scale of the disaster – Tinsley received three years and Meakin half that.

The Romanian accident, which happened on 13 January 1917, is shrouded in mystery because of its location and the tight censorship of the Romanian and Russian authorities. It bore several similarities with a later disaster at St-Michel-de-Maurienne in France (see p.285) – a heavily overloaded troop train ran out of control, leading to a fire that

TRAGEDY AT CIUREA, 1917
It is thought that the devastating crash was partly
caused by soldiers in the overcrowded carriages
accidentally damaging brake pipes.

killed many of the victims. The accident occurred at Ciurea — in a
remote eastern part of Romania near what is now the border with
Belarus — and involved Russian troops and Romanian civilians fleeing
a brutal German advance. Romania had entered the war late on the
side of the Allies, and after early success was soon overrun by German
forces. To escape the enemy, a huge train of 26 carriages packed with
wounded Russian soldiers, as well as refugees, left the small town of
Bârnova bound for Ciurea. A survivor, Nicolae Dunanreanu, wrote
of the scramble to get on the train:

> ... everywhere, people — and particularly soldiers — clambered on to the
> roofs, steps, and buffers, gripping each other in mad desperation. There
> was not even the smallest corner free, one could not even get both feet
> on a step, nor a buffer, and these desperate people seeking a relative or
> fleeing from the enemy who occupied more than half the country could
> not guess that a greater disaster awaited them.

The two stations were separated by an incline that averaged 1 in 40,
but with sections as steep as 1 in 15. It became apparent shortly after
starting the descent that the train's brakes were not working properly
— it later emerged that passengers had broken the connecting pipes
between carriages by stepping on them as they crowded onto the

DISASTER IN THE ALPS
The remains of a 19-carriage train carrying over 900
French troops lie at the bottom of a gorge near the
village of St-Michel-de-Maurienne, France.

train. The two locomotives did not have sufficient braking power between them, and consequently the train hurtled ever faster down the slope. Despite the efforts of the train crew – who took the emergency measure of putting the locomotive in reverse, and tried to sand the track to increase adhesion – the coaches were derailed as they entered Ciurea station, causing destruction on a vast scale. The final death toll is thought to have exceeded 1,000, although wartime secrecy – and the remoteness of the area in which the accident occurred – meant that no precise figure has ever been ascertained. There is no doubt, however, that it was by far the worst railway accident ever to occur in Europe as a whole.

Later that year, an accident occurred in France that would prove to be the worst railway disaster within Western Europe. It was caused by elementary mistakes made by railway officials working under the strain of wartime loads and – crucially – under the orders of the military, who ignored the officials' warnings. A very long train of 19 carriages was being hauled over the Alps on the night of 12 December 1917, carrying more than 900 French troops on their way home for Christmas. The men had fought in Italy and were anxious to get home quickly for their leave. Having travelled through the Mont Cenis tunnel, a crucial link between the two countries, the train waited at Modane on the French side for more than an hour as other services were allowed onto the overburdened line. The train was also being delayed because of the lack of a second locomotive, which was vital not just to provide extra power up the gradients, but to assist with braking on the descents. Only three carriages had air brakes, while the rest had either crude, hand-operated brakes, or none at all.

As the delay lengthened and the *poilus* (French infantry) became rowdy, the train driver, Girard, came under pressure to proceed down the incline. He refused unless a second locomotive could be found, but the only one available had been allocated to an ammunition train. Girard was overruled by the local military traffic officer, Capitaine Fayolle, who told the driver that he would be thrown into the *fortresse* (prison) if he refused. It was a classic case of military personnel failing to understand the limitations and safety requirements of the railway. As a result, the inevitable happened. With such a huge load and inadequate braking power, the train began to speed out of control. When the brakes were applied, the friction was so great that they heated up and caught fire. This sowed panic among the passengers, some of whom jumped off the speeding train. Travelling at around three times the speed limit of 40kph (25mph), the train jumped the rails at a bend near the village of St-Michel-de-Maurienne. Several carriages plunged into the gorge below, while others burst into flames. Relieved of its burden, the locomotive stayed on the tracks – and Girard, who was not initially aware of having lost his load, survived.

The death toll was initially announced as 424, but is now thought to have been 457. Other estimates put the number as high as 675, since many of the dead were incinerated in the ensuing fire – which took a day to burn out – and several survivors later succumbed to their injuries in hospital. But it could have been even worse. Only the quick actions of a stationmaster prevented a train carrying Scottish troops towards Italy from

NUMBER OF UNIDENTIFIED DEAD AT ST-MICHEL-DE-MAURIENNE

135

crashing into the debris. Reflecting the sensitivity of such wartime incidents, it was not until 79 years after the accident, on 12 December 1996, that a memorial to the dead was opened at the site of the disaster.

Spain experienced its worst train disaster during World War II, despite the country's neutrality. The accident occurred on 3 January 1944, near the village of Torre del Bierzo in the León province, when three trains collided inside a tunnel. Like the Romanian and French disasters, the cause was a runaway train speeding down an incline, resulting in a fire that claimed most of the lives. The overnight Galician mail express failed to make a scheduled stop at Albares due to a broken braking system. The stationmaster at Torre del Bierzo, the next station down the line, ordered sleepers to be placed on the line to slow the train down, but his efforts were to no avail. The train ran towards a tunnel where it hit another train that was in the process of being moved out of its path. Unaware of the crash, a coal train with 27 loaded wagons then approached the tunnel from the opposite direction and ploughed into the wreckage. The ensuing fire burned for two days, preventing the injured from being rescued and making identification of most of the victims impossible.

Strict censorship under the regime of General Franco meant that the accident received very little publicity at the time, and the official RENFE (the Spanish rail operator) file on the accident was lost. There were many illegal travellers on the train heading for a post-Christmas market, and although the official death toll was 78, research has shown that the real figure was closer to 500.

World War II was also the backdrop for Italy's most serious accident, which brought a death toll far in excess of any other rail disaster in the country. Again, wartime conditions were the underlying cause. The accident happened at Balvano, a small town inland from Salerno on the Bay of Naples. The area was under occupation by Anglo-American forces that had battled their way up from Sicily, and food and other basics were in short supply. Many townspeople jumped on freight trains illegally to travel into the countryside to obtain supplies, either for themselves or to sell on the black market. One such steam-hauled train left Salerno on the wet and cold evening of 2 March 1944, heading for farms inland in the Apennine mountains. Hundreds of people jumped onto the flat wagons at each successive stop, and sheltered under tarpaulins and whatever else they could find. The train stopped in a tunnel near Balvano, where it was forced to wait nearly 40 minutes for another service to come down the hill. This was to prove fatal for hundreds of the 650 or so illegal travellers. Wartime shortages meant that the only fuel available for the engine was poor-quality coal, which emitted a high level of carbon monoxide. The incline in the tunnel caused the fumes to spread downwards; the death toll was enormous, and has been estimated at between 450 and 500. Those who survived had mostly been in the rear wagons, which were not in the tunnel when the train stopped. The alert was sounded by a brakeman, who ran back to the nearest station shouting "they are all dead", before collapsing from the effects of the fumes. A colonel in the US Army who helped in the aftermath of the disaster later wrote: "The faces of the victims were mostly peaceful. They showed no sign of suffering. Many were sitting upright or in positions they might assume while sleeping normally". Death had come quietly and quickly.

Fortunately, the scale of these disasters is unlikely to be repeated in the modern era. Train technology — such as advances in braking efficiency — and the enforcement of regulations mean that train travel is far safer now. Generally, trains are not as overcrowded as in previous years, and fire is rarely a hazard given that steam locomotives are no longer used. Moreover, carriages are no longer made of wood, and are designed and built to be strong enough to withstand the forces of crashes — so even when accidents do occur, the survival rate tends to be higher. Nevertheless, with high-speed trains travelling at nearly 320kph (200mph) every day in Europe, the possibility of a tragedy on a large scale remains — as evidenced by the July 2013 accident at Santiago de Compostela in Spain, in which 79 people lost their lives.

The Hejaz Railway

R AILWAYS CAME LATE TO THE MIDDLE EAST. By the end of
the 19th century, there were just a few lines operating in the
crumbling Ottoman Empire. Their military and political value had
been recognized by far-sighted rulers, however, and this was the
catalyst for the construction of a railway deep in the desert of the
Hejaz region of what is now Saudi Arabia – a line that would be made
famous in the West by Lawrence of Arabia.

As with many pioneering railways, the idea for its construction was
mooted long before work commenced. German-American civil
engineer Charles Zimpel proposed a line from Damascus to the Red
Sea in 1864, and numerous similar lines were also suggested in the last
third of the 19th century. However, it was the proposal in 1897 by
Muhammad Insha Allah, an Indian Muslim teacher and journalist,
that attracted the attention of the Sultan of the Empire, Abdulhamid II.

Abdulhamid was the conservative leader of the failing Ottoman
Empire, ruling from Constantinople (now Istanbul). Soon after his
accession, in 1876, the empire had lost two fifths of its territory, including
European holdings such as Bulgaria and Greece, effectively ending
Ottoman influence in Europe. Following this loss, the Sultan resolved to

strengthen his hold over the remaining
Asian part of the empire, which included the
Arabian Peninsula. The political influence of
the empire was waning, but Abdulhamid
hoped to reinforce its religious significance.
The proposed railway offered an opportunity
to consolidate his own position as Caliph,
leader of all Muslims: the new line would
ensure a fast, cheap way for pilgrims to travel
to Mecca. Funding for the railway was
obtained largely through Muslim support
due to its religious significance.

LAWRENCE OF ARABIA
British Army officer T.E. Lawrence became
familiar with the Middle East during his career
as an archaeologist. He led the Arab Revolt in
1916–18, which all but destroyed the Hejaz Railway.

THE HEJAZ RAILWAY

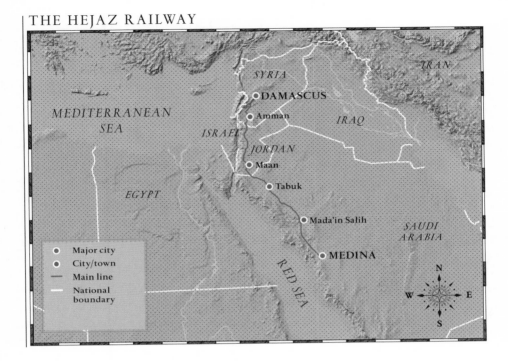

Work started on the 1,500mm- (4ft 11^{11}/$_{16}$in-) gauge railway in late 1900 under the auspices of a German engineer, Heinrich Meissner, who drove the project for eight years. Initially, it was beset by problems and progress was slow. The original surveys were unsatisfactory and had to be redone. The labourers, mostly conscripts, worked in appalling conditions – poor treatment that resulted in a mutiny. Recognizing the lack of progress, the Sultan took a softer approach and Meissner began to impose a more acceptable regime, attracting experienced foreign workers from Belgium, France, and Germany in particular. In the later stages, however, Christians were not allowed to work on the southern end of the railway because of religious sensibilities, but by then trained Turkish Muslim engineers were available.

Three teams were created: for reconnoitring, surveying, and construction. The reconnoitring team, which made a preliminary assessment of the route, experienced the most difficulties: they went into the desert mounted on camels and horses, venturing into unmapped land and facing hostile tribes, and so were accompanied by a cavalry detachment. The second team, the surveyors, used the maps created by the reconnoitring group to set out a detailed route for the

"The engineers had to build a railway through this precipice, the 'belly of the demon'"

DOMINICAN FRIAR, TRAVELLING ON THE HEJAZ RAILWAY IN 1909

construction gangs to follow. Construction was carried out by a special railway battalion with four divisions, each one focused on a particular task: the advance party marked out a trace for the track and prepared the earthworks; the second division put down the ballast; the sleepers were laid by the third group; and the rails were tied in by the fourth.

Such a disciplined and organized process allowed rapid progress despite the difficulties of the terrain and other obstacles. It was not just the heat, which could reach 50°C (122°F) in the middle of the day (matched by cold nights in winter), or the remoteness of the land, but the sheer scale of the operation: 1,600km (1,000 miles) of track had to be laid to reach the original target – the holy city of Islam, Mecca.

The scarcity of water was the worst problem faced by the builders of the line, which followed old pilgrimage trails. These had occasional wells and pools where rainwater collected, but, for the most part, the vital liquid was stored in cisterns installed along the line and replenished by wagons transported down the newly constructed railway. While lack of water was a perennial problem, ironically flash floods washed away parts of the line in the rainy season. To limit such damage, many sections of the railway were built on embankments.

Sand drifts across the tracks were another obstacle. When construction reached the desert of the southern Arabian Peninsula, there was little vegetation to prevent sand being driven onto the railway by the wind, and it was therefore necessary for the line to be protected by sandbanks made of stone and clay.

The greatest irony was the shortage of fuel. Coal mined in Turkey proved too smoky, and so fuel was imported from Wales at great expense, then mixed with the local black stuff. Since steam locomotives can run on oil, the solution was in fact near at hand. As James Nicholson, author of the line's history, puts it, "In view of the fact that the Ottomans at that time also controlled the Eastern Province of what is now Saudi Arabia, they would have been surprised to discover just how easily all their fuel needs could have been met by what lay beneath the sands".

The workers, who numbered 7,000 at the peak of construction, lived in small tents that had to be moved forward constantly as the line progressed. Labourers lived on a diet of bread, biscuits, or rice with only occasional additions of meat. There were no fresh vegetables or fruit, so vitamin deficiency diseases, such as scurvy, were common. Cholera outbreaks were not unusual and caused widespread panic, with workers fleeing the camps, which delayed progress.

As the railway approached Medina, plans were still in place to extend the line to Mecca. However, opposition to what was called "the iron donkey" was strong among the local tribes, who did not want to see it reach Mecca. Their objections were not solely stimulated by religion: many local tribesmen made their living from operating the camel caravans for pilgrims. This resistance culminated in a revolt in January 1908, when Abdulhamid's political position was already weak. As a result the planned extension of the line to Mecca was scrapped. Instead, Medina, the second holiest city in Islam, became its terminus.

The last stretch of track from Al-'Ula to Medina was the most difficult to lay in terms of the terrain, but work speeded up with the arrival of extra workers. The rapid conclusion of the project was partly

FIRST TRAIN FOR MEDINA
A crowd gathers to send off the first train carrying passengers on the Hejaz Railway from Damascus to Medina on the pilgrimage to Mecca in 1909.

to ensure that the line's opening coincided with the anniversary of the Sultan's accession to the throne on 1 September 1908. The deadline was met and there were celebrations in Medina, but the Sultan did not attend: his popularity was by this time so low that he feared his absence from Constantinople might result in a coup.

Despite the Sultan's mounting political difficulties, the Hejaz Railway enjoyed eight years of normal operations, carrying many thousands of pilgrims to and from Medina. However, the line's fate was always bound up with regional and, indeed, global political considerations, and World War I was to turn the railway into a battleground.

The Ottoman Empire entered the war in 1914 on the side of the Germans. The British were keen to ensure that the Turks did not launch attacks elsewhere, and so encouraged the Arabs in the Peninsula to rise against them. The Hejaz Railway was an obvious target, and in June 1916 the tribes began attacking the line. However, the Arabs needed explosives and better equipment, and that is where T.E. Lawrence – Lawrence of Arabia – entered the fray. Despite ranking only as captain and holding a desk job in Cairo, he persuaded his superiors to send him across the Suez Canal to support the uprising led by Prince Feisal, one of the sons of Sharif Hussein, the Emir of Mecca.

Feisal's irregular troops had already launched several successful attacks on the line when Lawrence joined them in early 1917. He led several more raids, both attacking trains and sabotaging the track. The strategy, an early use of guerrilla tactics, was not to close the line, but rather to tie up Turkish troops in its protection. Very few of Lawrence's troops were killed in these raids – depicted so powerfully in the David Lean film *Lawrence of Arabia* – but thousands of Turks lost their lives and the strategy proved successful. Gradually, Lawrence and Feisal worked their way up the line and gained control of the railway as the Turks fled north. This meant that Medina, and the Turkish troops defending it, were cut off from the rest of the Ottoman forces.

Lawrence and Feisal eventually joined up with the British forces under General Allenby for a final assault on Damascus. Feisal's army, which included Lawrence, was given the task of cutting off the junction that led from the Syrian city of Daraa to the Mediterranean port of Haifa (now in Israel). The last, decisive attack on the Turks in Damascus in September 1918 was successful, but Medina was still occupied by Turkish troops who did not surrender until January 1919, arguably the last action of World War I.

LAWRENCE OF ARABIA **AND THE ARAB REVOLT**
Arab soldiers attacking a train on the Hejaz Railway in
the film *Lawrence of Arabia*. Despite the notoriety he gained
for his exploits, Lawrence insisted it was the Arabs' war.

As Lawrence recognized in his account of the battle over the Hejaz,
Seven Pillars of Wisdom, the Turks were courageous and became adept at
repairing the line. Following the war, and the division of the Ottoman
Empire into states under British or French control, the operation of
the line was split between the two European colonial powers. The
Allies and the retreating Turks had destroyed much of the southern
section of the railway, but several parts remained open for traffic.

The best-used sections were freight services on the branch line
between Damascus and Haifa and, until the start of the Syrian conflict,
there was a passenger train from Damascus to Amman (the capital of
Jordan). Saudi Arabia is also building a new network of lines to cater
for the Haj and its freight needs, and there has even been talk of
reopening the entire Hejaz Railway, but this may prove too expensive,
and unnecessary now that many pilgrims travel to Mecca by air.

The eight years from 1908 to 1916 were to be the only time at which
regular services operated along the whole railway. Even then, conditions
were uncomfortable for the pilgrims, as services were overcrowded and
slow. The journey, however, which took just over a day, was a vast
improvement on the old 40-day overland trip. It proved a brief heyday
for one of the world's most ambitious railway construction projects.

Streamliners

In the age of aviation and the motor car, locomotive designers sought to lure passengers back to the railways with a new generation of high-speed, modern designs. First applied to the marquee passenger expresses of the US, the term "streamliner" came to describe the steam, diesel, and electric locomotives that were sculpted for speed.

Aerodynamic styling designed by famous steam locomotive engineer Sir Nigel Gresley

LNER NO.4468
MALLARD **(1937)**
A Class A4 Pacific built by London and North Eastern Railways, No.4468 *Mallard* holds the world record for the fastest speed achieved under steam traction. On 3 July 1938, it hauled seven coaches at a speed of 202kph (125mph), thanks to its aerodynamic bodywork and highly efficient steam circuit.

Streamlined valances hide running gear

ETAT ZZY 24408 (1934)
Built by French car maker Bugatti, ZZY 24408 was one of several "Autorail Rapide" express rail-cars used in France. Despite a number of innovations – such as drum brakes, four petrol engines, oil-damped suspension, and a central cupola for the driver – the model was withdrawn in 1953 due to the expense of its fuel.

PPL NO.4094D (1939)
No.4094D was a "fireless" shunter run by Pennsylvania Power and Light Co. Instead of a firebox and boiler, it had a reservoir charged with steam from an external source. It was used in settings where pollution or fire risk had to be eliminated, such as gas power stations or chemical works.

NW NO.611 (1950)
With rigid wheelsets and lightweight driving rods to enable its relatively small driving wheels to reach 177kph (110mph), No.611 is a Norfolk and Western J-class steam engine. NW's flagship model, the class hauled both passenger and freight trains.

"Kylchap" chimney contains four nozzles for improved engine efficiency

2m- (6ft 8in-) diameter driving wheels

DB CLASS 602 (1970)
Originally built in 1957 as a diesel-hydraulic VT 11.5 passenger train for the Trans-Europ Express, Deutsche Bundesbahn's Class 602 was a 1970 refit with 1,600-kw (2,200-hp) gas turbine engines. The new class was capable of 200kph (124mph), but high fuel costs led to its withdrawal in 1979.

HOKURIKU SHINKANSEN E7 (2013)
This model of Japanese *Shinkansen* bullet train (see pp.364–71) was launched in November 2013 in Rifu, Miyagi, Japan. These trains operate at speeds of around 320kph (200mph).

Australia's Gauge Bungle

THE CHEQUERED HISTORY of railways in Australia is in many respects a case study of how not to manage a railway network. In contrast to many other countries, where the railways acted as a great unifier and were built in a standardized way that assisted their expansion, the state-run railway companies in Australia seemed to take an almost perverse enjoyment in making life difficult for freight carriers and people wishing to travel long distances across this vast country. In no other country in the world has the issue of the gauge of the various lines so dominated the history of the railways and resulted in so much damage to the development of the rail network.

Given that in its infancy Australia was the destination of so many British convicts, deported there in the 19th century, it is perhaps unsurprising that its first railway line was operated by convict-power. In 1836, an 8-km (5-mile) narrow-gauge line was built across the Tasman Peninsula in Tasmania to the Port Arthur prison settlement, enabling visitors to avoid a stormy sea passage. Convicts who had first been press-ganged into building the track were then required to haul the little open-top wagons that plied the line, enjoying a slight rest on downward sections, where they could hop aboard for the ride. Passengers paid the not-inconsiderable fare of one shilling. However, this human-powered arrangement could hardly be called a railway, and it was not until 1854 that the first proper lines were opened.

Constructed almost simultaneously, the nation's first lines set a pattern of disconnected services that would plague Australia's railway system throughout its history. In South Australia, an 11-km (7-mile) horse-drawn line opened in May 1854 between Goolwa on the lower Murray River and Port Elliot, and four months later the nation's first steam service began in Victoria, between Melbourne's Flinders Street Station and Sandbridge (now Port Melbourne). Both these lines used the 1,600mm (5ft 3in) broad gauge, as used in Ireland, but a line opened in New South Wales the following year using the 1,435mm (4ft 8½in) standard gauge. This was the start of Australia's failure to coordinate its railways, resulting in — according

THE NUMBER OF
DIFFERENT RAIL
GAUGES USED IN
AUSTRALIA

22

AUSTRALIA'S MAIN LINES

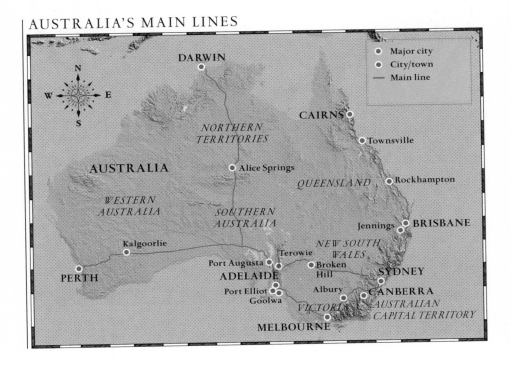

to rail enthusiast and former deputy prime minister Tim Fischer —
a veritable confetti of gauges, with 22 different track widths being used
across the nation. Following the opening of these first lines, early
attempts were made to coordinate the use of gauges. However, these
only added to the confusion. Amazingly, the New South Wales line was
first converted to the broader width and then back to standard gauge in
the belief that this would match neighbouring Victoria. However,
Victoria and South Australia claimed that, in fact, changing to standard
gauge would be too expensive, as they had bought rolling stock in broad
gauge. And thus, as a historian of rail transport in Australia put it, "the
glorious bungle began". To exacerbate matters, the three remaining
states, Queensland, Tasmania, and Western Australia — all of which
were separate British colonies until the creation of the Commonwealth
of Australia in 1901 — each chose the 1,067mm (3ft 6in) narrow gauge,
enabling cheaper construction but adding to the gauge confusion.

In the last quarter of the 19th century, the railways began to expand
rapidly, mostly due to the demand for freight conveyance. The overseas
export market was the catalyst, with the consequent need to carry ore
from the country's mines, and agricultural produce from the vast

BRIDGE ON THE GHAN RAILWAY
The Ghan transcontinental railway runs from Darwin
to Adelaide – a 2,979-km (1,851-mile) journey that has
only been possible since 2004, when the entire track
was finally converted from narrow to standard gauge.

interior, to Australia's ports. But any attempt to create a national network
– or even merely to create links across state borders – was hampered by
the gauge issue. In effect, the six Australian states each built a railway
network resembling that of an individual country, with very few
connections and little cross-border traffic.

For example, when the rails of New South Wales and Victoria met at
Albury in 1883, in theory linking Melbourne and Sydney, the different
gauges meant that passengers had to change trains, and goods had to be
transhipped for onward despatch. The same happened between Sydney
and Brisbane, when the lines between Queensland and New South
Wales met at Jennings in the same year. Even at borders between states
where there was no break of gauge, "huge time-wasting barriers were
created to stop any kind of seamlessness", according to Fischer. The
only two adjoining states with the same gauge – Victoria and South
Australia – changed locomotives at the border because each state had
bought different types of engine that could not fit onto the other state's
network. This lack of standardization proved costly, as it hindered

savings from bulk-buying of equipment. Coastal shipping took up the slack, handling most passenger and freight traffic between states, even though maritime transport was a slower method of travel.

The question of whether all the railways should adopt standard gauge had been debated as early as 1890. However, it was not until Australia became an autonomous nation in 1901 that the gauge issue was addressed, by the new federal government. Before then, the various colonial administrations had decided that the cost of standardization would be too high, making differences in gauges — known as "breaks of gauge" — inevitable. In 1917, the government built the standard-gauge Trans-Australian Railway between Kalgoorlie in Western Australia and Port Augusta in South Australia, but several breaks of gauge were required to reach connecting stations — at Kalgoorlie to reach Perth, and at Port Augusta and Terowie to reach Adelaide. Similarly, when the line between Sydney and South Australia was later completed in 1927, breaks of gauge were required at Broken Hill, where the line switched to narrow gauge, and at Terowie to reach Adelaide.

The nationwide rail system had expanded to some 40,000km (26,000 miles) — relatively small for so large a country — by the end of World War I. As in other countries, railways lost market share between the wars as they faced growing competition from road transport, even in the key freight market. Starved of much-needed investment from their state owners, the railways then had to cope with the added loads of wartime, following Australia's entry into World War II in September 1939. The railways were used intensively for the war effort, carrying both troops and freight, but afterwards a pattern of neglect began to threaten their very existence. Facing even greater post-war competition from road transport, and with the emerging airlines picking off long-distance passengers, there was talk of abandoning the system. In the words of one historian of the Australian railways: "they might have succumbed to the direst predictions of the critics and become nothing more than streaks of rust across the countryside..."

THE DISTANCE THE
TRANS-AUSTRALIAN
RAILWAY RUNS
WITHOUT A BEND

478 KM
(297 MILES)

THE LONGEST
STRAIGHT TRACK
IN THE WORLD

RAILWAY ACROSS THE NULLARBOR
The Trans-Australian railway crosses the Nullarbor Plain, named for its lack of trees. This transcontinental Sydney–Perth line opened in 1970, after the gauges in South and Western Australia were standardized.

However, the attempt to develop a standard-gauge network would continue for much of the 20th century. The first concerted effort had been made in 1932, with the completion of a standard-gauge railway between Sydney and Brisbane, but it was not until after World War II that real efforts were made to create a network across the whole country using the same gauge. In the 1950s, a plan was drawn up to create a national network of standard-gauge lines, but progress was slow because of the cost. It was not until 1962 that the Sydney–Melbourne route, the busiest long-distance line in the country, was standardized, and three years later the Sydney–Perth route followed suit. The Melbourne–Adelaide railway was converted to standard gauge in 1995, and the Adelaide–Darwin line followed nine years later.

There is no doubt that the gauge "bungle" cost Australia and its railways dearly. Changing trains is both unpopular with passengers and costly for freight. The Australian experience is in great contrast to that other vast country developed thanks to immigration – the US, where the railways were the principal catalyst for growth. But thanks to the Australian government's programme of standardization and modernization – including the introduction of diesel trains and the closure of heavily loss-making branch lines – the railways survived and, in places, even began to flourish, although they have never been as vital a part of the economy as in many other countries.

The experience of Australia is in sharp contrast to its neighbouring country and fellow ex-British colony, New Zealand. Although the origin of the railways was similar – the first lines were built by provincial governments, with the first one opening in 1863 – central government took over in 1876. From then on, New Zealand's railway system was developed in an integrated manner, using just one gauge.

The government of the dominion of New Zealand deliberately expanded the railways to provide a unifying force for the sparsely populated nation, which consists of two main

THE JOY OF TRAINS
The New Zealand government promoted rail transport not only for industrial purposes but for leisure activities too.

NZ RAILWAY REFRESHMENT ROOM
The refreshment rooms at provincial New Zealand railway
stations often became the social heart of the townships
they served, offering hearty meals at decent prices.

islands. As the author of a history of New Zealand railways, Neill
Atkinson, put it: "since the late nineteenth century, the state used its
expanding rail network to promote not just the development of
agriculture, industry, forestry, and mining, but to further policies in
areas as diverse as education, town planning, and recreation. Trains
ferried school children to the classroom, suburban workers to
factories and offices, sportspeople to competitions, and thousands of
picnickers and punters to beaches, parks, and racetracks".

Railway stations soon became the hub of their communities. Each
station's "Railway Refreshment Rooms", sold appetizing, cheap food
and beverages served "in the legendarily thick New Zealand Railway"
cups, bowls, and plates. The railways became an integral part of New
Zealand's economy and culture, and, by the early 1920s, more than 28
million journeys were made annually by rail in a country of a little
more than one million people. The railways were, in the words of a 1938
advertisement for New Zealand Railways, "the industry that made
New Zealand – the people's railways for the people's profit". The
contrast with Australia could not have been greater.

High-speed Steam Trains

THE CRUDE "TEA KETTLES ON WHEELS" built by pioneers such as George Stephenson in Britain and Peter Cooper in the US were transformed over the first 100 years of the railway as steam-train technology leapt forward. The period between the world wars, in particular, saw great engineers of the time turn steam locomotives into sophisticated powerhouses.

An interesting analysis undertaken in 1889 by early "trainspotters" E. Foxwell and T.C. Farrer provides a comparative analysis of the speeds of trains across the world. In general, the compilers were greatly disappointed by the slowness of most trains. For their research, the pair included only "expresses", which they defined as averaging at least 46kph (29mph) – hardly speedy travel, but even so, not many qualifying trains were found. There were no such services in several major railway nations – including India and the whole of South America – and only a few in Australia. Foxwell and Farrer found that the countries with the highest proportion of fast services were France and the Netherlands, which interestingly used mainly British locomotives. In Germany, an average of 56kph (35mph) was rare, while in Italy there was only one express – a daily service between Milan and Venice. Services in Sweden – then still a poverty-stricken agricultural country – were "poor", but Denmark had several good trains. Hungary, meanwhile, was praised for allowing the Orient Express (see pp.190–97) to average 51kph (32mph), which was faster than in neighbouring Austria. In the US, the only trains that qualified as expresses were in the east, including the best service in the world – a train that ran the 64-km (40-mile) trip between Washington, DC, and Baltimore at an average of 85kph (53mph). Otherwise, Foxwell and Farrer were disappointed at the speed of many services in the US, finding that even those with famous names, which often contained words like "Flyer", barely qualified as express trains, averaging only around the 48-kph (30-mph) mark. The problem, they found, was that tracks in the US often had to go through the centre of towns, where the trains had to travel very slowly because of potentially dangerous level crossings.

LEADING THE WAY
Engineers board a steam locomotive on a French
railway in 1870. The French led the race for greater
speed, calling their high-speed services "exprès"
trains (literally "with purpose").

This intrepid pair of timetable-watchers returned to their task a
decade later and found that considerable improvements had been
made. By the start of the 20th century, France led the way with 20
daily expresses averaging at least 90kph (56mph) and a series of fast
international services running from Paris that covered much of
Western Europe, including Vienna and Warsaw. In Germany and
Britain, too, expresses routinely averaged 80kph (50mph) or more.

Part of the reason for these increases in speed was a trend that had
begun around the time of Foxwell and Farrer's first survey — rival
railway companies would vie for the fastest journey time between two
points. The first such contest took place in Britain, in a bid for the best
time between London and Scotland. Two parallel lines, the East Coast
and West Coast main lines, travelled between these two destinations.
The companies that ran these services had a tacit agreement that
journey times between London and Edinburgh would be 9 hours by
the East Coast, and 10 by the longer West Coast route, which also had
to contend with steeper gradients. But in June 1888, the two West
Coast companies—the London and North Western and the Caledonian,
which together provided a joint service — announced that they would
cut the extra hour from their service. A few weeks later, just ahead of
the Scottish grouse-shooting season — which started on 11 August and
represented a lucrative period for the London–Scotland operators —

THE SCENIC ROUTE
A poster for the London-to-Scotland
West Coast line c.1910. Competition
with the East Coast line reduced
journey times by several hours.

the East Coast companies (the Great
Northern, the North Eastern, and
the North British) retaliated. They cut
half an hour from their timetable by
limiting stopping times, reducing the
journey time to 8 hours and 30 minutes.

The North Western (the main
company on the West Coast route)
responded quickly, vowing to slash
the journey time to 8 hours – a full
20 per cent reduction on its previous
10-hour schedule. The East Coast
companies hit back in this dramatic
game of poker, promising a journey time of 7 hours and 45 minutes.
As the battle reached its height, people gathered at the point of
departure to see off the rival trains, and their performance was
reported in the manner of weekend football games. Signallers along
the routes took special care not to slow down these prestigious
trains, and teams of workers ensured that the tracks were up to
standard. Eventually, the East Coast companies peaked with a run of
just 7 hours and 30 minutes later that summer, but the contest
concluded soon after as the rivals came to agree on a standard
journey time at 8 hours and 30 minutes.

Seven years later, in the summer of 1895 – following the completion
of the Forth Bridge, which greatly reduced journey times to the
north of Scotland – an even fiercer and ultimately more dangerous race
broke out. This time the trains ran by night, and the "race course" was
extended to Aberdeen – over 800km (500 miles) from London by rail,
and about 160km (100 miles) further than Edinburgh, the previous
terminus. For added excitement, the trains from the two rival lines
were forced to share the final section of track after the Kinnaber
junction, 61km (38 miles) south of Aberdeen. The first train to reach
this point was the clear winner. The contest lasted for 17 days in August
1895 and attracted huge crowds at the departure and arrival points.

Rival companies engaged in various underhand methods, such as not stopping at intermediate points, travelling with just two or three carriages to keep the weight down, and simply ignoring the timetable altogether. By the end, the times were incredible, with the East Coast service a mere 8 hours and 40 minutes. The West Coast companies finally managed to beat this by 8 minutes with an average speed of 101kph (63mph). However, the affluent passengers arriving for the season's grouse shooting did not welcome being turfed out of their comfortable carriages at Aberdeen at 5am, rather than 7am, which had been perfectly timed for breakfast.

Concerns over safety and cost caused the contest to peter out. Furthermore, the following summer a major disaster occurred at Preston on the West Coast line due to excessive speed. An inexperienced driver failed to slow the train as it passed through the station, where a curve demanded a speed restriction of 16kph (10mph). Unlike most trains passing through Preston, the service was scheduled to run through without stopping, and the train jumped the tracks at 72kph (45mph). There was only one fatality, but the accident alerted passengers and the railway companies to the risks of focusing purely on speed.

By 1900, the Great Western Railway (GWR), the biggest of the British companies in terms of mileage, was leading the race for speed. In 1904, one of its new locomotives, *City of Truro*, was clocked at 164kph (102mph) on a downhill stretch in Somerset. Although the exact speed is disputed, it is generally considered one of the first times in the world that the 160kph (100mph) barrier was breached. This occurred during a campaign by GWR to establish itself as the premier railway company in Britain. The company's ambition led to competition with the London and South Western (LSWR) company over traffic from liners sailing to and from the US. Transatlantic ocean liners had traditionally docked at the English port of Southampton, with passengers then travelling onwards to London by train. However, to save time, since travel by land

"… the travelling was so curiously smooth that […] it was difficult to believe we were moving at all…"

CHARLES ROUS-MARTEN, ON THE *CITY OF TRURO*'S RECORD-BREAKING RUN is so much faster than by sea, ships also began docking at the port of Plymouth – over 240km (150 miles) west of Southampton. Though further from London, passengers could rapidly cover the remaining distance by train, shaving nearly a day off the total journey. The LSWR had traditionally served Plymouth, but now the GWR also wanted a slice of the action. A full-scale war broke out as rival companies ran trains with no particular timetable, simply picking up passengers from ships as they arrived and steaming to London as quickly as possible. This was to have tragic consequences on 30 June, when a special service that had left Plymouth just before midnight attempted to travel through the city of Salisbury at more than twice the 48kph (30mph) speed restriction and came off the rails. Of the 43 passengers on board, 24 were killed. While these special services were later run with more care, the race between the two companies continued until 1910.

In the US, the race for the fastest time between New York and Chicago lasted many years. It had begun in 1887, when the Pennsylvania Railroad introduced the *Pennsylvania Limited* – an all-Pullman affair boasting a barber's shop, valet, and maid service. Two years later the New York Central Railroad responded with a train that covered the 701km (436 miles) between New York and Buffalo (on the Canadian border) in 7 hours, at an average speed of 98kph (61mph). Then in 1902, the Central hit back with the launch of the *Twentieth Century Limited* express train, which covered the near-1,600-km (1,000-mile) distance between New York and Chicago in 20 hours – a reduction of 4 hours on the usual time. In response, the "Pennsy", as it was known, renamed the *Pennsylvania Limited* the *Pennsylvania Special*, and managed to complete the journey in the same time as its Central rival. A battle ensued, with each company repeatedly trying to reduce the journey time in a series of much-publicized initiatives. However, these grand contests proved too costly for either company, and eventually a gentlemen's agreement of a 20-hour journey time was reached.

Train races of this kind largely died down until the 1930s, when they were revived as a last-gasp attempt to help steam technology see off competition from rival methods of traction. Steam engines had improved remarkably between the wars thanks to several illustrious engineers. The greatest of these was Frenchman André Chapelon, whose rigorous scientific analysis and emphasis on efficiency were widely imitated, leading to radical improvements in locomotive performance. In Britain, a contest broke out in 1937 between the two consolidated companies – Britain's many companies had been merged into just four in 1923 – serving the Scottish route. William Stanier, chief engineer at the London, Midland, and Scottish (LMS), built the Princess Coronation class of high-speed locomotives, which are widely recognized as the best British locomotives ever produced. On a specially arranged press trip, the first engine of the class reached 183kph (114mph), a speed that was intended to better the effort of its rival, the London and North Eastern Railway's (LNER) streamlined A4 Pacifics. The LNER claimed that an A4 had reached 181kph (113mph), but when the company learned the record had been beaten, it planned a record run in great secrecy. This was eventually undertaken in 1938 when *Mallard*, a streamlined A4, reached 202.6kph (126⅞mph) in a specially organized run on a straight piece of downhill track south of Grantham. This record for steam locomotives would never be surpassed, although a German Class 05 locomotive had come close two years earlier when it reached 200.4kph (124½mph) between Hamburg and Berlin. In the US, the use of high-speed diesels (see pp.224–31) on prestigious routes spelled the end of steam, and, by the 1970s, steam power in continental Europe had mostly been displaced by large-scale electrification.

RECORD-SETTER
In 1905, the steam locomotive PRR 7002 set a record time for the *Pennsylvania Special* service from New York to Chicago.

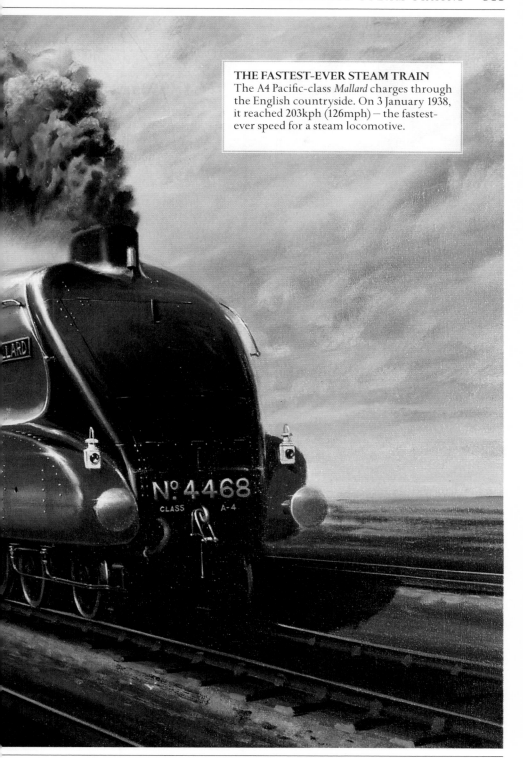

THE FASTEST-EVER STEAM TRAIN
The A4 Pacific-class *Mallard* charges through the English countryside. On 3 January 1938, it reached 203kph (126mph) – the fastest-ever speed for a steam locomotive.

Going Diesel: from the *Fliegende Hamburger* to the Future

S TEAM ENGINES WERE DIRTY BEASTS – difficult to maintain, temperamental, and inefficient – so a search for alternatives started early. Experiments with electric traction led the way, but once the internal combustion engine had been invented, attempts to apply it on the railways were bound to follow. The first internal combustion engines tried out on trains were fuelled by petrol, but it did not prove efficient and was expensive, especially for large engines.

German engineer Rudolf Diesel invented and patented the eponymous Diesel engine in 1892. Instead of a spark plug, it used air heated by high compression to ignite the fuel. Two main types of diesel engine are now in use: one provides power directly; the other, the diesel-electric, uses a diesel engine to power a generator, which then provides electricity for propulsion. Both have been used extensively.

Following Diesel's invention, experiments with locomotives began almost at once. However, there were numerous technical obstacles to overcome before they could be put into practical use, and, apart from a few appearing on a small Swedish railway, diesel engines were not introduced until after World War I.

Efforts to build functional diesel locomotives continued through the 1920s. Despite some success on the US and Canadian railways, the real pioneer was Germany, which began experimenting with powerful diesel engines for rail propulsion. The result was a two-car unit called the *Fliegende Hamburger* ("Flying Hamburger"), which represented a considerable advance for rail technology in both speed and efficiency. The Germans had, in fact, already established the world's rail speed record with a bizarre-looking four-wheel coach powered by a petrol aircraft engine with an aeroplane-type propeller at the back. It was built by BMW and reached 230kph (143mph) on a test run in June 1931, but a host of technical difficulties ensured it never saw regular service.

By contrast, the *Fliegende Hamburger* did become a widely used model on several routes, first going into service under this name in the winter of 1932–33. It covered the 286km (178 miles) between Berlin and Hamburg in 2 hours and 20 minutes – an average speed of 122kph (76mph) – which required cruising speeds of around 160kph (100mph)

THE *FLIEGENDE HAMBURGER*
The streamlined design of the *Fliegende Hamburger* improved the train's speed and efficiency by reducing wind resistance, but also created an enduring design style.

to maintain the timetable, making it by far the fastest rail service in the world. The train had a remarkable streamlined design, like a Zeppelin airship, the result of wind-resistance tests in a wind tunnel. Although Hitler preferred cars, which he saw as the transport of the future, the *Fliegende Hamburger* became part of his propaganda exercise to show the superiority of the "Thousand-Year Reich". The success of the *Fliegende Hamburger* soon led to the design being used on other services: two years later, a similar service was introduced on the Berlin–Cologne route, with an average speed of 132kph (82mph), and a *Fliegende Frankfurter* ("Flying Frankfurter") service followed. These diesel trains represented a radical technological development, but were laid up in World War II because of fuel shortages and only saw service again briefly after the war.

It was in the United States that diesel technology was developed more widely and successfully than elsewhere. Its development took place against the background of a need to compete in a nation where cars and later planes were eroding rail's market share. The US railroad companies had been taken over by the government during World War I because of their incompetence and refusal to cooperate with one another. They emerged from state control eager to improve what they offered, by using prestigious trains such as the *Pennsylvania Special* and *Twentieth Century Limited* as their trademark services.

By the late 1920s, however, these services had begun to seem slow, and their proprietors were desperately seeking a new technology to speed the trains up. This was particularly true for the railroad companies whose services crossed the vast swathes of the West. With car use still not widespread and aviation in its infancy (both the Model T Ford, the first affordable American automobile, and the first commercial domestic flight, between Boston and New York, were launched in 1927) and planes still posing a safety risk, the railroad companies began to look to diesel as the answer to their problems.

These new diesel trains were a different kind of train to the steam-hauled services. Consisting of perhaps half a dozen or eight cars, they were exclusively for passengers and provided a high degree of comfort. They were built of light stainless steel and alloys, which made them look sleek – especially compared to the heavy, conventional steam trains – and they ran fast between major cities, with limited stops to improve journey times.

While some diesel locomotives had already been introduced by various US railroads, these were confined to shunting since the powerful diesel engines were thought too heavy to be economical compared with traditional steam. Petrol engines continued to be tried on some trains, such as the three-car *Blue Bird* trains of the Chicago Great Western that ran between the Twin Cities (St Paul and Minneapolis) and Rochester, Minnesota — but again, they were simply too expensive to operate.

A key technical breakthrough for diesel engines was made by General Motors, the automobile company, which used alloys rather than steel to give a better power-to-weight ratio. The new, lighter engine attracted the attention of Ralph Budd, the head of the Chicago, Burlington, and Quincy Railroad — the Burlington, as it was known — at the Chicago Fair of 1932. Budd, one of the few railway visionaries of the interwar period, realized the more powerful engine's potential to revolutionize long-distance rail travel. After seeing the engine at the fair, he commissioned a new type of streamlined diesel locomotive whose sleek and elegant looks were an attraction in themselves. Called the *Pioneer Zephyr* (the name Zephyr, meaning light west wind, came from Chaucer's *Canterbury Tales*, which Budd had been reading), it was launched amid much fanfare in May 1934 with a record-breaking

BURLINGTON *PIONEER ZEPHYR*
The streamlined American *Zephyrs* gave the German trains a good run for their money in terms of speed and mimicked their gleaming, aerodynamic shapes.

"Dawn to Dusk Run" between Denver, Colorado, and Chicago. The 1,600-km (1,000-mile) trip was covered at an average of 126kph (78mph), remarkable by US standards and almost as good as the German diesels. However, a lot of special measures had been taken: patrol staff were placed on all 1,689 level crossings along the route to stop car traffic well ahead of the train, and the train was limited to just three carriages to reduce the weight. Famously, Budd reported that the fuel for the train was far cheaper than coal, costing a mere US$14.64 (£3) — although, at 4 cents per 3.8 litres (1 gallon), that meant 1,386 litres (366 gallons).

While such fast speeds could not be achieved on regular journeys, the train was far faster than any before and became the pioneer for a host of services that transformed American long-distance train travel in the years running up to World War II. A veritable family of *Zephyrs* and other trains sprang up on routes across the expanses of the West and along the East Coast, operated by these elegant new streamlined diesels. The Burlington, spurred on by Budd's enthusiasm, introduced in quick succession the *Twin Cities Zephyr,* between the twin cities and Chicago, and the *Mark Twain Zephyr* to St Louis.

The Union Pacific's pioneer train went on a nationwide tour in 1934 before entering active service as the *Kansas Streamliner.* Renamed the *City of Salina* in 1936, it could run at more than 145kph (90mph) for long distances, averaging a stunning 148kph (92mph) on its run across the Nebraskan plains. The *pièce de résistance* of the period was the record-setting coast-to-coast journey by the *City of Portland*, a Union Pacific six-car sleeper train, which travelled the 5,230km (3,250 miles) between New York and Los Angeles in 56 hours and 55 minutes — nearly a day faster than the regular coast-to-coast service. Moreover, the fuel cost

506—Santa Fe's "Super Chief" Traveling thru the Orange Groves, California

TRAIN OF THE STARS
The Santa Fe *Super Chief,* which was launched in 1936 and ran between Los Angeles and Chicago, was known as the "train of the stars" because it was said to be Hollywood actors' favourite mode of transport.

AVERAGE SPEED OF THE *FLIEGENDE HAMBURGER*	AVERAGE SPEED OF THE *CITY OF SALINA*
# 122 KPH (76 MPH)	# 148 KPH (92 MPH)

was only $80 (£20), compared with $280 (£56) for coal. This was only a trial run, however, and a non-stop coast-to-coast service was never established as passengers had to change trains at Chicago or St Louis.

These modern diesels later acquired observation cars and other amenities to satisfy their affluent clientele. A fabulous variety of food and drink was on offer and for a while the trains became the envy of the world, with the companies competing to provide the best facilities. These trains were the apogee of America's rail system, indeed, they were probably the best the world had ever seen, but by the 1950s, as flying became safer and cheaper, they began to be phased out. Diesel remains, however, the main form of traction on US railways to this day, with only a very small proportion of electrified railways. Indeed, the typical image of American rail is of freight trains more than 100 wagons long, being hauled by three or four powerful diesel locomotives.

Elsewhere in the world, diesels began to replace steam locomotives soon after World War II. Diesel multiple units, in particular, were a great way of saving money on branch lines. These had engines under the floor of the carriage, so that there was no need for a locomotive, and they could be driven from either end, obviating the need to turn around. The French even developed a rubber-tyred diesel train called the *Micheline*, which was used extensively on minor routes.

However, electrification was often chosen over diesel. While it is initially more expensive, electric haulage is ultimately cheaper, cleaner, and offers faster acceleration. On many suburban services, steam trains were replaced directly with electric trains rather than diesels. Nevertheless, with only Switzerland operating a 100 per cent electrified network, diesel remains an important form of traction, in particular for heavy freight and on little-used lines where the cost of electrification is not worthwhile. Diesel trains will be with us for a long time yet.

Diesel Power Meets Electricity

Diesel-electric traction emerged as the economically and functionally superior successor to steam power in the 1940s. Power is derived from a diesel engine (the "prime mover"), but is transformed into electricity by a generator that powers motors in the bogies, which in turn propel the train.

MARYLAND AND PENNSYLVANIA NO.81 (1946)
No.81, a General Motors EMD NW2-class shunter, was one of the first diesel-electrics to see widespread use. Popular due to its low cost and versatility, this small yet powerful class remains in service in small numbers even today.

Twin exhaust stacks

13m (44ft) in length

Two dual-axle bogies in a "B-B" arrangement

Power output of 750kw (1,000hp)

GN NO.201 (1947)
This RS-2 class diesel-electric switcher was built by ALCO, and was one of 20 purchased by the Great Northern Railway (US) to replace its coal-fired locomotives. Its 12-cylinder engine yields a power output of 1,100kw (1,500hp).

CNL NO.6505 (1949)
The EMD F7 diesel-electric was designed for freight, but was also used for passenger trains by some operators. Economical to operate and maintain, the pictured unit runs on the Conway Scenic Railroad (US) heritage line.

SP NO.6051 (1954)
One of nine EMD E9 diesel-electric passenger locomotives run by the Southern Pacific Railroad, No.6051 hauled services out of Los Angeles. Capable of a 2,400-hp (1,790-kW) power output, it was retired in 1969 and restored to its original "daylight" red-orange paint scheme.

ERIE LACKAWANNA NO.3607 (1967)
No.3607 was a General Motors EMD SD45, a six-axle diesel-electric freight locomotive with a power output of 2,680kw (3,600hp). More than a thousand units were produced between 1965 and 1971, a small number of which are still in operation on US railways.

4.4m (14ft 6in) in height

Total weight of 112 tonnes (124 tons)

BRITISH RAILWAYS D200 (1958)
An English Electric Type 4 Class 40, D200 was one of the first wave of diesel-electrics to ply the rails in Britain. With a top speed of 140kph (90mph), the class had been intended for passenger expresses, but was relegated to slower passenger and freight services.

NS NO.9628 (1996)
Norfolk Southern Railway (US) still operates a fleet of 1,090 General Electric Dash 9-40CW diesel-electric locomotives, the first of which was introduced in 1996. The class is powered by a 16-cylinder engine that is limited to a power output of 3,000kw (4,000hp) to improve running costs.

World War II:
Atrocities on the Line

A LTHOUGH THE RAILWAYS' ROLE IN WORLD WAR II was not quite as fundamental as it had been during the World War I (see pp.270–75), they were nevertheless a vital part of the logistics of war. With petrol in short supply and a lack of modernized roads in many conflict areas, the railways carried troops and supplies far and wide. However, the railways were also involved in two of the greatest war crimes of the World War II: the Holocaust, which resulted in the deaths of two thirds of all the Jews in Europe at the hands of the Third Reich, and the construction of the Burma to Siam (now Thailand) Railway, for which the Japanese used prisoners of war. These two events portray a darker side that is often left untold in railway histories, but vividly, if hauntingly, demonstrates the power of the railways and their significance to those who controlled them.

Approximately six million Jews were killed by the Nazis in the Holocaust, along with millions more from other groups such as Slavs, Poles, Romanies, communists, and homosexuals. Most of the victims were taken to death camps by train, and the sheer volume and speed of the deportations would not have been possible without intensive use of the railways. Any other method of transport would have presented insuperable problems – to have devoted so many trucks to the task would have damaged the Germans' war effort, and marching victims along roads might have revealed the true horrors of the Nazi's plans to the wider population.

The first of these trains were used principally to move German Jews to ghettos and ran between Germany and Poland (and then further east to Riga in Latvia). The grim despatch of Jews and other sections of the population to the concentration and death camps began in the spring of 1942, and the flow intensified over the following two years. These deportations were carried out in a systematic manner on an industrial scale, as part of the "Final Solution" agreed at the notorious Wannsee conference in January 1942. Efficiency was seen as essential and required the active involvement of numerous German government ministries, including the Reich Security Main Office (RSHA), the Transport Ministry, and the Foreign Office, as well as the corresponding organizations in other allied or occupied states who were required to hand over their citizens. Many railway workers were involved, too.

The deportations were mostly carried out in freight wagons. Some victims, notably those from the Netherlands and Belgium, were transported in third class passenger cars, partly to maintain the subterfuge that they were merely being re-homed. Conditions on the trains were appalling: the freight wagons were supposed to be filled with up to 50 people, but in fact, due to a shortage of wagons, they sometimes had as many as 150 occupants, which meant standing room only. Trains could carry a maximum of only 55 wagons each, as anything longer would travel too slowly. There was no food or water on the journey and only a bucket latrine. The only ventilation was through a barred window and consequently many people suffocated. In the summer, the temperature could be unbearably hot and victims baked, while in the winter the temperature plummeted and victims froze. The trains were given the lowest priority on the railway network and consequently journeys were

AUSCHWITZ II - BIRKENAU
Trains carrying deportees entered this extermination camp in Poland on a specially built branch line that extended right up to the gates of the camp.

often delayed while more important military convoys were allowed through. This meant that the deportees were sometimes held in sidings for days and the average time for journeys, which should have taken a day or so, was four and a half days. The longest journey involved the deportation of Jews from the Greek island of Corfu, who were taken by boat to the Greek mainland and then transferred to a train. The train was held up several times and consequently took 18 days to reach Auschwitz. By then, many of the occupants were already dead. Given the conditions, length of the journey, and the lack of food and water, deaths in transit were common and most trains arrived containing several corpses.

One of the least known but cruellest parts of the deportation process was the fact that the victims were forced to buy tickets for the journey, a full one-way fare for adults, with children being charged half price. This scheme generated an astonishing amount of revenue, calculated at around 240 million Reichmarks (around £50 million, or US$201 million). At the peak of the process, there were up to 10 trains per week arriving at the camps. For the Nazis, it was the very efficiency of this mode of transport that made the extermination of so many people possible. The despatch of trains only began to slow down when the Allies invaded France in the summer of 1944 and the operation ceased entirely as the Third Reich began to fall apart in the spring of 1945. In the 21st century, several railway companies have apologised for their role in these wartime deportations, including Dutch railways Nederlandse Spoorwegen in 2005 and French SNCF in 2011.

During the Holocaust the railways conveyed millions to their deadly destinations. Meanwhile, in Asia it was the railway line itself that was the scene of another war crime. When the Japanese overran Singapore, the main British naval base in Southeast Asia, in February 1942, they captured more than 80,000 British, Indian, and Australian troops. Along with 50,000 existing prisoners, many were sent to work on the construction of the Burma to Siam Railway, which was intended to provide the Japanese with a vital supply line as they advanced westwards, towards India.

As there was no adequate existing road or rail links between the two countries and the sea route was vulnerable to attack from Allied ships and submarines, a railway seemed the obvious solution. To

BRIDGE BUILDING
Prisoners build at bridge Tamarkan, 55km (34 miles) north of
Nong Pladuk in Siam. The scaffolding was made from bamboo,
but the bridge, completed in April 1943, was made of steel.

build the 483-km (300-mile) line, which went through harsh
mountainous territory and tropical rainforest, the Japanese used
forced labour of up to 330,000 men, mostly made up of press-ganged
locals, but also including more than 60,000 Allied PoWs. The line was
started simultaneously from both ends, Thanbyuzayat in Burma and
Nong Pladuk in Siam, in June 1942. There was a constant shortage of
materials and most of the equipment, including tracks and sleepers,
was brought from dismantled branches of other local railways. The
human cost was, however, appalling and the line became known as
the "Death Railway". Dutch merchant sailor Fred Seiker described
his experience as PoW on the railway labour force:

> You carried a basket from the digging area to the top of the embankment,
> emptied it and down again to be filled for your next trip up the hill. Or
> you carried a stretcher – two bamboo poles pushed through an empty
> rice sack – one chap at each end, and off you went. Simple really. But in
> reality this job was far from easy. The slopes of the embankments
> consisted of loose earth, clambering to the top was a case of sliding and
> slithering with a weight of earth in attendance. This proved to be very
> tiring on thigh muscles and painful, often resulting in crippling cramp.
> You just had to stop, you could not move. Whenever this occurred the
> Japs were on you with their heavy sticks, and beat the living daylight out
> of you. Somehow you got going again, if only to escape the blows.

Working hours were typically 7:30am to 10pm and the food rations were just 200g (7oz) of rice per day, often with no vegetables, let alone meat. Robert Hardie, a British doctor who was captured in Singapore, described in diaries published posthumously in the 1980s how the Japanese would line up the sick that he was tending and demand that a dozen of them should be sent to the work camp. He wrote: "One is under constant pressure to provide men to work under this Nipponese system: for certain groups of men are given certain work to do in a certain time. If many go sick in a group, the others have to work all the harder and longer". Hardie also recounted the repeated refusals of his captors to provide even basic medical supplies, as well as their indifference to the spread of diseases, such as cholera, malaria, and dysentery. The death rate was particularly high in the final months of the railway's construction as the Japanese were desperate for the line to be completed.

Despite the weakness of the men due to starvation and disease, their sheer numbers and the pressure from their Japanese guards ensured that the line was completed remarkably quickly, in just 16 months. On 17th October 1943, the two sections of the line met,

HELLFIRE PASS
The most difficult section of the line involved cutting through rock in a remote area of Siam. The work was extremely arduous, especially given the lack of adequate tools, and became known as Hellfire Pass.

"It didn't matter how many men died, the railway would be built. And it was built at a terrific cost"

JOHN LESLIE GRAHAM, BRITISH POW

17km (11 miles) south of the Three Pagodas Pass at Konkuita in Siam. By this time the death toll was estimated to have reached more than 100,000, a figure that included a quarter of all the Allied prisoners. The railway immediately became a vital part of the Japanese line of communication after their navy lost control of the South China Sea during the summer of 1942. However, as an essential bridge to the Burmese railway system was never completed, the supply route still entailed transporting some goods via ferry.

The story of the Burma to Siam Railway reached a wider audience through the 1957 David Lean film *The Bridge on the River Kwai*, which was based on a book by Pierre Boulle. The story refers to Bridge 277, built over a stretch of river that was then called Mae Klong. The tale is largely fiction, since it shows the bridge ultimately being destroyed by sabotage. In reality, the bridge remained in working condition, despite the men's attempt to undermine it by mixing the concrete poorly and encouraging termites to use wooden supports as nests. Although the film was criticized as unrealistic and failing to depict accurately the appalling conditions which the men lived and died under, it nevertheless helped to ensure that the memory of this terrible project lasted longer than the line itself. Much of the railway was damaged during the war and it never fully reopened. A few sections, such as the line between Kanchanabur and Nong Pladuk, did reopen in the 1950s, but most of it was abandoned, submerged under water by the Vajiralongkorn dam, or reclaimed by the jungle. Today a daily tourist train runs along the surviving 209-km (130-mile) section, while other parts have been converted to a walking trail. Three large cemeteries honouring those who lost their lives building the line can be found along the route, along with an Australian-built memorial and museum at Hellfire Pass, and several smaller memorials.

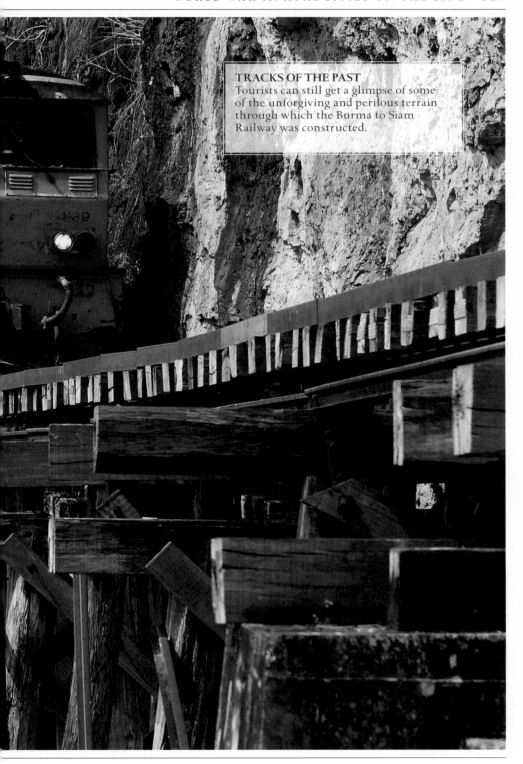

TRACKS OF THE PAST
Tourists can still get a glimpse of some of the unforgiving and perilous terrain through which the Burma to Siam Railway was constructed.

The Iron Road Today

KYUSHU SHINKANSEN 800
ELECTRIC, 2011

In the immediate postwar years the railways suffered a period of decline. The car had become the pre-eminent form of passenger transport, and the lorry dominated the freight business. Motorways and highways were being built across the world, and they were intended to replace the railways. The plane had also become affordable, and both international and domestic services were proliferating globally. Railway closures were inevitable, starting with branch lines and rural tracks, then spreading to the main lines themselves. In the United States, the decline of passenger railways was particularly swift, and for a while it seemed as if they would barely last into the 21st century.

Then everything changed. The oil crisis of the mid-1970s, together with congestion on the roads and environmental concerns regarding exhaust emissions, suddenly brought the train back into fashion. In Japan, high-speed "bullet" trains were introduced, which travelled faster than any car, and networks of similar lines were built in France and Germany, and later in China and Spain. Moreover, when the long-mooted 50-km (31-mile) Channel Tunnel linking France and Britain was finally given the go-ahead, it was built to carry trains because a railway was the only practical way of travelling in such a long tunnel. Similarly, to relieve the pressure of congestion on Europe's Alpine roads, a series of lengthy modern rail tunnels are now being built under the mountains. In 2006, China completed the highest railway in the world – the Qinghai–Tibet line, which offers a far easier journey than the highly dangerous road – and is currently building the largest high-speed network in the world.

The railways are therefore booming in the 21st century. Light rail systems, metros, high-speed lines, and newly electrified tracks are being built across the world. The 19th-century invention has found new friends in the 21st century and is enjoying a fantastic renaissance thanks to its ability to transport masses of people quickly and cheaply.

Brezhnev's Folly

OF ALL THE MANY MADCAP SCHEMES in the history of the railways, one takes the prize for being not only the craziest but also the most costly. That winner is the 3,700-km (2,300-mile) Baikal-Amur Mainline, a branch of the Trans-Siberian (see pp.180–89) that dwarfed the original railway both in difficulty and cost. It was one of the most ambitious of numerous megaprojects dreamed up by the Soviet regime to demonstrate the superiority of Communism (others included the space programme and a plan to reverse the flow of several Siberian rivers, which was fortunately abandoned). The BAM, as the railway became universally known, took three quarters of a century to complete and cost US$14 billion (£8.5 billion), but its worth still remains in doubt.

The idea behind the BAM was to provide an alternative route to the existing Trans-Siberian, which ran from European Russia to the Asian Pacific. The Soviet regime first mooted the railway as a strategic alternative in the 1930s Stalinist era, following disputes with China and Japan over a section of the Trans-Siberian that crossed Chinese territory to reach Vladivostok. Even the Amur Railway, a longer route over exclusively Russian territory that was completed in 1916, was considered too close to the Chinese frontier and therefore vulnerable to attack. To counteract the perceived threat, Stalin's government passed a secret decree to construct a new line running parallel to the existing Trans-Siberian but around 800km (500 miles) further north. No details of the route were set out other than the termini at Tayshet, where the line diverged from the Trans-Siberian, and Sovetskaya Gavan, on the Pacific Ocean north of Vladivostok.

The land crossed by the proposed new railway was virtually uninhabited, as most of the population of Siberia had settled within 160km (100 miles) of the Trans-Siberian, so the reasons for undertaking this vast project were (the Sino-Japanese menace notwithstanding) questionable. The Soviet government had started publishing five-year plans setting out its economic targets, and its Second Five-Year Plan, for 1933–37, emphasized the economic advantages of building the BAM. It "will traverse little-investigated regions of eastern Siberia and bring to life an enormous new territory and its colossal riches – amber, gold, coal – and also make possible the cultivation of great tracts of land suitable for agriculture", the plan stated.

BAIKAL-AMUR MAINLINE

Surveyors were dispatched to the Siberian wastes to prospect the land. Working under a reign of terror, several were executed for not doing their job properly in the view of the regime, while others ended up in the construction gangs. These were made up of prisoners – mainly political – sent to the Gulag (the government's corrective labour camps) by Stalin's increasingly repressive regime. Tayshet became infamous as a camp for Gulag prisoners working on the railway after Alexandre Solzhenitsyn described it in *The Gulag Archipelago*. Published first in the West in 1973, the book drew the world's attention to the atrocities that took place in Soviet forced labour camps under Stalin. Hundreds of thousands of prisoners were sent to camps in Siberia and forced to work on the line in appalling conditions – far worse than those endured on the Trans-Siberian. Russians knew that being sent to the "Bamlag" – the camps of the BAM Gulag – was a death sentence, as prisoners were subjected to unendurably harsh conditions and systematically starved.

The northern latitude of the track meant that most of the terrain it traversed was permafrost – a leftover of the freezing temperatures of the Ice Age – which presented particular difficulties for track-laying. Once railway workers started digging through the insulating surface layer of soil to the permafrost, ice that had been frozen for millennia thawed and did not refreeze, even in winter. Instead, the land turned marshy and unstable. Waiting for the ground to settle would have delayed work by years, so tracks were laid regardless, resulting in rail breaks and derailments. Disturbing the permafrost also led to an increase in seismic activity in the region.

Not surprisingly, little progress was made on the line. On top of permafrost and earthquakes, the mountainous region north of Lake Baikal posed insurmountable difficulties. Weather conditions were extreme, with only 90 frost-free days a year, and winter temperatures as low as −60 °C (−76 °F), meant that mechanical equipment did not work and special cold-resistant steel had to be used for the rails. These factors, combined with a starving labour force, meant that by the outbreak of World War II, when work was halted, only a couple of short sections at each end had been completed.

Remarkably, as soon as the war ended in 1945, work resumed on this vain project, which Stalin seemed intent on completing. The workforce was now made up of Japanese and German prisoners of war, who were treated more harshly even than the pre-war domestic convicts. It is

CONDITIONS IN THE GULAG
This ink drawing by a Gulag inmate gives a sense of the conditions endured by forced labourers working on the BAM – cold, hungry, and worked to the bone.

"BAM will be constructed with clean hands"

LEONID BREZHNEV

estimated that of 100,000 German PoWs sent to the Ozerlag camp near Lake Baikal, only 10 per cent survived to be repatriated in 1955; the Japanese prisoners suffered similar rates of mortality. A conservative estimate of the death toll of the two groups is 150,000 – and all for nothing, since barely 725km (450 miles) of the line had been completed by the time work was again halted following Stalin's death in 1953.

The demise of Stalin and his repressions might have signalled the end of the BAM project. Nikita Khrushchev, Stalin's successor, showed no interest in the railway, and the Gulag camps that had provided its labour were closed. By the 1960s, however, interest was revived, with a series of ostensible new reasons to build it: the line would relieve congestion on the Trans-Siberian, open up gas fields in western Siberia, and provide a new route for burgeoning container traffic between the Far East and Europe. Moreover, vast copper deposits had been discovered at Udokan, 400km (250 miles) east of Lake Baikal.

It was Leonid Brezhnev, the uninspiring and deeply conservative leader whose stern demeanour characterized Soviet rule in the 1970s, who decided to restart the scheme. Now a new type of cheap labour was to be used: volunteers of the "All-Union Leninist Youth League" (the Komsomol). The project was turned into a propaganda exercise, in the hands of the Komsomol, not only to demonstrate the advantages of the Communist way, but also to enthuse a whole generation of young people with that ideal. By helping to build the line, the volunteers would become lifelong supporters of the regime. Building the BAM became a rallying cry for Socialist propaganda as well as a path to victory over the obstacles that nature and the elements posed against humankind, making it a struggle that had to be won, at whatever cost – and that cost was to prove enormous.

In 1972, after much secret preparation, the Komsomol announced that work on the railway would restart immediately and the BAM would be completed in 10 years (later extended by two years to 1984). The project was given priority over other Soviet schemes and a nationwide appeal for volunteers was issued. While some young people may have turned up at the recruitment offices for idealistic reasons,

WORKERS' PRIZE
Idealistic young Komsomol workers on
the BAM were rewarded with medals
and praise, as well as material goods
such as cars and housing.

there were practical incentives too: volunteers were promised priority allocation of housing and cars, both of which were in short supply in Soviet Russia, and for those interested in a political career, working on the BAM was essential for their CVs. The pay was good too, compared with jobs back home. However, even those who started off with genuine enthusiasm were soon disillusioned. They were well treated, but once they discovered the sheer scale of the project and the incompetent way in which it was being run, it dawned on them that the railway was no advertisement for the Communist system – quite the opposite. They realized, as geologists and other scientists had long known, that creating a railway in northern Siberia was not a good idea.

There were innumerable practical difficulties. The recruits were given little training for what was a skilled task, no detailed route had been prepared, and the physical conditions were even worse than expected. Attempts to continue work in winter, because of the ideological need for rapid progress, were counterproductive. Although work was stopped when temperatures reached −20 °C (−4 °F), even above that temperature bulldozers stopped functioning and axes shattered. Any lessons learned from previous attempts to work in the permafrost seemed to have been forgotten, and once again whole sections of track gradually sank into the morass, while station and warehouse buildings constructed on shaky foundations collapsed.

Conditions on completed sections of the line were so bad that trains had to go extremely slowly and derailments were frequent. One 188-km (117-mile) section between Tayshet and Tynda that opened early took eight hours to traverse. With the tunnels also proving far more difficult to dig out than expected, the opening of the line was inevitably delayed: the 10-year target had always been a fantasy. The 15-km (9-mile) Severomuysky Tunnel, east of the lake, caused almost insuperable problems. When digging began in 1977, water from an underground lake flooded it. Although an ingenious solution was eventually found – liquid nitrogen was injected into the tunnel walls, freezing the water

GLORY TO THE CONSTRUCTORS OF BAM RAILWAY!
Brezhnev's decision to finish building the BAM in the 1970s
was a monumental propaganda exercise, intended to inspire
a new generation of workers with the ideals of Communism
and gain their support for the regime.

while the tunnel was lined with a concrete shell – it took 26 years to complete. In the meantime, two very steep bypasses were built, both adding considerably to the eventual journey time. Nevertheless, the Communist authorities – intent on using the line for propaganda purposes – stuck to the 1984 opening date with a ceremony that featured the hammering fast of a golden spike to tie in the final rail. It was a complete sham. No foreign journalists were invited, as it would have been obvious that the line was far from complete.

In the end, the BAM was officially opened three times. Brezhnev had died in 1982, but Mikhail Gorbachev, who succeeded him in 1985, continued with the scheme. It was by then soaking up one per cent of the nation's total annual GDP. Seven years after the first ceremony, Gorbachev announced that the line was open and boasted that it would form a new link between Russia and Japan. Even then, the intractable Severomuysky Tunnel was still not complete and several sections could only accommodate slow trains used to supply materials for constructing the line. Russia's post-Soviet president Vladimir Putin announced the line's completion in 2001, and the tunnel finally opened in 2003.

The BAM has not lived up to Brezhnev's expectations. The promise of opening up a vast agricultural region was always a delusion, since the Siberian climate is so harsh. It did not relieve pressure on the Trans-Siberian, since it is the section west of the junction at Tayshet, which is shared with the BAM, that is under greatest pressure. Nor has it provided a practical alternative route between Asia and Europe.

Just as the Trans-Siberian contributed to the downfall of the Tsarist regime, the BAM and the excessive resources devoted to it helped to bring down Communism. Most of the half a million Komsomol volunteers and other workers who built the line returned to their home towns deeply sceptical of the ideals of Communism and its grand projects. Indeed, many were infuriated that the cars and housing they had been promised were denied to them, a failure that led to demonstrations in the post-Soviet era, with ex-BAM workers demanding that their vouchers for volunteering be redeemed.

Far from carrying people to the promised land of a 21st-century future, as the slogans had promised, the BAM clearly went nowhere. The BAM became, in the Soviet era, the butt of popular jokes, symbolizing failure and the powerlessness of the Soviet leaders. As Christopher J. Ward wrote in *Brezhnev's Folly*, a history of the line:

A FREIGHT TRAIN THUNDERS THROUGH SIBERIA
BAM trains pass through the virtually uninhabited snowy
wilderness of northern Siberia. Passengers are few, but
container traffic is gradually increasing.

By repeating ad nauseam claims of BAM's economic, social, and cultural
significance, the Komsomol, the Communist Party, and the Soviet
government held an unwavering belief that the USSR's youth needed
this message to avoid a loss of collective faith. Ironically, however, the
realities of the railway helped to intensify such a loss of faith in the Soviet
political and economic system in general.

Today, however, there are a few signs that the railway may have
been worth at least some of the effort. Russian Railways, the state-
owned company, plans to increase container traffic on the line,
which is now carrying more minerals from Siberian mines too, and
there has been further recent investment, including the construction
of the Kuznetsovsky Tunnel, at a cost of US$9 million (£5.5 million)
for less than 4km (2½ miles), to give better access to the Pacific, as
well as improvement of parts of the line that were slow due to steep
gradients. However, the BAM will still go down in history as one of
the craziest civil engineering projects ever attempted and forever be
known as "Brezhnev's folly".

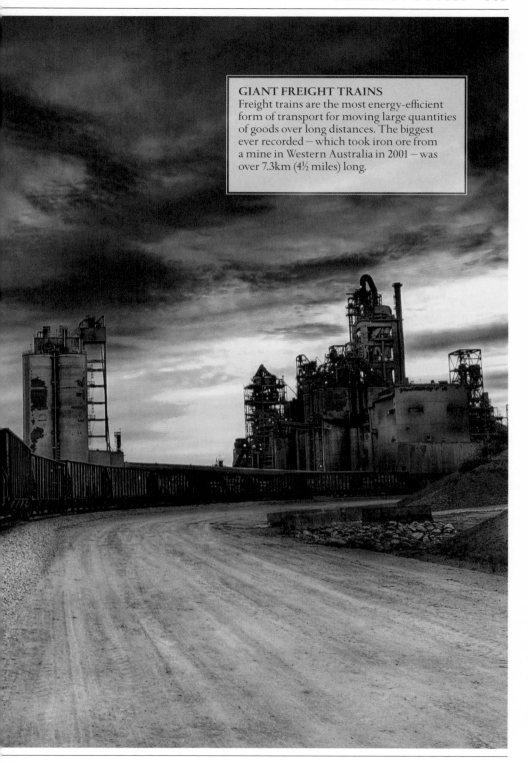

GIANT FREIGHT TRAINS
Freight trains are the most energy-efficient form of transport for moving large quantities of goods over long distances. The biggest ever recorded – which took iron ore from a mine in Western Australia in 2001 – was over 7.3km (4½ miles) long.

Railways Lost and Found

A LMOST AS SOON AS THE RAILWAYS WERE BUILT, sections started to become redundant and were closed. Some lines, built by railway companies to meet a need that turned out not to exist, were never profitable and were soon abandoned; others, built to serve a particular mine or factory, lost their purpose when the works in question closed. The rapid demise of some superfluous early railways was inevitable. In Britain, 320km (200 miles) of track had already closed by World War I, either because the lines were never viable or because of competition from rival routes. The first significant closure was the 27-km (17-mile) line between Chesterford and Six Mile Bottom in Cambridgeshire, built by the Newmarket and Chesterford Railway. It was closed in 1851 after a more direct route was created. Unusually, the line closed outright rather than being kept open as a freight route, a profitable alternative for many early lines. Other countries simply built too many railways. France had more railways than it needed, thanks to government support for railway construction in the 1860s, and many of the lines did not survive into the 20th century. Ireland, despite enduring the terrible famine of the 1840s that resulted in the death and emigration of 3 million people, built a network of lines that never made economic sense, given the country's sparse population. At the 1920s peak, it boasted 5,540km (3,440 miles) of railways serving a population of 4 million. It was hardly surprising much of this network closed in the 1930s, especially as car use increased.

In a way, it was remarkable that more lines did not close in this period, one reason being that railway companies had to seek government permission to close lines in many countries, including the US and Britain. Permission was rarely granted since terminating a service was inevitably unpopular and attracted negative publicity for politicians, meaning that many little-used lines remained open. In Britain, an 1844 Act required railways to run at least one service a day to serve poorer travellers. This resulted in a phenomenon known as "parliamentary trains", with companies operating the minimum number of trains necessary to circumvent the costs of closure. Some of these "ghost trains" run to this day. Even rather hopeless lines could be kept open to avoid controversy. Renowned chronicler of the

Victorian railways Jack Simmons wrote of the Bishop's Castle Railway in mid-Wales, for example, which became insolvent five years after its completion in 1861 and yet remained in operation until 1935.

Relatively few railways closed around the world in the interwar period. In part this was because of local opposition to closure, as the railways were now an established form of public transport – usually the only one until the advent of buses. Railway companies were reluctant to sanction closures too, as it was hard for them to predict the effect of closing branch lines on the network as a whole. Railway economics are complex, and managers had to determine whether passengers on a branch line would continue to use the system if their local service was no longer provided before deciding if the revenue they contributed overall made it worth keeping an unprofitable branch line open. This is a continuing conundrum.

In Britain, which boasted over 32,000km (20,000 miles) of railways at their peak before World War I, there were few closures in this period, despite growing competition from buses and cars. Just 386km (240 miles) of track were shut and another 1,600km (1,000 miles) restricted to freight services. Only the most extreme cases succumbed: the Invergarry and Fort Augustus branch line in the Scottish Highlands, which was completed in 1903 but never reached Inverness as intended, was closed in 1933 because it was carrying only six people per day. Closures remained the exception, however, until after World War II.

In the US, one type of train suffered major closures in the interwar years. This was the interurban (see pp.56–57), an extended tramway that linked neighbouring towns on tracks alongside roads. Built cheaply, they sprang up across the nation in the 1910s, usually operating a single carriage, akin to a bus on tracks. At their peak in 1913, these crude railways covered 24,000km (15,000 miles), but they were badly hit by competition from cars. Closures started immediately after World War I and accelerated in the Depression after 1929, meaning most interurban lines had a lifespan of barely 20–30 years – very short for the cost of the infrastructure. A remarkable 10,250km (6,350 miles) were abandoned in the early 1930s, and by the end of World War II

THE LENGTH OF US RAIL TRACK CLOSED BETWEEN 1916 AND THE PRESENT DAY

258,000KM
(160,000MILES)

only a few lines survived. All but a handful had shut by 1960. As George Hilton and John Due, authors of *The Electric Interurban Railways in America*, put it: "the interurbans... never enjoyed a prolonged period of prosperity... they played out their life cycle in a shorter period than any other important American industry".

In almost every country with a significant railway system, there were line closures in the post-war period, and the US was no exception, closing lines in great numbers. Major railway companies realized their profits would now come from freight rather than passengers, given the growing competition for suburban journeys from cars and for long-distance travel from planes. Closures required permission from the Interstate Commerce Commission, the federal agency that regulated the railways. By the early 1960s, all the main companies were petitioning the commission to close lines, and by the end of the decade there was a veritable stampede to end passenger services. Many companies used subterfuge to force the commission's hand, using old rolling stock, reducing services, and even demolishing stations to make lines appear uneconomic. Once permission to close was forthcoming, the companies were ruthless about implementing closure. So eager were they to get out of the passenger business, they stopped trains running the minute authorization came through – so commuters of the Chicago, Aurora, and Elgin railway who had taken the train into town on the day closure was confirmed had to make their own way home. The Louisville and Nashville Railroad dumped its last 14 passengers in Birmingham, Alabama, 645km (400 miles) short of their destination; only after protests was a bus provided to get them to their final destination.

The pace of US closures became so frantic that the government intervened, creating the state-owned and subsidized rail company Amtrak in 1971 to safeguard the remaining passenger services. It is an irony that the US, which tends to eschew state intervention, still has a nationalized railway system. Although it went from a peak of 410,000km (254,000 miles) in 1916 to 152,000km (94,000 miles) today, it is still the biggest railway system in the world, although it is mainly used for freight. Amtrak carries a mere 30 million passengers annually, compared with roughly 1.2 billion in Britain and 1.1 billion in France, both countries with far smaller populations.

In Britain, pressure to close lines came to a head in 1963 with the setting out of a radical plan by the chairman of the British Railways Board, Richard Beeching. He found that the railway network was very unbalanced, with half of the country's 29,000km (18,000 miles) of track carrying only 4 per cent of passengers. His solution was radical. The now infamous Beeching Report, known by its detractors as Beeching's Axe, resulted in the closure of 8,000km (5,000 miles) of track and a third of the 7,000 stations. While many lines that were clearly not viable were axed, some major routes were terminated too – subsequently a great cause of regret.

THE BEECHING REPORT
Richard Beeching, author of the report that drastically reduced Britain's railway network, became a hate figure for railway advocates.

In other countries, closures were carried out incrementally, less radically than in the US and more slowly than in Britain. France lost half of its 59,000-km (37,000-mile) network in closures that started in the 1930s until, to protect the remaining lines, the government nationalized the system in 1938. In Eastern Europe, Communist regimes retained their rail systems more-or-less intact as few people could afford cars, but extensive closures took place after the Iron Curtain fell in 1989. However, in recent years the closure process has been reversed in some countries and railway mileage has increased, with the reopening of mothballed lines and the construction of new, principally high-speed lines.

All these closures had one surprising, beneficial side-effect – the creation of a preserved railways industry based on steam trains. Countries where steam trains had until recently remained in service, including Poland, China, and India, attracted enthusiasts; in other countries, volunteers preserved sections of old lines and now operate tourist services on them. The first railway in the world to be preserved as a heritage railway was the British Talyllyn Railway, a 4-km (7-mile)

"Beeching's report marked the end of our romance with the train, and the rise of the car"

IAN HISLOP, EDITOR OF *PRIVATE EYE* AND RAILWAY ENTHUSIAST

narrow-gauge railway opened in 1866 to carry slate down a Welsh valley from quarries to the coast. When its closure was announced in 1951, a group of volunteers kept the line open. The railway heritage movement has spread around the world since then, and some of these lines even operate regular services that connect with the main line. Old lines are being reopened all the time, among them the Welsh Highland Railway, which reopened in 2011 and now, together with the Ffestiniog line, provides an 80-km (50-mile) route across north Wales. In France, too, there are around a hundred such preserved lines, covering 1,200km (750 miles) of track. These railways attract 3 million visitors a year, and include a section of 60-cm (2-ft) narrow-gauge lines used on the Somme front in World War I (see pp.278–87). The US also has a big preservation movement. Its most scenic railway is the Durango and Silverton Narrow Gauge Railroad, a 73-km (45-mile) line through Colorado. The route was built in 1881–82 by the Denver and Rio Grande Railway to exploit silver and gold mines in the San Juan Mountains. The remaining section is one of the few in the US that has seen continuous use of steam locomotives since the 19th century.

Some of the most spectacular railways in the world have been brought back into use after being abandoned. In Ecuador, a 450-km (280-mile) line between the port city of Guayaquil and the highland capital, Quito, has been restored and its steam locomotives are now a major tourist attraction, recreating one of the greatest rail journeys in the world. Thanks to these preserved railways and the volunteers who work on them, the steam engine will remain a source of admiration for generations to come.

DURANGO AND SILVERTON RAILROAD
The Durango and Silverton Narrow Gauge Railroad owes its preservation in part to its Hollywood success: it has featured in numerous movies, among them *Viva Zapata* and *Butch Cassidy and the Sundance Kid*.

WHITE PASS AND YUKON RAILROAD
Built in 1898 during the Klondike Gold
Rush, the WP&YR suspended operations
in 1982, when the mines closed, but was
resurrected as a tourist route from Skagway,
Alaska, to Carcross, Yukon, in 1988.

Vive le Channel Tunnel

THE OPENING OF A TUNNEL LINKING Britain and France in 1994 was the culmination of more than 180 years of debates, discussions, and delays. The first proposal for a tunnel under the English Channel (although not a rail one) had been made as far back as 1802, by one of Napoleon's engineers. At that time, the journey from London to Paris took about four days (or several weeks if the Channel winds were unfavourable) but the British military, politicians, and even the press were not keen on the idea of a tunnel, fearing that it would leave the island nation vulnerable to attack. Over the next half century, various schemes were mooted, on both sides of the Channel, but they came to nothing. The first serious attempt at digging a rail tunnel was promoted by a Victorian entrepreneur, Sir Edward Watkin, in 1881. Exploratory tunnels were dug at Dover in England and Sangatte in France, but work was abandoned in 1882, largely due to political pressure from the still-unconvinced British.

By the early 20th century, more advanced tunnelling machines and the development of electric traction had made the idea of a rail tunnel a more realistic proposition. However, by this time a fit of xenophobic hysteria had seized most of the British military establishment, who were adamant that foreign powers would use the tunnel as a corridor for invasion. In fact, Marshal Foch, the Allies' Supreme Commander in the last year of World War I, declared that a tunnel could have shortened the conflict by two years. Nevertheless, these delays in building a tunnel simply meant that the competition kept on speeding up. By 1852, the

EARLY DESIGNS
This 1876 engraving shows plans for a single-track rail tunnel under the English Channel.

journey time between London and Paris had been reduced to 12 hours by sea and rail, and 60 years later it took a mere 7 hours. In the 1930s, the glamorous *Flèche d'Or* (Golden Arrow) train-ferry service reduced the journey time to just over six and half hours and by that time there was also a regular air service between Croydon, just outside London, and Le Bourget, northeast of Paris.

Although military hysteria dissipated after the end of World War II in 1945, progress on a tunnel remained slow, particularly at the British end. In 1963, the British government finally endorsed the building of a tunnel. By this time, the commercial outlook was promising as the number of travellers from London to Paris was increasing steadily (1 million per year in 1960 and 2.5 million by 1978). However, the British were still rather lukewarm about the project and had not yet agreed a new rail line to link the tunnel to London and beyond. British Rail (BR) suggested a variety of routes but each one was more expensive than its predecessor. In the end, the cost of the new rail link provided an excellent excuse for the government to cancel the project in early 1975, just as tunnelling was about to begin. This about-turn, which was in fact necessitated by Britain's perilous financial situation, naturally infuriated the French and reinforced their suspicions that Britain was not really serious about a Channel tunnel.

However, the idea for a tunnel refused to go away, and within four years Sir Peter Parker, the chairman of BR, together with his counterparts from the SNCF in France, had resurrected the project by proposing a single-track tunnel – inevitably called the "mousehole" – running "flights" of trains back and forth across the Channel. This somewhat ramshackle idea did not progress, but the principle of building a Channel tunnel received a boost from an unlikely source – eurosceptic British Prime Minister, Margaret Thatcher. The "Iron Lady" decided that a tunnel could proceed under the Channel, as long as it was privately, not publicly, funded. Along with French President François Mitterand, Thatcher set up a working group and then invited bidders to submit their proposals. Thatcher disliked railways, so her natural preference was for a road-based, or at least a "drive-through" scheme – a bias she shared with Mitterrand – but in the end a scheme involving dual rail tunnels won out. By the end of 1985, the Channel Tunnel Group/TransManche Link, a consortium of five French and five British contractors plus five banks, had been awarded the contract to build the tunnel.

The whole operation was still fiendishly complicated. It took two more years for the Channel Tunnel Act, which officially rubber-stamped the scheme, to pass through the British Parliament (although the French procedure took mere days) and the world's investment community was by no means enthusiastic about the tunnel's financial prospects. Financial negotiations were hampered by the geographical spread of the various banks involved and the sheer number of contractors involved in the scheme made the construction process equally complex. However, the balance of power between the interested parties was transformed in early 1987 with the appointment of Alastair Morton as full-time British joint chairman of Eurotunnel, the company that actually held the contract to build the tunnel. During Morton's nine years at Eurotunnel he saved what was a fundamentally uneconomic venture from disaster by dealing with the British government, the contractors, and the 200 banks eventually involved. He also grappled with BR and SNCF, who would be the main users (to add further complexity, BR was being prepared for privatization at the time). After protracted negotiations about the technology the tunnel would use and the type of links the tunnel would provide, a complicated international consortium was formed combining railway companies from France, Britain, and Belgium.

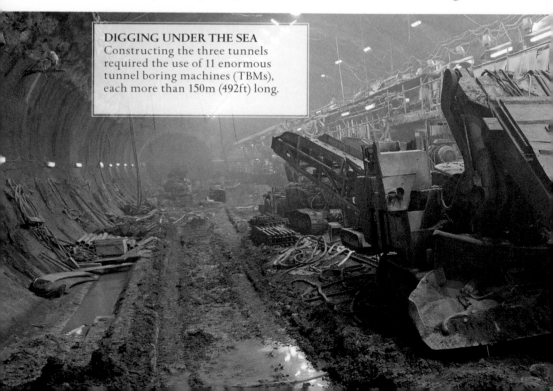

DIGGING UNDER THE SEA
Constructing the three tunnels required the use of 11 enormous tunnel boring machines (TBMs), each more than 150m (492ft) long.

Tunnelling commenced at long last in December 1987, when the British started digging a service tunnel that would be used for maintenance and emergencies. Starting with the service tunnel was a good way of testing the tunnelling conditions, foreshadowing any geological or practical issues before work on the main rail tunnels began. The French commenced their end of the service tunnel a couple of months after the British and then, in June 1988, two rail tunnels were started simultaneously from both sides. Thus the Channel Tunnel was, and remains, in fact three tunnels – two rail tunnels separated by a service tunnel. It was the biggest engineering project ever undertaken by France or Britain, requiring 15,000 workers at its peak. However, progress was slower than predicted, causing costs to spiral. In fact, there were no fewer than three major financial crises while the tunnel was under construction and the cost of the project exceeded its budget by more than 80 per cent. Nevertheless, on 4 December 1990, the two tunnelling teams finally shook hands mid-Channel. Amazingly, the tunnels were only 330mm (13in) out of alignment, despite each travelling 15km (9 miles) from opposite ends.

Completing the tunnels was just the beginning of the process, however. As one observer put it: "turning the tunnels into a piece of complex, safe, and sophisticated transport infrastructure was to prove an altogether different challenge", involving as it did power supply, lighting, ventilation, communication, maintenance provision, and fire detection and suppression equipment. The trains themselves were also incredibly complex, as they had to cope with different power supplies and signalling systems not just in Britain and France, but also in Belgium, where some trains would terminate. Safety fears also meant that every piece of equipment had to receive a separate operating certificate for each country, at an estimated cost of over £400 million (US$645 million), with a further £200 million (US$322 million) lost in the resulting delays. However, the stringent safety requirements have proved their worth: there have been only three serious fires in the Channel Tunnel – all started on shuttles carrying lorries – that closed the Tunnel for short periods, but caused no loss of life.

In the end the tunnel was delayed by a year, far less than many much smaller projects. The contractors handed over the project to Eurotunnel in December 1993, and the "Chunnel" – a nickname that fortunately hasn't stuck – was officially opened by Queen Elizabeth II and President Mitterand in May 1994. Freight trains began travelling through the Tunnel a month later and rail passengers were welcomed in November, on the service now known as Eurostar. On 22 December 1994, the Channel Tunnel achieved a world first with the inaugural car shuttle service, known as Eurotunnel Le Shuttle, from Folkestone to Calais.

However, in one major respect the project was incomplete when the Channel Tunnel opened in 1994. Providing a fast line to the tunnel was relatively easy for the French, since all it took was building a branch line to Calais from their new fast line from Paris to Lille and Brussels. By contrast, neither BR nor the British government could overcome the difficulties inherent in building an entirely new line from London to Folkestone. BR had never designed a new railway line, and all the routes it suggested threatened the rich heartland of Kent, as well as numerous marginal constituencies in South East London. As a result, the Eurostar trains on the British side of the tunnel had to travel

NUMBER OF TONNES OF SPOIL REMOVED DURING TUNNELLING

10,000,000
(11,023,000 TONS)

EUROSTAR
When the Channel Tunnel opened, trains on the French side could travel up to 300kph (186mph). On the British side, the top speed was only 160kph (100mph).

along tortuous, winding tracks that had been laid a century earlier. The rails were strengthened and the route was provided with new signals and upgraded power supplies, but still, the trains were noticeably much slower in England than in France.

It took until 1996 before work began on a high-speed line for the British part of the route – a line now called High Speed 1 (HS1). Even when work finally began, it was far from straightforward. The project was beset with financial and construction problems. Excavation of the route revealed many ancient relics, which thrilled archaeologists, but caused further delays. Eventually, the first section of the high-speed route through Kent opened in 2003, reducing the journey time between London and Paris by 20 minutes.

The second section of the route, from the North Downs in Kent to a new terminal at St Pancras station in London, was an even bigger engineering problem. It involved tunnelling under the River Thames, navigating marshes in east London, building an enormous new station at Stratford, and rebuilding St Pancras station. The biggest headache, however, was constructing an 18-km (11-mile) tunnel to St Pancras that would avoid the existing sewers, main railway lines, and underground system. Finally, on 13 November 2007, the link was finished, and Eurostar transferred its passenger services from Waterloo to St Pancras. The switch of termini marked an historic moment, linking Britain's first high-speed line to its equivalent in Europe and finally completing the Channel Tunnel project more than 200 years after it had first been proposed. It is the world's longest undersea rail tunnel – 37.9km (23½ miles) of the 50.4-km (31⅜-mile) tunnel runs under the Channel – and has been described by the American Society of Civil Engineers as "One of the Seven Wonders of the Modern World".

Building Tunnels

Tunnelling is the most costly and labour-intensive of all engineering enterprises and, in the early days of the railways, it was also the most dangerous. Working long shifts lit by candlelight in cramped conditions, navvies (see pp.84–89) risked serious injury or loss of life as they burrowed underground using only basic tools. From the mid-19th century their picks, hand-drills, and explosives were gradually replaced by tunnel-boring machines (TBMs), the first of which was used after 1862 to dig the Fréjus Rail Tunnel beneath the Alps (see p.106). Since then, strict safety regulations have reduced risks considerably, and the introduction of computer control has increased the machines' efficiency.

The tunnel's girth is determined by the cutting wheel's diameter – 8–9m (26–29ft) for the Channel Tunnel

Immersed tunnels

Suitable for routes that cross shallow bodies of water, immersed tunnels on the seabed are a cost-effective alternative to boring beneath it. The first tunnel to be built in this way was the Bay Area Rapid Transit (BART) tunnel in San Francisco, US, in the late 1960s. Sections of the tunnel are floated to the tunnel site, sunk into a pre-cut trench on the seabed, and secured with layers of gravel, concrete, and backfill.

BART TUNNEL SECTION UNDER CONSTRUCTION

TUNNEL-BORING MACHINE (TBM)
CHANNEL TUNNEL, c.1990s

Also known as "moles", TBMs are equipped with different cutting devices according to the geology of the tunnelling area, from soft clay to mixed earth and shale or bare rock. The Channel Tunnel TBMs that cut through chalk marl under the English Channel to link Britain and France (see pp.348–53) were also designed to deal with high water pressure.

The cutting wheel rotates as hydraulic rams drive the machine forwards

The 11 Channel Tunnel TBMs — each weighing 1,100 tonnes (1,210 tons) — were assembled on site

How it works

TBMs consist of several connected systems that are operated in different phases of construction to bore and line the tunnel, lay the rails, and convey waste material away from the site. The cutting wheel can be up to 19.3m (63ft) in diameter, while the TBM apparatus can be as much as 150m (490ft) in length.

Mechanized segment feeder moves concrete rings into position

Cutting wheel rotates, gouging material from face

Screw-conveyor carries debris away from tunnel site

STEP 1: TUNNELLING PHASE
During the tunnelling phase, the rotating cutting wheel is pressed into the tunnel face at a predetermined rate. Debris is transported away from the cutting face by a screw conveyor (for shale or rock, pictured here) or a series of pressurized pipes (for earth or clay).

Material is analysed to verify stability of tunnelling area

Tunnel debris supports cutting wheel and tunnel face

Concrete rings are cemented together to line the tunnel

STEP 2: RING-BUILDING PHASE
The cutting apparatus stops to allow the ring-building phase to commence — the installation of concrete rings, which provide a watertight and strengthening lining for the tunnel. The rings are cast above ground and moved to the construction site via rail.

Switzerland: the Best
of the Best

SWITZERLAND JOINED THE RAILWAY AGE relatively late, but, as in other countries such as Germany, the railways quickly became a unifying force and a vital part of the nation's prosperity. So much so that today Switzerland can lay claim to having one of the most efficient and well-used railway networks in the world.

Surrounded by mountains and beset by cold temperatures and copious snowfall in the winter, Switzerland did not seem like fertile territory for the iron road. Moreover, it did not even become a unified nation until 1848, following a brief civil war between the Protestant and Catholic cantons (states). The new Switzerland adopted a federal state system, similar to that of the US, and the new government decided that the country needed a proper, planned railway system. So, in 1850, two British engineers, Robert Stephenson and Henry Swinburne, were asked to oversee the development of a rail network. The pair suggested a basic, east-to-west line along the valleys between Geneva and Zürich, plus another line from Basel to Lucerne. Rather oddly though, the capital, Bern, was to be on a branch line. The cantons built these early lines, often with foreign investment and contractors. Stephenson and Swinburne's influence also meant that the Swiss adopted the standard gauge (1,435mm/4ft 8½in) and instituted British-style left-hand running on double-track lines, both of which are still used today.

The iron road's progress in Switzerland remained slow. Unlike most European countries, where the demands of traditional heavy industries such as mining or agriculture fuelled railway expansion, it was tourism that eventually became the catalyst for further development in Switzerland. From the mid-19th century, increasing numbers of visitors flocked to resorts in the scenic Alps and lakes. However, when pioneering travel agent Thomas Cook took his first tour party to Switzerland in 1863, there was still barely 650km (400 miles) of railway in the whole country. It was clear that the country's existing rail network could not cope with the demands of the tourist industry.

So, by the last third of the 19th century, the Swiss federal government was eager to see its railways develop more rapidly. Furthermore, the country's location in the centre of Europe made an efficient railway network in Switzerland highly desirable for its neighbours, too. They were eager to traverse Swiss territory to create both passenger and freight links across Europe, and were happy to invest in Swiss railways to make that possible. A treaty between Switzerland, Germany, and Italy in 1869 agreed a strategic link under the Gotthard Pass in the Alps. Completed in 1882, the Gotthard Tunnel (see pp.106–107) linked not just the cantons of Uri and Ticino, but also provided a valuable north–south route between Germany and Italy; the Simplon Tunnel (see pp.106–107), opened in 1906, also linked Switzerland to Italy.

Meanwhile, the railways continued to spread across the country, including Europe's first rack railway (see pp.108–109), which opened in 1871. Built to take tourists up the Rigi Mountain above Lake Lucerne, it used a rack-and-pinion system developed by Swiss engineer Niklaus Riggenbach. Three years later, the first 1m- (3ft 3⅜in-) gauge line opened from Lausanne to Bercher via Echallens, although this was actually built to serve an agricultural area rather than the tourist industry. By adopting a narrower gauge in less accessible or less populous areas, lines could be built much more economically, allowing railways (and also roadside tramways) to spread into the steepest and most remote corners of Switzerland.

SPANISH BUN RAILWAY
The first Swiss railway linked Zurich and Baden in 1847. It was nicknamed *Spanischbrötlibahn* ("Spanish Bun Railway") because affluent Zurich bankers used it to send their servants to fetch Baden's speciality buns.

THE ELECTRIC
ST. GOTTHARD LINE
SWITZERLAND

GOTTHARD LINE
The trans-Alpine Gotthard
Line proudly became
electrified in 1922.

After the initial railway boom of the late 19th century, some speculative railways went bust and many Swiss people became disenchanted with their railways being largely owned and operated for the benefit of foreign shareholders. Consequently, in 1898 a referendum on nationalizing the railways led to the formation of the Swiss Federal Railways in 1902 (officially known as SBB-CFF-FFS). Over the next few years, the SBB-CFF-FFS acquired approximately 50 per cent of the national trackage and embarked on a scheme to electrify the whole network. Given the country's lack of coal, the Swiss were early adopters of electric traction: the first electrically powered railway in Switzerland was a 1-m (3-ft 3⅜-in) gauge line between Montreux and Chillon in 1888. The Simplon Tunnel was also electrified from the start, and electric traction was used, too, for the *Jungfraubahn*, completed in 1912.

The two world wars accelerated the electrification process in Switzerland: during World War I coal shortages caused widespread travel disruption, while World War II affected Switzerland even more, despite its neutrality. The tourist trade on which many railways depended dried up, and some lines closed in the aftermath of the wars. However, the post-war government soon realized the value of Switzerland's transport infrastructure and began to invest in the railways, so much so that by 1960 the entire railway network in Switzerland was electric, making it the first country in the world to achieve this milestone.

During the latter half of the 20th century, car and lorry traffic in Switzerland grew inexorably, as it did elsewhere. With the building of modern highways through and under the Alps, much freight that was once rail-borne transferred to the road. By the 1980s, however, the Swiss public were increasingly concerned about the environmental damage caused by heavy lorries. This eventually led to two major national referendums on the railways. The first, in 1987, led to the Bahn 2000 project, which aimed to bring the Swiss rail network into the 21st century. This initiative resulted in the improvement of many lines and the construction of sections of high-speed track that are an integrated part of the existing infrastructure rather than, as in many other countries, entirely separate. A second referendum in 1992 approved, by a

IN THE SHADOW OF THE ALPS
The Matterhorn-Gotthard-Bahn (MGB)
is a narrow-gauge Alpine railway. This
branch line at Andermatt links to the
northern end of the Gotthard rail tunnel.

massive majority, a project called "AlpTransit" that regulated the number and capacity of trucks allowed across the Alps. It also prioritized improvements to the rail infrastructure over road-building, intending freight to be transferred onto the trans-Alpine railways. To facilitate this scheme two new railway tunnels were proposed — the 34-km (21-mile) Lötschberg Base Tunnel, which opened in 2007, and the 61-km (38-mile) Gotthard Base Tunnel, which is due to be completed 2016.

The 1980s also saw the introduction of an impressive integrated national transport timetable in Switzerland, co-ordinating rail, bus, and tram services. It means that almost every station in Switzerland has at least an hourly rail service that links to a national timetable plan, giving regular connections with all other routes and modes of transport. Oddly, although the transport services are coordinated by the government, its national rail company, SBB-CFF-FFS, owns just under 3,200km (2,000 miles) of track, with the remaining 750km (1,200 miles) being operated by around 80 different private or semi-nationalized companies. Despite this, the Swiss railway system is far more streamlined and has far less duplication than many other networks around the world, where competition between different companies resulted in unnecessary or inefficient lines being built.

Historically, the Swiss electorate, and generally their politicians, have been far more conscious of the implications of their public transport than most other nations. For example, the standard gauge rail network is the core of a wider transport system in Switzerland into which local trains (often 1-m / 3-ft 3⅜-in gauge), trams, and buses link

THE HEIGHT ABOVE SEA
LEVEL OF JUNGFRAUJOCH
STATION IN THE ALPS

3,454M
(11,332 FT)

THE HIGHEST
IN EUROPE

at all stations. Despite this integrated network, the Swiss still have one of the highest rates of car ownership per capita (about one for every two people), but they use them far less. In fact, Swiss people make more journeys via railway than any other nation, apart from Japan. On average, the Swiss travel 1706km (1,060 miles) per person annually by rail, while the Japanese travel 1,900km (1,200 miles). (The Swiss actually make more individual journeys than the Japanese, but these journeys are shorter.) Given that Japan is a

THE SWISS RAIL NETWORK

far bigger country with a very dense population, Switzerland's record is all the more remarkable. The key to that success is that the rail network is part of a genuinely integrated public transport system designed to make non-motorized travel easier and more efficient for its citizens. Reliability and punctuality have proved crucial, too, supported by consistent government investment in the railways. Not only is the rail network extensive and well managed, but the cost of rail fares is also highly competitive. In addition to the usual range of discounted season and zonal tickets, it is possible to purchase a national, all-modes (rail, bus, tram, boat) travel card that costs around £3,500 (US$5,630) per year — a bargain by the standards of many other countries.

Today, a growing Swiss population is placing the rail network under increasing strain and the railways require considerable investment to keep pace with demand. The Swiss, however, seem up to the task: in Zurich, for example, an expensive series of tunnels has been planned to allow trains to pass through the city more quickly and to link expanding suburbs. Railways, it seems, have become ingrained in the culture and success of Switzerland, and the importance of the iron road shows no signs of waning.

SIGNATURE STRUCTURE
The Glacier Express crosses the imposing
Landwasser Viaduct, in Graubunden,
Switzerland, along the Albula railway.
The limestone bridge rises 65m (213ft)
above the Landwasser River.

Going Faster: Bullet Trains and High-speed Lines

BY THE 1960s, THE RAILWAYS were competing against cars, lorries, and aeroplanes. Politicians and civil servants thought the railway age was coming to an end – an outmoded form of travel that belonged to the 19th rather than the late 20th century – and governments chose to invest in motorways and roads that provided the convenience of door-to-door travel instead. Car ownership soared, lorries started hauling freight, and commercial flights took off, heralding the dawn of the jet age. To counter these trends, railway services needed modernization. It was the Japanese who led the way with the ground-breaking *Shinkansen* ("new mainline"), known in the West as the bullet train. It started a trend for high-speed railways that would spread – albeit rather slowly – around the world.

Japan's geography and pattern of settlement contributed to the genesis of the bullet train, as it had to the development of Japan's railways in the first place. The country consists of four main islands, but less than a fifth of the land mass is habitable, so most of the population of 126 million is confined to a relatively small part of the country. It was this density of population in lowland regions that created the right conditions for high-speed rail development. In fact, while the high-speed aspect of the *Shinkansen* is emphasized, the new lines evolved mainly because the existing network was running out of capacity.

Japan came late to the railway age. The island state had shunned the rest of the world until 1868, when the new Meiji administration sought to modernize the country, opening its doors to the railways. The first line, which covered the 29km (18 miles) between Tokyo and Yokohoma, opened in 1872, and the Japanese adopted trains with enthusiasm. The engineers of the line used the narrow gauge of 1,067mm (3ft 6in), the same as in New Zealand as the islands had similar topographies. Later plans to convert to standard gauge to increase traffic on the railways were opposed by military powers; instead, lines were extended.

The railways boomed in the final few years of the 19th century, and by 1907 there were nearly 7,250km (4,500 miles) of railway in operation, all owned by the state-run Japanese Imperial Railways. Development continued steadily between the first and second world wars. By 1945,

INAUGURATION OF THE TOKAIDO *SHINKANSEN*
The Tokaido *Shinkansen* was launched in Tokyo just in
time for the 1964 Olympics. The bullet train reduced the
journey time between Tokyo and Osaka to 4 hours and
became the prototype for high-speed trains worldwide.

the total mileage had reached 26,000km (16,000 miles), nearly a quarter
of which was owned privately, with the rest under the control of the
renamed Japanese National Railways.

By the 1930s, Japan's first trunk route, the Tokaido line, which linked
Tokyo with a series of major cities that included Nagoya, Kyoto, Osaka,
and Kobe, was already becoming heavily congested. An entirely new
route between Tokyo and Osaka was proposed that would cover the
640-km (400-mile) journey in four hours – an unheard-of speed for a
railway at the time. Work started in 1941, but was more or less abandoned
after the Japanese attack on Pearl Harbor triggered the Pacific War.

The Japanese economy took some time to recover from defeat in the
war, but by the mid-1950s the Tokaido line was again running at
capacity and the plan for the Tokaido *Shinkansen* was revived. Shinji
Sogō, the president of the state-run railways, lobbied hard to persuade
the government that the railway line would be viable, as at the time it
seemed that cars and planes would make railways redundant. It was the
need for extra train routes that stimulated the *Shinkansen*'s development,
but to compete with cars it was built on motorway principles, with few
stops and fast journey times. The high speed was a by-product of the
need for capacity rather than an end in itself – a principle that applied
to most high-speed systems around the world. Of course, the high-

PASSING MOUNT FUJI
In what has become an iconic image of the meeting of the modern and the ancient world in Japan, the *Shinkansen* bullet train passes in front of snow-capped Mount Fuji.

speed aspect helped to attract passengers away from their cars, and also made it possible for rail to compete with aviation over distances of up to 800km (500 miles), thanks to its city-centre-to-city-centre routing.

It was decided that Japan's new line would carry only fast electric passenger trains and would use the standard 1,435mm (4ft 8½in) gauge to provide greater capacity and enable use of technology from other railways. Despite difficult terrain and cost overruns – the eventual cost of 380 billion yen (around £400 million or US$1.1 billion at the time) was twice the original budget – the line was completed five years after work started in 1959. By contemporary high-speed standards, the line was slow, with an average speed of 209kph (130mph), but thanks to its dedicated track and limited stops the journey time was radically reduced. While the conventional express took 6 hours and 40 minutes between the two main cities, Tokyo and Osaka, the *Shinkansen* made the trip in 4 hours when it started operating just before the 1964 Tokyo Olympics. The *Shinkansen* changed business patterns too, by making day trips between Tokyo and Osaka possible. Shinji Sogō's faith in the railway was fully justified. An immediate success, the service carried 100 million passengers in less than three years; by 1976, it had carried one billion. Today, the Tokaido *Shinkansen* carries 143 million passengers annually.

It was not an easy ride, however. The service suffered teething troubles, including pain to passengers' ears when trains crossed in the tunnels that accounted for 72km (45 miles) of the route, and a more embarrassing problem: the air currents generated in the tunnels blew water up from the toilet bowls, much to the users' discomfiture. Eventually, it was decided to pressurize the trains to solve these problems, which proved expensive but was successful. Interestingly, despite the *Shinkansen*'s popularity, Japanese National Railways faced opposition to building the network it had envisaged. Noise and cost were both concerns, but eventually, in the 1970s, several new lines as well as extensions to the Tokaido line were built. Today, there is a network of 3,540km (2,200 miles). The fastest trains on the Sanyo line travel at 300kph (186mph), a speed that has become the norm across the world for high-speed lines.

NUMBER OF PASSENGERS CARRIED BY BULLET TRAINS EACH YEAR

325 MILLION

JAPANESE HIGH-SPEED RAIL NETWORK

Around the world, it was some years before another country followed Japan's lead. Although railway managers were keen to increase speeds from the 90–110kph (60–70mph) that was standard for express trains by the 1960s, governments remained doubtful as to whether the "old technology" of train travel was worth investing in. In Germany and France, train speed trials took place, demonstrating that trains could easily reach speeds of 200kph (124mph) for long periods, and attempts were made to speed up services on existing lines. In France, the Paris–Toulouse route was upgraded in 1966 to support 200kph (124mph) running through improvements to tracks and signalling. In Britain, a new diesel service branded InterCity 125 was introduced on routes from London after 1976. However, all used existing lines, which limited their speed as other, slower trains shared the tracks.

To avoid line-sharing, France decided in the 1970s to create a dedicated bullet-style service called the *Train à Grande Vitesse* (TGV); like the *Shinkansen*, the TGV has become a world-renowned brand. At the time, capacity on the key Paris–Lyon route was reaching its limits and it was decided to build a new line, separate from the existing railway except at the city entrances, where tracks were shared with conventional services. The

TGV uses the same gauge as regular trains so it can run on high-speed and standard tracks for flexibility. The French had created high-speed trains that had beaten the world record several times, reaching an impressive 422kph (262mph) on an experimental track in 1969. Clearly, such speeds would only be possible on a dedicated track, so in 1976, construction of the first *Ligne à Grand Vitesse* started. The Paris–Lyon line was completed in 1981, when the first TGVs started running at a top speed of 270kph (168 mph), later increased to 300kph (186mph). The service was an instant success, challenging air travel between the two cities. France embarked on a network of high-speed lines emanating from Paris. The *Est*, which opened in 2007, operates at 320kph (200mph).

France's high-speed network covered 1,907km (1,185 miles) in 2013, but has now been surpassed in distance by Spain. In 2005, Spain announced a plan to ensure that 90 per cent of the population would live within 50km (30 miles) of a station served by the Spanish *Alta Velocidad Española* (AVE) network. Spain's first high-speed line, between Madrid and Seville, was completed in time for the Seville Expo '92. It used standard gauge as opposed to the 1,680mm (5-ft 6in) Iberian gauge used by other Spanish services. This led to a technological development that allows the latest high-speed trains to change gauge without stopping so they can continue journeys off the high-speed network. By 2013, Spain operated half a dozen routes out of Madrid and, with Barcelona also a hub, a total of 2,000km (1,285 miles) of high-speed line had been opened, with a further 1,100km (684 miles) under construction.

After France, Germany was the second country in Europe to develop high-speed lines. It opted for a different model by creating high-speed sections rather than whole new routes, so the trains switch frequently between conventional and high-speed lines. Germany launched its Intercity-Express (ICE) in 1991, operating at a top speed of 280kph (174mph) on the Hannover–Würzburg high-speed railway.

Since 2000, a number of new high-speed rail services have started operating in East Asia. In South Korea, the Korea Train Express was launched in 2004 along the Seoul–Busan corridor, linking the country's two biggest towns. It uses trains built by Alstom, the same company that builds the TGV in France. Taiwan has a high-speed railway running more than 322km (200 miles) along the west coast of Taiwan, from the national capital Taipei to the southern city of Kaohsiung, using technology based primarily on Japan's *Shinkansen*. However the biggest network by far is in China (see pp.372–79).

TGV AND THALYS HIGH-SPEED TRAINS
Connecting France, Germany, and Benelux, TGV
and Thalys trains depart from stations in Paris
before joining dedicated high-speed lines.

Safety has been a major factor in the success of high-speed trains: although there have been three major accidents involving high-speed trains, none occurred at full speed on dedicated lines. In Germany in 1998, a wheel broke at 200kph (124mph) and came off the rails at a bridge – resulting in the derailment and destruction of the full set of 16 cars and the death of 101 people. In China in 2011, due to a signalling error, a train travelling at 100kph (62mph) hit a stationary train on a viaduct, killing 40 people. At Santiago de Compostela in Spain in 2013, a train came off the rails at 195kph (120mph) on a curve with a speed limit of 80kph (50mph), and smashed into a concrete wall, killing 79 people. Despite these accidents, the overall safety record of high-speed rail is better than for any other form of transport.

By 2013, there were nearly 16,000km (10,000 miles) of high-speed line around the world, with plans for lines in countries including Ukraine, Turkey, and Belarus. In the US, an 837-km (520-mile) line from San Francisco to Los Angeles has been approved by the California state government, but budget constraints and protests have delayed construction. In Britain, the proposal for HS2, a 530-km (330-mile) high-speed network joining London with several major cities at a cost of £50 billion (US$82 billion), has also met with fierce opposition. While some new schemes might be controversial, the advantages of high-speed rail are uncontested, and its place in the future of transport, is assured.

China, the New Pioneer

CHINA WAS PROBABLY THE ONLY COUNTRY in the world to have joined the railway age and then, briefly, to have left it again. Despite this false start, China now boasts by far the most extensive system of high-speed dedicated lines anywhere on the globe, a network that China is bent on expanding to become the backbone of the nation's transport infrastructure. China is also home to the world's highest railway: the Qinghai–Tibet line.

The first railway line in China was built by Jardine, Matheson & Co., a European-owned trading firm looking to improve access between Shanghai and the nearby port of Woosung. The line was just 16km (10 miles) long, but its construction in 1876 was mired in controversy: the deeply conservative Chinese officialdom was reluctant to allow the laying of railways, fearing it would ruin the livelihood of the vast numbers of those who carried goods for a living. One Chinese official at the time, Yü Lien-yuan, worried that the resulting unemployment would foment unrest:

> several tens of millions, who earn their living by holding the whip or grasping the tiller, will lose their jobs. If they don't end up starving in the ditches, they will surely gather [as outlaws] in the forests.

Another official was concerned that coal would run out, arguing that "when one uses coal with such profligacy, coalfields would soon disappear". In addition to these doom-laden visions, there was much antagonism towards foreigners and foreign-owned concerns at this time. Imperialist shows of might, such as the Opium Wars, lived in very recent memory, and foreign powers had been taking advantage of China's weakness: several European governments, as well as the Japanese, had set up missions along the coast that were effectively a way of obtaining access to China's riches without paying taxes on them. As such, Chinese officials took a dim view of the Shanghai– Woosung railway, and its European-sponsored construction never received official sanction. Just one year after the railway opened, Shen Pao-Chen, the governor of the region through which the railway ran, ordered the line to be ripped up and had the equipment shipped to Taiwan, where it was abandoned to the elements.

THE WORLD'S HIGHEST RAILWAY
A train passes through the Kunlun Mountains on the Qinghai–Tibet Railway, the world's highest rail line, which reaches 5,072m (16,640ft) above sea level.

It was not until 1881 that a permanent railway line would open in China. Originally intended to be mule-hauled, the line was a 10-km (6-mile) standard-gauge railway running from a coal mine to a canal at Hsukochuang, about 160km (100 miles) east of the capital, Beijing. A British engineer, C.W. Kinder, was responsible for the construction, as well as for commissioning China's first locomotive, the *Rocket of China*. These events, however, did not herald a railway revolution. The government remained reluctant to endorse this ground-breaking method of transport, despite its success across the world, and very few lines were built in the 1880s. It took the disastrous defeat in the Sino-French War of 1884–85 to make the Chinese realize that modernization was essential and that railways could be a catalyst for development. Kinder's line was extended by 32km (20 miles) in the direction of Beijing. However, in what can be seen as a measure of the role of superstition in Chinese government structures, a mysterious fire in the Imperial Palace was seen as a sign of celestial displeasure and the line was never completed.

By 1894, when the Sino-Japanese war broke out, little progress had been made and China had a mere 500km (320 miles) of railway, compared with 280,000km (175,000 miles) in the US. However, defeat in the war finally stimulated a railway boom in China. While Beijing became the centre of the network, many other lines were built to serve mines in relatively remote areas. By the time of the Xinhai Revolution of 1911, which created the Republic of China, there were 9,500km (6,000 miles) of track, a significant increase, but still a relatively small statistic for the most populous country in the world. It was, at the time, half the size of the railway network in India – a similarly impoverished, but smaller, nation.

Growth of the railways slowed during the period of the Republic as a result of a series of civil wars and the occupation of China by Japan in the late 1930s. Many lines were destroyed in these various conflicts, and by the end of World War II this vast nation still had only 22,500km (14,000 miles) of workable railway. After gaining control of the country for the communists in 1949, Mao Zedong invested heavily in the railway network. Lines were repaired and new ones built, even in difficult mountainous territory. This progress continued after Mao's death in 1976, and by the end of the 20th century China finally had a network covering most of the country. One major gap, however, remained – a line connecting Tibet with the rest of China.

Tibet is remote and separated from the rest of the country by the Kunlun Mountains in the north and the Nyenchen Tanglha range in the east. The main Tibetan plateau is a huge, high landmass stretching 2,400km (1,500 miles) from east to west, and 800km (500 miles) from north to south. It is home to the largest subarctic permafrost region in the world – which, to put it mildly, is not ideal railway territory. All land routes to the vast plateau cross mountain passes that climb higher than any peak in the US. As author Abrahm Lustgarten describes in *China's Great Train*, the roads:

> twist and wind through steep gorges loaded like cannons with unstable rock and snow at their peaks and flushing with torrents of interminable water in their troughs.

A China–Tibet rail link was seen as a way to cement China's control over this long-disputed area, known by the Chinese as the Tibetan Autonomous Region. Historically part of China, Tibet had declared its independence following the collapse of the Qing dynasty in 1912, but had been reclaimed by the communist-controlled government in 1951 and occupied by soldiers from the People's Liberation Army. Ever since the communist revolution, the government had harboured

APPROACHING LHASA
A train charges along the 929-m (3,047-ft)-long Lhasa River Railway Bridge, 2km (1¼ miles) from the terminus of the Qinghai–Tibet Railway.

ambitions to build a railway line to Lhasa, the capital of Tibet, to help establish control over the territory. However, technical difficulties and lack of money had stood in the way of the project. International experts argued that the railway simply could not be built, having observed the difficulties of laying railway tracks on permafrost during the construction of the Baikal Amur Mainline in eastern Russia (see pp.330–37).

Tibet accounts for an eighth of China's land mass and yet in 2000 it was still the only region in the country without a rail link connecting it to the more developed east. The Chinese government instituted a "Go West" campaign and the proposed line to Tibet became an important part of that strategy. At the time, Tibet was an undeveloped agrarian region with little connection to the outside world, but there was a possibility that mineral resources could be exploited with the help of the proposed railway.

A precursor to the Tibetan railway was completed in 1984: an 800-km (500-mile) railway heading west from Xining (the capital of Qinghai province and the traditional gateway to Tibet) to Golmud, also in Qinghai province. The plan to continue the line through to Lhasa, however, would not be agreed until over a decade later. In 1999, President Jiang Zemin launched a campaign to develop western China, which was lagging behind the booming east, and the Tibet railway became a key part of that strategy. However, there remained some dispute over the best route for the railway. Golmud, which had been founded in the 1960s as a labour camp for mainly Tibetan prisoners, was now a small city and offered the shortest route to Lhasa. This route involved crossing hundreds of miles of permafrost, however, and there were concerns that the technology to ensure that this could be done was not available. The most obvious alternative route was one from Yunnan province in southern China, but this would be twice the distance of the Golmud route, and so twice as expensive. Eventually, it was decided that it was possible to overcome the permafrost problem, and work started on the 1143-km (710-mile) line between Golmud and Lhasa in 2001. A railway constructed in the 21st century benefitted from many previously unavailable techniques, but the difficulties of working at such high altitude in a remote region still surpassed that of most previous railway projects, and the labour force required was enormous – over 100,000 workers migrated to Tibet to build the railway at the start of the project. One major challenge was that some sections had to be built on ground that was not quite permafrost – the top layers of soil melted during the summer and so became unstable. To accommodate this, long sections of track were elevated on what were effectively bridges, held up by deep, pile-driven foundations. In addition, passive heat exchangers were installed to cool the track and the surrounding soil.

The human cost of the venture was high, with many workers succumbing to altitude sickness. According to Lustgarten, "Tibetans in nearby villages would see railway officials burying dead workers on the hillsides outside the [Fenghuoshan] tunnel", but the official explanation for the deaths was food poisoning. No casualty statistics have been released by the authorities, who deny that there were any deaths from altitude sickness.

The work began at both ends of the line, and track-laying was completed within four years – the fitting out of signalling and other equipment took another year. Just five years after work started in July 2006, the line opened with much fanfare. The overall cost was around $4 billion – although this may be an underestimation given the difficulties of precisely working out the costs of the scheme. On its completion, the Qinghai–Tibet line beat numerous records in railway construction. It is the highest railway in the world: the Tanggula Pass, at 5,072m (166,640ft), surpasses its spectacular counterpart in the Andes, Peru (see pp.196–201), built almost a century before, by around 250m (820ft). Tanggula station is also the world's highest railway station, and the 1.2-km (¾-mile)-long Fenghuoshan tunnel is also the highest railway tunnel in the world at 4,905m (13,435ft) above sea level.

The railway has a capacity of up to eight passenger services per day in each direction. Since the air in Tibet is thin, the carriages on Lhasa trains have special air conditioning systems to keep oxygen levels healthy, and each seat has its own emergency breathing apparatus. The windows are especially large to give travellers the best view, and are protected against the high levels of ultra-violet light on the Tibetan plateau. With all these dangers, passengers are required to obtain a Health Registration Card before travelling from Golmud to Lhasa, and each train has a doctor on board in case of emergencies.

China's belated railway expansion has continued with the construction of a huge network of high-speed lines. Up until 1993, China's trains were still very slow, averaging just 48kph (30mph), prompting a number of "speed up" campaigns to counter competition from roads and aviation. The result was a series of services that could run at up to 161kph (100mph) by the end of the decade. The government, however, had even greater ambitions: the construction of a whole new set of lines in order to radically improve rail services and the nation's infrastructure. A programme was thus devised to build the world's biggest network of high-speed lines, defined as more than 200kph (124mph). Some existing lines were upgraded, but for the most part entirely new lines were constructed – each one faster than the last. The "Mid-to-Long-Term Railway Network Plan" proposed the construction of a national, high-speed rail grid composed of four north-south corridors and four east-west corridors, which, together with upgraded existing lines, would total 12,000km (7,500 miles).

The first of these dedicated lines, the Qinhuangdao-Shenyang High-Speed Railway along the Liaoxi Corridor in the northeast, opened in 2003 with a line speed of 200kph (124mph), which was upgraded to 250kph (155mph) by 2007. Others soon followed, some opening in time for the 2008 Olympics. One of these was the Beijing–Tianjin Intercity Railway linking northern China's two largest cities and designed for trains running at a speed of 350kph (217mph).

In October 2010, China opened its fifteenth high-speed rail, the Shanghai–Hangzhou line, and the following year the key Beijing–Shanghai line, which had a design speed of 380kph (236mph), became operational. This gave China over 8,000km (5,000 miles) of dedicated high-speed track, more than double that of any other country.

These impressive advances received a setback in July 2011 with a disastrous crash at Wenzhou in which two high-speed trains derailed. The crash cast a

NUMBER OF BRIDGES ON THE GOLMUD-LHASA LINE

675

TOTALLING
161KM
(100 MILES)

HIGH-SPEED ROLLING STOCK
A fleet of high-speed bullet trains awaits servicing
at a maintenance base in Wuhan, Hubei province,
one of China's busiest transportation hubs.

long shadow, and for a time construction slowed. The programme
threatened to be delayed, or even shelved, as passenger numbers
dwindled in response to the accident, and the top speeds of trains
were reduced. However, by 2012, the programme had resumed and
passenger numbers climbed again.

In 2013, China's 1,580 high-speed train services transported
1.3 million passengers daily, and these impressive statistics are
only going to grow. The government plans to have a 25,750-km
(16,000-mile), high-speed network by 2020 — at a cost of US$300 billion
(£184 billion) — giving China a high-speed rail system extending many
times the distance of any other country. This achievement, along
with the expanding number of metro lines in towns across the
country — and the record-breaking Tibet railway — establishes China
as indisputably the 21st century's principal railway pioneer, so far.

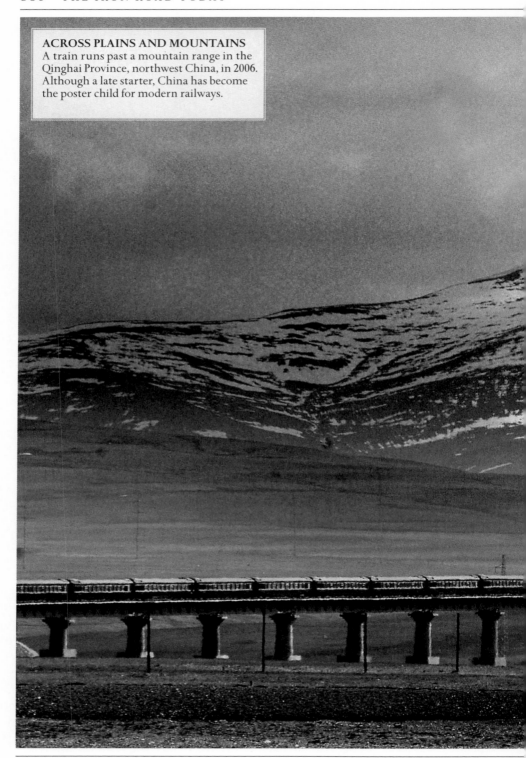

ACROSS PLAINS AND MOUNTAINS
A train runs past a mountain range in the
Qinghai Province, northwest China, in 2006.
Although a late starter, China has become
the poster child for modern railways.

The Railway Renaissance

THE STORY OF THE RAILWAY would have been remarkable even if, with the advent of the car and plane, it had simply been consigned to history. In that, it would have resembled the trajectory of so many other innovations: birth, brief heyday, gradual decline, and then oblivion. However, despite a period of decline, the railway has proved pessimistic predictions wrong by enjoying a 21st-century renaissance, and a future that looks assured.

This resurgence of the train has not simply been the result of far-reaching technological developments, although improvements have certainly been made. Railway carriages are rather more comfortable than those of the 19th century, and freight wagons are sturdier and better designed for rapid unloading with the spread of containerization. Signalling is much improved, too, and there have been other sophisticated adaptations to make the railways faster and more efficient. Despite these advances, train travel in the 21st century would still be immediately recognizable to George Stephenson and other pioneers. Tracks are still usually set 1,435mm (4ft 8½in) apart, and passengers are still transported in carriages that stop at stations and are controlled by external signals.

Of course, the function of the train today is different. While the railway was once a monopoly supplier of long-distance transport, it is now more of a niche industry – but a very important one. Never again will the railway serve every village and small town. The heyday of the iron road providing the only fast and cheap way of travelling between many places is over; those little village stations and rural halts are lost forever. Nor will railways dominate the freight market as they once did. Gone, too, are the parcel yards and goods depots once found at every station, wiped out by the lorry and the van.

The railways had to overcome a very difficult time: there was a point in the post-war period when railways were regarded as irrelevant (see pp.340–47). The French railway writer Clive Lamming even gave this phenomenon a name – "*ferropessimisme*", the notion that the decline and marginalization of the railways was inevitable. But the railways are still very much a part of modern life and pessimists have been proved wrong. Many countries are now bemoaning the fact that key lines were closed down and major stations turned into shopping malls or housing developments. Across the world, the railways are flourishing and will continue to do so for the foreseeable future, because rail is still a very convenient form of travel for passengers and an extremely efficient way of transporting goods.

There are several key markets in which rail travel offers great advantages to passengers. Intercity rail journeys of 500–650km (300–400 miles) – or further with high-speed lines – may take longer than a flight, but passengers are able to relax or work on the train and, unlike far-flung airports, train terminals are located in the heart of the city. Local commutes are also more efficient by rail, whether train or metro, as these trips are usually faster and more reliable than driving, and unaffected by traffic. Trains also offer the best way to enjoy scenic routes, and in some cases, as with the Trans-Siberian (see pp.180–89), are one of the only viable means of transport across remote areas.

Rail is also very well suited to moving large amounts of very heavy, non-urgent freight, such as aggregate and stone, which otherwise damage roads. Trains have a competitive advantage too, when transporting loads long distances: they are cheaper than convoys of trucks, which require several drivers and may need to stop overnight. Developments in containerization have also made loading and unloading far easier.

The railways have made a remarkable recovery from their post-war nadir, when it seemed their glory days were at an end and that the train would soon go the way of the schooner or the stagecoach. They survived, in most countries at any rate, because of their competitive edge in several markets, and because road transport has its own limitations. In an age of uncertainty over oil supply, railways remain a reliable and relatively cheap form of transportation.

The railways, however, do not stand still. They are continually adapting and evolving – and expanding. In response to competition, services have been speeded up and facilities improved; redundant lines and services have been abandoned; and

A 1994 US STUDY SHOWED THAT FREIGHT LORRIES EMIT AROUND

8 TIMES

MORE AIR POLLUTION THAN TRAINS

major developments can still be expected. One such example is the wider adoption of in-cab signalling to replace external signals; this is safer and more efficient, allowing more trains on the track, but will require considerable investment. Moreover, and more significantly, brand-new and reopened lines are springing up in many places.

There are a huge number of significant projects in the offing, many costing billions, or tens of billions, of pounds. Aside from China (see pp.372–81), Saudi Arabia is probably responsible for more major rail and metro developments than any other country. Its 1500-km (900-mile)-long North–South Line will enable freight to travel from Al Jalamid (in the phosphate belt in the north) to Az Zabirah (in the bauxite belt in the centre of the country), and then eastwards to the processing and port facilities at Raz Az Zawr.

Also in the pipeline is the ambitious Landbridge Project, which is intended to run from the west to east coasts of Saudi Arabia, linking the Red Sea and the Persian Gulf, thus greatly reducing the time required to transport freight from the Gulf. It involves building 960km (600 miles) of new line to connect the capital city, Riyadh, to Jeddah on the west coast, while upgrading existing links between Riyadh and the city of Dammam on the east coast. In addition, 130km (80 miles) of track will run north–south along the coast to connect Dammam and Jubail. These links will create a useful new route for sending raw materials and manufactured goods between Europe and North America on one side, and East and South Asia on the other.

As well as these bold initiatives, the Saudi government is building a Mecca-to-Medina line (the Haramain High Speed Rail) to carry pilgrims for the Haj, redolent of the Hejaz Railway (see pp.288–93). Other proposals include the Riyadh metro, to serve six routes, and the Saudi–Bahrain Railway Bridge.

All of these projects involve building lines across difficult desert terrain, often in remote areas, echoing many of the great construction projects covered in this book. It is clear that Saudi Arabia is embracing the railways in a way that is astonishing for a country that is home to the world's largest oil reserves, with a wealth built on fuelling cars.

THE PROJECTED COST OF THE RIYADH METRO IN SAUDI ARABIA

US$23 BILLION

VISIONS OF THE FUTURE
This digital projection of a terminus along the
Haramain High Speed Rail in Saudi Arabia shows
the platforms shielded by fabric roofing. The ambitious
designs for the main stations will enable massive capacity.

There is no shortage of exciting forthcoming developments and
projects worldwide. Russia is planning to improve the Trans-Siberian
(see pp.180–89) and the Baikal-Amur Mainline (see pp.330–37), and
has visions of building a line across to America. It would certainly
beat any other project for sheer ambition and, indeed, cost.

The renaissance of rail is arguably most remarkable in Africa – a
continent that has never properly exploited the advantages of rail
transport. Now, thanks in many instances to investment from China,
several major lines have been brought back into use and others are
being constructed. A plan to build an 2,800-km (1,800-mile) line
across central Africa, linking the capital of landlocked Rwanda,
Kigali, with the Kenyan port of Mombasa, looks set to proceed with
Chinese money at a cost of £8.5 billion (US$13.8 billion). The railway
will partly make use of an existing colonial-era line in Kenya and
Uganda, but the section from the Ugandan capital, Kampala, through
to Kigali will be entirely new. Connections through to other parts of
Kenya and Uganda are also envisaged.

In West Africa, work is starting on a line in order to facilitate the
export of minerals. The line would link Niamey, the capital of another
landlocked nation, Niger, with the huge port of Abidjan in Ivory Coast,
via Ouagadougou, the capital of Burkina Faso. Nigeria also has plans to

renew and expand its railways, and is seeking to reinstate commuter services in its biggest city, Lagos. In South Africa, a new 80-km (50-mile) mass rapid transit system, the Gautrain, was fully opened in 2012, linking Johannesburg, Pretoria, Ekurhuleni, and O.R. Tambo International Airport. There will never be a Cape to Cairo line (see pp.214–23), but Africa will become more rail-oriented than it has ever been.

The growth of the railways is a worldwide phenomenon. In the autumn of 2013, the railway development website, railway-technology.com, listed nearly 450 major railway projects across the world, including more than 100 in Asia and 33 in Australasia. As mentioned previously, there are plans for high-speed lines in numerous countries where previously rail investment had stagnated or declined. High-speed rail is a rising new market as it attracts travellers away from short-haul flights and onto the more environmentally sustainable railways. It offers not only the prospect of reduced journey times between city centres, but also a far more pleasant travel experience.

Meanwhile, the other great boom in railway development has been the urban metro, and this shows no sign of abating. In the summer of 2013, there were 188 metro systems across the world in no fewer than 54 countries, ranging from Teresina in Brazil to Yerevan in Armenia.

A FAILED ENTERPRISE
The underused, overpriced Sydney Monorail
ran for 25 years, before being scrapped in 2013 to
make way for a light rail system.

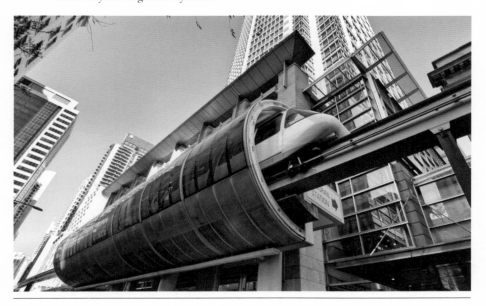

Perhaps the most surprising adherents are to be found in car-obsessed Dubai, the largest city in the United Arab Emirates, which opened a metro line in 2009. The city has already opened a second line, with plans for three more in the wake of its success.

Trams, or "light rail", are also enjoying a global revival. Old systems are being renovated and many cities, even in the car-dominated US, are opening new lines. In the US, a new type of housing, "transit-oriented development" (high-density development centred around a transit stop), is proving popular as it allows people to commute easily to work, without having to drive.

Rail travel has succeeded by seeing off the alternatives. For a time other technologies were variously put forward as having greater potential to improve transport, including numerous bizarre monorail schemes. The most prominent of these was "maglev" – magnetic levitation (see pp.388–89). Magnetic force is used to elevate the "train" slightly above the special track and then magnets are used to provide forward thrust. The result was a very smooth ride at far higher speeds than conventional trains, along with better acceleration and braking. Despite many decades of research and development, and the introduction of a few systems, there are still currently only two maglev systems in operation – one in Japan and the other in China. The Chinese maglev, shuttling passengers between Shanghai and the airport, takes just seven minutes 20 seconds to cover 30km (18½ miles) and reaches a speed of 430kph (268mph). However, the cost of development, the potential risks (there has been one major accident on a German test track, resulting in 23 deaths), and the fact that conventional rail is already a tried and tested technology used across the world, has meant that maglev expansion has been stymied. While there are proposals for lines in several countries, it is clear there is no immediate prospect of this technology replacing rail.

In what has proved to be a real shock to many transport planners (and past futurologists), the railways have not only survived to see the 21st century, but are, in fact, booming. As oil becomes scarcer and concerns about environmental impact grow, rail transport will only appear more attractive. Rail offers convenience, safety, and speed, as well as compatability with personal technology: travellers can use mobile devices or work on laptops, using time otherwise wasted behind the wheel. The train is becoming more, not less, suited to life in today's world. The 21st century will be the second age of the train.

Maglev Trains

Unlike conventional trains with their track-and-wheel interface, maglev (magnetic levitation) trains literally float on air, using powerful magnets to suspend trains at a constant level above a steel rail or "guideway" and electromagnetic force to propel the trains. Due to a lack of friction, maglev trains are quiet and stable, can accelerate and decelerate fast, and both trains and guideway suffer little wear and tear. However, due to incompatibility with existing railways, maglev technology has seen limited adoption – the only working commercial systems are in Japan and China. The maglev infrastructure is expensive to build, but once in place operating costs are low and the trains can achieve very high velocity: maglev trains hold the world speed record for rail transport.

Alternative Systems

The SCMaglev (Superconducting Maglev, named for the train's powerful magnets) is the latest in a series of high-speed maglev trains developed in Japan. It makes use of electrodynamic suspension (EDS) on U-shaped rails for levitation and propulsion. It has undergone successful trials, though has not yet progressed to commercial use.

THE SCMAGLEV IS THE FASTEST PASSENGER TRANSPORT TRAIN IN THE WORLD, REACHING 581KPH (361MPH) ON A TEST TRACK IN 2003.

Train runs on a T-shaped monorail which makes derailment almost impossible

How it works

Existing commercial maglev systems use electromagnetic suspension (EMS), in which magnets in the train are activated for both levitation and propulsion by an electric current in the track. This current can be adjusted to determine the train's speed, while electronic sensors monitor the gap between train and guideway.

LEVITATION

Powerful electromagnets on the undercarriage of the train, which wraps around the T-shaped guideway, are attracted by levitation and guidance coils mounted in the rail.

Guide magnets on train maintain an 8–12mm (⅜–½in) gap

Battery-powered support magnets on train

Guideway's electromagnetic coils (stators) and train's support magnets attract each other to levitate train

PROPULSION

The polarity of propulsion coils in the rail changes constantly, attracting and repelling magnets on the train. The frequency is reversed to stop the train.

GUIDEWAY

TRAIN

Guideway's alternating current attracts then repels train's magnets to propel train

Direction of magnetic field, reversed to brake

TRANSRAPID MAGLEV

German company Transrapid, the leader in maglev trains, has been honing its electromagnetic suspension (EMS) since the 1960s. Seen here on its test track, the Transrapid train went into commercial operation in 2004 on China's Shanghai Maglev, which travels the 30km (18½ miles) from the airport to the financial district in 8 minutes at 400kph (250mph).

Lack of engine makes maglev trains light and energy-efficient: air cooling the propulsion system uses more power than levitation

C-shaped undercarriage contains the train's support magnets for levitation

Glossary

ADHESION The frictional grip between the wheel of a train and the rail of a track.

AIR CUSHION A "spring" of air used in modern suspension systems.

AIR BRAKE A braking system that uses compressed air as its operating medium.

AMERICAN A steam locomotive with a *wheel arrangement* of 4-4-0.

ATLANTIC A steam locomotive with a *wheel arrangement* of 4-4-2.

BALDWIN A US *locomotive* manufacturer that was in business from 1825 to 1971.

BALLAST The bed of stone, gravel, or cinders on which a rail track is laid.

BANK A steep section of a track that a train requires additional engines to climb.

BERKSHIRE A steam *locomotive* with a *wheel arrangement* of 2-8-4.

BLASTPIPE The exhaust pipe of a steam *locomotive* that diverts steam from the cylinders into the *smokebox* beneath the *chimney* to increase the draught through the fire.

BOGIE The undercarriage assembly of a train, incorporating the wheels, suspension, and brakes. Called a *truck* in the US.

BOILER Cylindrical chamber in which steam is produced to drive a steam *locomotive*.

BOXCAR See *van*.

BRANCH LINE A secondary railway line that branches off a *main line*.

BROAD GAUGE Rails spaced more widely than the *standard gauge* of 1,435mm (4ft 8½ in).

BUFFER A device that cusions the impact of rail vehicles against each other.

BUFFER STOP / BUMPER POST The post at the end of a track that halts a train from travelling any further.

CAB The control room of a *locomotive*, housing the engine crew.

CABOOSE A railway car used by railway workers to monitor track conditions. It is usually attached to the end of a train.

CANT The angle of elevation of a rail, relative to vertical or to its partner rail.

CHALLENGER A steam *locomotive* with a *wheel arrangement* of 4-6-6-4.

CHIMNEY The vertical exhaust funnel of a train. Called a *smokestack* in the US.

COMPOUND LOCOMOTIVE A steam *locomotive* that uses two sets of cylinders, the second powered by exhaust steam from the first.

COUPLER / COUPLING The mechanism that connects and holds *rolling stock* together.

COUPLING ROD A rod that transmits power from a driven axle to the wheels.

COWCATCHER A metal frame projecting from the front of a *locomotive* designed to clear the track of obstructions.

CUTTING A channel dug through the hillside to enable a rail track to maintain a shallow gradient.

CYLINDER The core of a steam engine in which a *piston* moves back and forth under the pressure of expanding and condensing steam.

EMBANKMENT A raised pathway across a depression in the landscape that enables a rail track to maintain a shallow gradient.

ENGINE The power source of a *locomotive*, driven by steam, electricity, or diesel.

EXPRESS TRAIN A train that passes certain stations on its route without stopping, in order to arrive at its final destination faster.

FIREBOX The compartment within a steam engine where fuel is burnt to provide heat.

FIREMAN / STOKER / BOILERMAN A worker responsible for keeping the *firebox* of an *engine* fed with coal.

FREIGHT / GOODS Materials or products transported for commercial gain.

GANDY DANCER A track maintenance worker.

GAUGE The width between the inner faces of the rails.

GONDOLA An open-top peice of *rolling stock*, used to transport loose materials, such as ore and coal.

HANDCAR A small, open railroad car propelled by its passengers, often by means of a hand pump. Known as a *pump trolley* in Britain.

HUDSON A steam *locomotive* with a *wheel arrangement* of 4-6-4.

INTERCHANGE The practice by which railway companies transport *freight* from other organisations over their tracks.

INTERLOCKING TOWER See *signal box*.

INTERMODAL Moving either *freight* or passengers by more than one type of vehicle.

JUBILEE A steam locomotive with a *wheel arrangement* of 4-4-4.

JUNCTION A place where multiple train lines split or converge.

LANTERN A portable lamp with a fuel source. Used by early railroad workers to provide light and to signal to other workers at night.

LEVEL CROSSING A location where a railroad crosses a road or path at the same elevation.

LEVEL JUNCTION A railway junction where multiple lines intersect, crossing the path of oncoming rail traffic at the same elevation.

LIGHT RAIL Small, fixed railroads, typically operating within urban environments e.g. streetcars and trams.

LOCOMOTIVE The engine-powered vehicle that either pulls or pushes a train along the tracks.

LOOP A railroad formation where tracks cross over themselves as they ascend a mountain.

MAIN LINE An important line between major towns or cities.

MARSHALLING YARD A railroad yard where freight wagons are loaded and unloaded, arranged, and organized into trains.

MIKADO A steam *locomotive* with the *wheel arrangement* 2-8-2.

MONORAIL A railway system based on a single rail. Often elevated, and built in urban environments.

NARROW GAUGE A railway with a gauge narrower than the standard 1,435mm (4ft 8½ in).

NAVVIES The specialist manual labourers who constructed the majority of the railways in the 19th century.

PACIFIC A steam *locomotive* with a *wheel arrangement* of 4-6-2.

PANTOGRAPH A metal arm that connects to an overhead line, providing power to an electric train.

PASSENGER TRAIN A train with carriages intended to transport people. These trains travel between stations at which passengers may embark or disembark.

PASSING LOOP A position on a single-track railway, where trains travelling in opposite directions can pass each other. Called a *passing siding* in US.

PASSING SIDING See *passing loop*

PISTON A component of an internal-combustion engine which moves up and down against a liquid or gas to provide motion.

POINTS / RAILROAD SWITCH A section of railway which allows a train to move from one track to another.

PRAIRIE A steam locomotive with a *wheel arrangement* of 2-6-2.

RAILROAD CAR A covered railroad vehicle used for carrying passengers or cargo.

ROLLING STOCK Used by railroad companies to refer to the entire collection of vehicles which run on their railway. As a more general term refers to any complete locomotive or carriage.

ROUNDHOUSE Buildings used to service and store trains. Many used to be arranged around a *turntable*.

SIDING A section of track off the main line used for storing rolling stock.

SIGNAL BOX A control room in which the movement of trains are controlled by means of signals and blocks, ensuring trains travel safely and to schedule. The US term is *interlocking tower*.

SLEEPER A train that can provide beds for all its passengers, particularly for overnight or long-distance journeys.

SLIP COACH The practice of uncoupling carriages from an *express train*, and braking them to a halt at a station. This allowed passengers to disembark without halting the main train.

SMOKEBOX A component of a steam engine. The smokebox would collect smoke from the *firebox*, after it had heated water to provide steam, and release it though the *smokestack* or *chimney*.

SMOKESTACK See *chimney*

STANDARD GAUGE Rails spaced 1,435mm (4ft 8½ in) apart.

STATION MASTER The individual in charge of running a station.

STEAM ENGINE An engine that uses steam, produced by heating water with burning fuel, to perform mechanical work.

SUBWAY See *underground*

TENDER A carriage containing the necessary fuel and water needed to power a steam train's engine.

THROUGH COACH A rail carriage that switches *locomotive*s mid-journey, removing the need for passengers to switch trains. Used particularly on long-haul journeys.

TRACK The permanent fixtures of rails, *ballast*, fastenings, and underlying substrate that provide a runway for the wheels of a train.

TRACTION The act of drawing or pulling a load. Can also refer to the adhesive friction of a train to a track.

TRUCK See *bogie*.

TURNTABLE A device for rotating rail vehicles so they can travel back in the direction they came from. Largely obsolete today.

UNDERGROUND A railway that operates underground, typically in a major city. Known as a *subway* in the US.

UNIT TRAIN A train that carries only one type of goods.

VAN A flat-bottomed freight wagon with sliding doors on each side. Known in the US as a *boxcar*.

WATER COLUMN See *water crane*

WATER CRANE A track-side device for quickly refilling the water tank of a steam *locomotive*. Known in the US as a *water column*.

WHEEL The wheels of trains are typically cast or forged with an affixed tyre of hardened steel.

WHEEL ARRANGEMENT A system for classifying how wheels are placed under a *locomotive*, such as the *Whyte notation*.

WHEEL FLANGE A component of a train wheel. The flange extends the wheels to the interior of the train track, preventing the train from running off the rails.

WHYTE NOTATION A system classifying *wheel arrangment* by counting first leading wheels, then driving wheels, then trailing wheels (e.g. 0-2-2).

YARD An area with multiple tracks and sidings for the storage, maintenance, and loading and unloading of rolling stock.

YELLOWSTONE A steam *locomotive* with a *wheel arrangement* of 2-8-8-4.

ZIGZAG / SWITCHBACK A method of track construction on steep inclines. A train ascends the track in a zigzag fashion.

Bibliography

This is very much a selective bibliography, mainly mentioning books I have used as source material, since there are literally tens of thousands of books on the railways. Many of these are very detailed and written for a specialist audience, and have consequently not been included in this list. The list is, therefore, aimed at the general reader who wants to know more on the subjects covered in this book, rather than at a specialist audience.

I have, of course, made extensive use of my own series of six railway history books, all published by Atlantic. *The Subterranean Railway* (2004, updated 2013) is the story of the London Underground, *Fire and Steam* (2006) covers the story of Britain's railways, and *Blood, Iron and Gold* (2008) shows how the railways changed the world. *Engines of War* (2010) demonstrates the importance of railways in wartime while *The Great Railway Revolution* (2012) is the story of American railroads; *To the Edge of the World* (2013) is the history of the world's longest railway, the Trans-Siberian.

GENERAL

Erwin Berghaus, *The History of the Railways*, Barrie & Rockliffe, 1964

Anthony Burton, *Railway Empire*, John Murray, 1994

Anthony Burton, *On the Rails*, Aurum, 2004

Christopher Chant, *The World's Railways*, Grange, 2002

Basil Cooper, *A Century of Train*, Brian Trodd Publishing, 1988

Nicholas Faith, *Locomotion*, BBC Books, 1993

Nicholas Faith, *The World the Railways Made*, Bodley Head, 1990

Tim Fischer, *Trains Unlimited*, ABC Books, 2011

Geoffrey Freeman Allen, *Railways Past, Present and Future*, Orbis Publishing, 1982

Geoffrey Freeman Allen, *Railways of the Twentieth Century*, Winchmore, 1983

Geoffrey Freeman Allen, *Luxury Trains of the World*, Bison, 1979

Jim Harter, *World Railways of the Nineteenth Century: A Pictorial History in Victorian Engravings*, Johns Hopkins University Press, 2005

Clive Lamming, *Larousse des Trains et des Chemins de Fer*, Larousse, 2005

Bryan Morgan, ed, *Great Trains*, Crown Publishers, 1973

O.S. Nock, *World Atlas of Railways*, Mitchell Beazley, 1978

O.S. Nock, *Railways Then and Now: A World History*, Paul Elek Ltd, 1975

O.S. Nock, ed, *Encyclopaedia of Railways*, Book Club Associates, 1977

Martin Page, *The Lost Pleasures of the Great Trains*, Weidenfeld and Nicolson, 1975

Steve Parissien, *Station to Station*, Phaidon, 1997

P.J.G. Ransom, *Locomotion: Two Centuries of Train Travel*, Sutton Publishing, 2001

Michael Robbins, *The Railway Age*, Penguin, 1965

Wolfgang Schivelbusch, *Railway Journey: The Industrialization of Time and Space in the Nineteenth Century*, Berg, 1996

John Westwood, *Railways at War*, Osprey, 1980

John Westwood, *The Pictorial History of Railways*, Bison Books, 2008

EUROPE

H.C. Casserly, *Outline of Irish History*, David & Charles, 1974

Nicholas Faith, *The Right Line: the Politics, the Planning and the Against-the-odds Gamble Behind Britain's First High-speed Railway*, Segrave Foulkes, 2007

Peter Fleming, *The Fate of Admiral Kolchak*, Rupert Hart David, 1963 (reprinted 2001 by Birlinn)

Murray Hughes, *Rail 300*, David & Charles, 1988

P.M. Kalla-Bishop, *Italian Railroads*, Drake, 1972

P.M. Kalla-Bishop, *Mediterranean Island Railways*, David & Charles, 1970

Allan Mitchell, *The Great Train Race: Railways and Franco-German Rivalry*, Berghahn, 2000

O.S. Nock, *Railways of Western Europe*, A&C Black, 1977

Brian Perren, *TGV Handbook*, Capital Transport, 1998

Albert Schram, *Railways and the Formation of the Italian State in the Nineteenth Century*, Cambridge University Press, 1977

Christine Sutherland, *The Princess of Siberia*, Methuen, 1984

Various authors, *Histoire du Réseau Ferroviaire Français*, Editions de l'Ormet, 1996

Various authors, *ICE: High-Tech on Wheels*, Hestra-Verlag, 1991

Arthur J. Veenendaal, *Railways in the Netherlands: A Brief History, 1834–1994*, Stanford University Press, 2001

THE AMERICAS

Dee Brown, *Hear That Lonesome Whistle Blow: Railroads in the West*, Touchstone, 1977

David Cruise and Alison Griffiths, *Lords of the Line: The Men Who Built the Canadian Pacific Railway*, Viking, 1988

Brian Fawcett, *Railways of the Andes*, Plateway Press, 1997

Sarah H. Gordon. *Passage to Union: How the Railroads Transformed American Life, 1829–1929*, Elephant Paperbacks, 1997

George W. Hilton and John F. Due, *The Electric Interurban Railways in America*, Stanford University Press, 1960

Stewart H. Holbrook, *The Story of American Railroads*, Bonanza Books, 1947

Theodore Kornweibel Jr, *Railroads in the African American Experience*, Johns Hopkins University Press, 2010

Oscar Lewis, *The Big Four*, Alfred A. Knopf, 1938

Albro Martin, *Railroads Triumphant*, Oxford University Press, 1992

Nick and Helma Mika, *The Railways of Canada: A Pictorial History*, McGraw-Hill Ryerson, 1972

O.S. Nock, *Railways of Canada*, A&C Black, 1973

Andrew Roden, *Great Western Railway: A History*, Aurum, 2010

David Rollinson, *Railways of the Caribbean*, Macmillan, 2001

D. Trevor Rowe, *The Railways of South America*, Locomotives International, 2000

John F. Stover, *American Railroads*, University of Chicago Press, 1961

Richard White, *The Transcontinentals and the Making of Modern America*, Norton, 2011

Oscar Zanetti and Alejandra García, *Sugar and Railroads: A Cuban History, 1837–1959*, University of North Carolina Press, 1998

ASIA

Ralph William Huenemann, *The Dragon and the Iron Horse: The Economics of Railroads in China, 1876–1937*, Harvard University Press, 1984

Robert Hardie, *The Burma Siam Railway*, Quadrant Books, 1984

Ian J. Kerr, *Engines of Change: The Railways that Made India*, Praeger, 2007

Ian J. Kerr, *Building the Railways of the Raj, 1850–1900*, Oxford University Press, 1995

Abrahm Lustgarten, *China's Great Train: Beijing's Drive West and the Campaign to Remake Tibet*, Henry Holt, 2008

Deborah Manley, ed, *The Trans-Siberian Railway: A Traveller's Anthology*, Century Hutchinson, 1987

Steven G. Marks, *Road to Power: The Trans-Siberian Railroad and the Colonization of Asian Russia, 1850–1917*, Cornell University Press, 1991

James Nicholson, *The Hejaz Railway*, Stacey International, 2005

O.S. Nock, *Railways of Asia and the Far East*, A&C Black, 1978

Peter Semmens, *High Speed in Japan*, Platform 5, 2000

Roopa Srinivasan, Manish Tiwari, and Sandeep Silas, *Our Indian Railway*, Foundation Books, 2006

Shoji Sumita *Success Story, the privatisation of Japanese National Railways*, Profile Books, 2000

John Tickner, Gordon Edgar, and Adrian Freeman, *China: The World's Last Steam Railway*, Artists' and Photographers' Press, 2008

Harmon Tupper, *To the Great Ocean*, Secker & Warburg, 1965

K.R. Vaidyanathan, *150 Glorious Years of Indian Railways*, English Edition Publishers, 2003

Christopher J. Ward, *Brezhnev's Folly: The Building of the BAM and Late Soviet Socialism*, University of Pittsburgh Press, 2009

Various authors, *Guide to the Great Siberian Railway*, 1900, David & Charles reprints, 1971

AFRICA

John Day, *Railways of South Africa*, Arthur Barker, 1963

M.F. Hill, *The Permanent Way: The Story of the Tanganyika Railways*, East African Railways and Harbours, 1958

George Tabor, *Cape to Cairo*, Genta, 2003

AUSTRALASIA

Neill Atkinson, *Trainland*, Random House, 2007

Tim Fischer, *Transcontinental Train Journey*, Allen & Unwin, 2004

C.C. Singleton and David Burke, *Railways of Australia*, Angus & Robertson, 1963

Patsy Adam Smith, *The Desert Railway*, Rigby 1974

Patsy Adam Smith, *Romance of Australian Railways*, Rigby, 1973

Index

Illustrations are in *italics*

A

accidents
  braking system improvements 139, 140
  Britain 140, 141, 143, 278–82, 307, 308
  driver error 141
  and "fishplate" joining rails 140
  France 43, 138–39, 140, 143, 284–86
  Germany 143, 371
  India 140
  Ireland 43, 139
  level crossings 142–43
  New Zealand 168
  and railway management 143
  Spain 142, 286, 287, 371
  and speeding 142, 143
  terrorist attacks 141
  tombstone technology 138–40
  United States 142–43
Africa
  Blue Train 177
  Cape of Good Hope to Cairo, plans for 214–21
  map 222–23
  military use 218–19, 220
  West Africa line proposals 385–86
Allen, Ralph 17
Alps 102–07, *103*
  AlpTransit project 107
  locomotive competition 104
  rack railway 105–06
  Semmering Pass line 102–05, *104*
  track-laying logistics 103–06
  tunnels 106–07, 193, 228, 357, 358, 360
Andes 198–203
Argentina 157, 267
Australia
  freight conveyance 297–98
  gauge size problems 296–302
  Sydney Monorail *386*
  Trans-Australian Railway *298*, 299, *300–01*
Austria
  balloon railway 73
  early network, horse-drawn 46
  map 50–51
  military use 60, 271–72
  Mödling Tram 227
  Semmering Pass line 102–04, 165

B

Beeching, Richard 342–43, *343*
Belgium
  cable railway 71
  early rail network 43–44
  map 50–51

station design 155, 158
braking system 139, 140, 144–45
Brazil, reversing engine 80
bridge design 168–69
Britain
  accidents 140, 141, 143, 278–82, 307, 308
  atmospheric railway 68–70, *68*
  Brighton electric railway 225, *226*
  cable/rope railways 71, *72–73*
  Channel Tunnel *295*, 348–53, *348*, *350–51*, *353–55*
  diesel and electric locomotives 224–25, *230*, *319*
  early investment 15–17, 23
  fraud 244–45
  Great Western Railway 86–87, 160, 162, 307–08
  heritage railways 343–45
  high-speed trains 305–08, 309, 369, 371
  Liverpool and Manchester Railway 14, 22, *23*, 25–29, 52, 60, 71, 232
  London and Birmingham line 29, 71, 85, 86
  London and North Western Railway (LNWR) 164–65
  London Underground 71, 130–37, *132–34*, *137*, 227, 229
  map 50–51
  Metropolitan Railway Company 131–36, *132–34*
  military use 60–61, 272–74, 278–82
  monorails 71–72, 164
  navvies 84–87
  "parliamentary (ghost) trains" 340–41
  privatization 143
  rail closures 340–41, 342–43, *343*, 345
  railway barons 163–65
  railway mania and expansion 52–54
  "scrip" share vouchers 52
  station design 154–55, 158, 353
  Stockton and Darlington line 22, 23–25, 52
  strikes 238–39
  terrorist attacks 141
Brunel, Isambard Kingdom 68–70, *68*, 154, 162
Budd, Ralph 315–16

C

cable/rope railways 71, *72–73*
Canada
  Canadian Pacific Railway 125–27, *126*
  station design 156, 158
carriages 146–51
  aristocracy, use of own 146–47
  compartments 146, 148, *148*
  corridor trains 151
  early travel discomfort 146–48
  Orient Express *see* Orient Express
  policing 150–51, *150*
  sleeping carriages, early 170–71
  ticket prices and comfort levels 146
  ticket-sharing scheme 164

Acknowledgments

The author would like to thank Nicholas Faith, author of *The World the Railways Made*, for drafting several chapters and advising on various aspects of the book, and Malcolm Bulpitt of the Swiss Railway Society for his draft of the section on Switzerland.

The publisher would like to thank the following for their kind permission to reproduce their photographs:

(Key: a-above; b-below/bottom; c-centre; f-far; l-left; r-right; t-top)

2 Matthew Malkiewicz: losttracksoftime.com. **5 Matthew Malkiewicz:** losttracksoftime.com. **11 Science & Society Picture Library:** NRM / Pictorial Collection. **15 Getty Images:** Lonely Planet Images. **18-19 Science & Society Picture Library:** Science Museum. **20-21 Science & Society Picture Library:** Science Museum. **22 The Bridgeman Art Library:** Institute of Mechanical Engineers, London, UK. **23 DK Images:** Courtesy of the National Railway Museum, York. **25 Science & Society Picture Library:** NRM. **26-27 Science & Society Picture Library:** NRM / Pictorial Collection. **28 Science & Society Picture Library:** Science Museum. **30-31 Science & Society Picture Library:** NRM. **32 Smithsonian Institution Archives:** NPG.75.13. **35 DK Images:** Courtesy of Railroad Museum of Pennsylvania. **36 Corbis:** Bettmann. **37-38 DK Images:** Courtesy of B&O Railroad Museum. **40 DK Images:** Courtesy of B&O Railroad Museum (cl, cr, bl). **41 DK Images:** Courtesy of B&O Railroad Museum (tl). **41 DK Images:** Courtesy of Railroad Museum of Pennsylvania (tr, cl, cr). **40-41b DK Images:** Courtesy of B&O Railroad Museum. **42 Getty Images:** Culture Club. **45 Topfoto:** ullsteinbild. **47 Alamy:** The Art Archive. **48 Getty Images. 53 Corbis:** Michael Nicholson. **54 The Bridgeman Art Library:** Sunderland Museums & Winter Garden Collection, Tyne & Wear, UK. **57 Science & Society Picture Library:** NRM / Cuneo Fine Arts (Artist copyright Estate of Terence Cuneo / The Bridgeman Art Library). **58 Traditionsbetriebswerk Stassfurt:** (bl). **58-59 Getty Images:** Fox Photos. **66-67 Corbis:** Horace Bristol. **61 AF Eisenbahn Archiv. 62 Library of Congress, Washington, D.C.. 65 The Kobal Collection:** United Artists. **66 Raggan Datta:** (bc). **68 DK Images:** Courtesy of Didcot Railway Centre. **72-73 Science & Society Picture Library:** NRM / Pictorial Collection. **74-75 akg-images. 77 Getty Images:** Hulton Archive. **79 Science & Society Picture Library:** Science Museum. **80 Getty Images:** Hulton Archive. **82 Getty Images:** The British Library / Robana (bl). **85 Science & Society Picture Library:** NRM. **86 Science & Society Picture Library:** Science Museum. **89 Getty Images:** Sovfoto / UIG. **90-91 Science & Society

Picture Library:** NRM. **92 Mary Evans:** Iberfoto. **93 Fotolia.com:** cityanimal. **96-97 Getty Images:** The British Library / Robana. **98 Alamy:** 19th era. **99 AF Eisenbahn Archiv. 102 AF Eisenbahn Archiv. 104 Alamy:** imagebroker. **107 Corbis:** Swim Ink 2, LLC. **108-109 Getty Images:** Roy Stevens / Time & Life Pictures. **110 Topfoto:** The Granger Collection. **113 William L. Clements Library, University of Michigan. 115 California State Library. 116 Mary Evans:** Everett Collection. **118-119 Corbis:** Michael Maslan Historic Photographs. **120 California State Library. 123 Corbis:** Bettmann. **124 Corbis:** James L. Amos. **126 Canadian Pacfic Railway. 128 The Bridgeman Art Library:** Private Collection / Peter Newark American Pictures (tl). **132-133 Science & Society Picture Library:** Science Museum. **134 Getty Images:** Hulton Archive (b). **137 Getty Images:** Keystone / Hulton Archive (tr). **139 National Museums Northern Ireland:** Collection Armagh County Museum (b). **140 Getty Images:** Jimin Lai / AFP (b). **142 Luped.com:** Roland Smithies (t). **144 DK Images:** Courtesy of Railroad Museum of Pennsylvania (bl). **144-145 akg-images:** North Wind Picture Archives. **147 Luped.com:** Roland Smithies. **148 SuperStock:** Christie's Images Ltd. **150 DK Images:** Courtesy of B&O Railroad Museum. **151 Getty Images:** MPI. **152 Corbis:** Underwood & Underwood (br). **152 Getty Images:** Digital Vision (bl). **153 Science & Society Picture Library:** NRM / Cuneo Fine Arts (bl). **156 Getty Images:** Popperfoto. **159 Getty Images:** Hal Morey. **160 Science & Society Picture Library:** Science Museum (c). **161 DK Images:** Courtesy of Railroad Museum of Pennsylvania (t). **161 Getty Images:** Fox Photos (b). **163 Corbis:** Underwood & Underwood. **165 AF Eisenbahn Archiv. 165 Getty Images:** Fotosearch. **166 Library of Congress, Washington, D.C. 168 Alexander Turnbull Library, Wellington, New Zealand:** EP-Accidents-Rail-Tangiwai rail disaster-01 (bl). **168-169 Science & Society Picture Library:** NRM. **170 Getty Images:** Chicago History Museum. **172 Corbis:** Bettmann. **174-175 AF Eisenbahn Archiv. 177 Getty Images:** MPI. **181 The Bridgeman Art Library:** Regional Art Museum, Irkutsk. **183 AF Eisenbahn Archiv. 184 Getty Images:** Sovfoto / UIG. **187 Getty Images:** De Agostini / E. Ganzerla. **188 Corbis:** Hulton-Deutsch Collection (bl). **190 Mary Evans:** Epic. **192 Getty Images:** Culture Club. **193 The Art Archive:** Kharbine-Tapabor / Collection IM. **194-195 Corbis:** Katie Garrod / JAI. **196 akg-images. 198 South American Pictures. 201 Topfoto:** Alinari. **202 Wikimedia:** Ernesto Linares. **204 Alamy:** Prisma Bildagentur AG (bl). **205 Getty Images:** Andrey Rudakov / Bloomberg (cl). **204-205 Marcelo Meneses / Ecuador Adventure:** (b). **208 AF Eisenbahn Archiv. 210-211 The Art Archive:** Culver Pictures. **212 Alamy:** imagebroker (cla). **212 DK Images:** Courtesy of B&O Railroad Museum (b). **213 Alamy:** Gerry White (cla). **213 Alamy:** David